Lean Software Development

The Agile Software Development Series

Alistair Cockburn and Jim Highsmith, Series Editors

Agile software development centers on four values identified in the Agile Alliance's Manifesto:

- Individuals and interactions over processes and tools
- Working software over comprehensive documentation
- Customer collaboration over contract negotiation
- Responding to change over following a plan

The development of Agile software requires innovation and responsiveness, based on generating and sharing knowledge within a development team and with the customer. Agile software developers draw on the strengths of customers, users, and developers, finding just enough process to balance quality and agility.

The books in The Agile Software Development Series focus on sharing the experiences of such Agile developers. Individual books address individual techniques (such as Use Cases), group techniques (such as collaborative decision making), and proven solutions to different problems from a variety of organizational cultures. The result is a core of Agile best practices that will enrich your experience and improve your work.

Titles in the Series:

Steve Adolph, Paul Bramble, Alistair Cockburn, and Andy Pols; *Patterns for Effective Use Cases;* 0201721848

Alistair Cockburn; *Agile Software Development;* 0201699699

Alistair Cockburn; *Crystal Clear;* 0201699478

Alistair Cockburn; *Surviving Object-Oriented Projects;* 0201498340

Alistair Cockburn; *Writing Effective Use Cases;* 0201702258

Anne Mette Jonassen Hass; *Configuration Management Principles and Practice;* 0321117662

Jim Highsmith; *Agile Software Development Ecosystems;* 0201760436

Jim Highsmith; *Agile Project Management;* 0321219775

Craig Larman; *Agile and Iterative Development;* 0131111558

Lars Mathiassen, Jan Pries-Heje, and Ojelanki Ngwenyama; *Improving Software Organizations;* 0201758202

Mary Poppendieck and Tom Poppendieck; *Lean Software Development;* 0321150783

Jean Tabaka; *Collaboration Explained;* 0321268776

Kevin Tate; *Sustainable Software Development;* 0321286081

For more information visit www.awprofessional.com/series/agile

Lean Software Development

An Agile Toolkit

Mary Poppendieck
Tom Poppendieck

Addison
Wesley

Boston • San Francisco • New York • Toronto • Montreal
London • Munich • Paris • Madrid
Capetown • Sydney • Tokyo • Singapore • Mexico City

The publisher offers discounts on this book when ordered in quantity for special sales. For more information, please contact:

Pearson Education Corporate Sales Division
One Lake Street
Upper Saddle River, NJ 07458
(800) 382-3419
corpsales@pearsontechgroup.com

Visit AW on the Web: www.awl.com/cseng/

Library of Congress Cataloging-in-Publication Data available

ISBN 0-321-15078-3
Text printed in the United States on recycled paper at RR Donnelley in Crawfordsville, Indiana
10 11 12 13—DOC—09 08 07 06
10th Printing September 2006

To Dustin, Andy and Brian, Karen and Becca

Contents

Foreword

BY JIM HIGHSMITH

In February 2001, when "Agile" was adopted as the umbrella word for methodologies such as Extreme Programming, Crystal, Adaptive Software Development, Scrum, and others, the industrial heritage of agile buzzed around in the background. Womack, Jones, and Roos's *The Machine That Changed the World*, Smith and Reinertsen's *Developing Products in Half the Time*, and Womack and Jones's *Lean Thinking* have resided on my bookshelf for years. The Agility Forum was founded by manufacturers in the early 1990s. The extensive literature on agile and lean industrial product development influenced my work on *Adaptive Software Development*.

But in *Lean Software Development*, Mary and Tom Poppendieck take lean industrial practices to a new level—they tell us how to apply them directly to software development. It is one thing to read about value stream mapping in a manufacturing plant but quite another to see how this idea applies to software development processes. It is one thing to read about Toyota's set-based decision making and another to apply those ideas to software design. Mary's manufacturing and industrial product development experience at 3M gives her insight into how these practices actually work, and her and Tom's information technology backgrounds gives them insight into how to apply the practices to software development.

Although Agile Software Development has roots that go back more than 10 years, as a movement it is only a couple of years old (in early 2003). Tying it to lean and agile industrial product development provides additional credibility to the principles and practices of Agile Software Development, but more importantly, it provides a wealth of ideas that can strengthen agile practices.

For example, the set-based decision making previously mentioned counters prevalent ideas about making design decisions. Traditional engineering (software and others) stresses analysis and early decision making so downstream activities can proceed. Set-based development stresses keeping multiple design options open in order to have as much information as possible, not only about a particular piece of the design, but also about the integration of all pieces. Set-based development helps optimize the whole rather than the pieces. Simple design and refactoring serve similar purposes for software developers—pushing off certain design decisions into the future when more information is available. Set-based development therefore provides a parallel that adds credibility to agile practices but also shows how to extend those practices.

Lean Software Development provides a wealth of information about applying lean techniques from an industrial setting to software development. In particular, it presents a toolkit for project managers, team leaders, and technology managers who want to add value rather than become roadblocks to their project teams.

Jim Highsmith
Flagstaff, Arizona
March 2002

Foreword

BY KEN SCHWABER

Agile processes for software development came into being during the 1990's. We constructed them based on experience, trial-and-error, knowledge of what didn't work, and best practices. I had used Scrum and Extreme Programming-like practices in my own software company during the early 90's. When I first formulated the detailed practices of Scrum, I made sure that I tried them on every sort of development situation imaginable before I published my first book about Scrum. In the absence of first-principles or a theoretical framework for Scrum and other agile processes, I wanted to make sure it really worked before I unleashed more snake oil on the world.

Others and I have made attempts to provide a theoretical underpinning to agile processes. I've referred back to my research in industrial process control theory, which friends of mine at DuPont's Advanced Research Facility helped me understand and apply. Jim Highsmith has referred to the principles of complex adaptive systems and complexity theory to explain, by analogy, the reasons why agile processes work.

Mary and Tom Poppendieck have provided us with a more understandable, robust, and everyday framework for understanding the workings of agile processes. I was with them at the XP2002 conference in Sardinia, Italy when Enrico Zaninotto, Dean of Faculty of Economics at the University of Trento, Italy gave his keynote talk, "From X Programming to the X Organization." In this talk, Enrico laid out the migration of manufacturing from the simple workshop through the assembly line to the modern use of lean manufacturing. He clearly demonstrated the economic imperatives underlying the current use of lean manufacturing. After the talk, Mary was obviously pleased at this validation. Enrico's talk brought together her background in manufacturing and product development with all of the collaborative work she had done with the lean construction movement and her knowledge of the Toyota production system.

This book is the consequence of the Poppendiecks' work to pull all of these movements and knowledge together. In doing so, they have provided a commonsense set of tools that underlie agile processes. People using agile processes can refer to the 22 tools that Mary and Tom describe to understand why and how the most common agile processes work, or to modify them based on a deep understanding of them, or to construct their own agile process. The tools in this book provide the framework.

I took particular pleasure in listening to Enrico and seeing Mary's and Tom's thinking gel. Our industry has long been burdened by the accusation that we should be able to "do it like manufacturing!" The manufacturing this referred to was the Frederick Taylor, Henry Ford assembly line. The systems development processes we constructed on Taylor's principles didn't work, and we didn't know why. Enrico laughed—"Modern manufacturing left the Taylor principles behind twenty years ago!"

No longer do we need to refer to such abstruse theory and science as complex adaptive systems to explain agile systems development. We can refer to the 22 tools set forth in this book and look to manufacturing and common sense for their rationale. We are finally starting to model software development on something that works for us!

Ken Schwaber
February 2003

Preface

I used to be a really good programmer. My code controlled telephone switching systems, high energy physics research, concept vehicles, and the makers and coaters used to manufacture 3M tape. I was equally good at writing Fortran or assembly language, and I could specify and build a minicomputer control system as fast as anyone.

After a dozen or so years of programming, I followed one of my systems to a manufacturing plant and took the leap into IT management. I learned about materials control and unit costs and production databases. Then the quality-is-free and just-in-time movements hit our plant, and I learned how a few simple ideas and empowered people could change everything.

A few years later I landed in new product development, leading commercialization teams for embedded software, imaging systems, and eventually optical systems. I liked new product development so much that I joined a start-up company and later started my own company to work with product development teams, particularly those doing software development.

I had been out of the software development industry for a half dozen years, and I was appalled at what I found when I returned. Between PMI (Project Management Institute) and CMM (Capability Maturity Model) certification programs, a heavy emphasis on process definition and detailed, front-end planning seemed to dominate everyone's perception of best practices. Worse, the justification for these approaches was the lean manufacturing movement I knew so well.

I was keenly aware that the success of lean manufacturing rested on a deep understanding of what creates value, why rapid flow is essential, and how to release the brainpower of the people doing the work. In the prevailing focus on process and planning I detected a devaluation of these key principles. I heard, for example, that detailed process definitions were needed so that "anyone can program," while lean manufacturing focused on building skill in frontline people and having them define their own processes.

I heard that spending a lot of time and getting the requirements right upfront was the way to do things "right the first time." I found this curious. I knew that the only way that my code would work the first time I tried to control a machine was to build a complete simulation program and test the code to death. I knew that every product that was delivered to our plant came with a complete set of tests, and "right the first time" meant passing each test every step of the way. You could be sure that next month a new gizmo or tape length would be needed by marketing, so the idea of freezing a product configuration before manufacturing was simply unheard of. That's why we had serial numbers—so we could tell what the current manufacturing spec was the day a product was made. We would never expect to be making the exact same products this month that we were making last month.

Detailed front-end planning strikes me as diametrically opposed to lean manufacturing principles. Process definition by a staff group strikes me as diametrically opposed to the empowerment that is core to successful lean manufacturing. It seems to me that the manufacturing metaphor has been misapplied to software development. It seems to me that CMM, in its eagerness to standardize process, leaves out the heart of discovery and innovation that was the critical success factor in our move to total quality management. We knew in manufacturing that ISO9000 and even Malcolm Baldrige awards had little or nothing to do with a successful quality program. They were useful in documenting success, but generally got in the way of creating it.

It seems to me that a PMI certification program teaches a new project manager several antipatterns for software project management. Work breakdown. Scope control. Change control. Earned value. Requirements tracking. Time tracking. I learned all about these when I was a program manager for government contracts at 3M, and was keenly aware of the waste they added to a program. We certainly knew better than to use them on our internal product development programs, where learning and innovation were the essential ingredients of success.

This is not to say that CMM and PMI are bad, but only that for anyone who has lived through the lean revolution, they tend to give the wrong flavor to a software development program. In this book we hope to change the software development paradigm from process to people, from disaggregation to aggregation, from speculation to data-based decision making, from planning to learning, from traceability to testing, from cost-and-schedule control to delivering business value.

If you think that better, cheaper, and faster can't coexist, you should know that we used to think the same way in the pre-lean days of manufacturing and product development. However, we learned that by focusing on value, flow, and people, you got better quality, lower cost, and faster delivery. We learned that from our competitors as they took away our markets.

May you lead your industry in lean software development.

Mary Poppendieck

ACKNOWLEDGMENTS

This book is in our words, but the ideas came from the agile community. Lean principles have had decades of success in lean manufacturing, logistics, and construction. These same principles, which are the framework of this book, are finally emerging as agile software development.

Many reviewers invested thoughtful hours reading and providing feedback that helped us refine our ideas and presentation, including Ken Schwaber, Jim Highsmith, Alistair Cockburn, Luke Hohmann, Martin Fowler, pragmatic Dave Thomas, Bill Wake, Rob Purser, Mike Cohn, and Martha Lindeman. Thanks to Glenn Ballard and Greg Howell from the Lean Construction Institute for their contributions. We also thank Kent Beck, Tim Ocock, Ron Crocker, and Bruce Ferguson for their contributions to the book.

Thanks to our employers, mentors, team members, collaborators and clients. Thanks to all who have attended our classes and tutorials, asked probing questions, and given us examples of lean principles that work (or do not work) in their worlds. Finally, thanks to the authors of the books and articles we cited, for their contributions to agile software development.

Introduction

This is a book of thinking tools for software development leaders. It is a toolkit for translating widely accepted lean principles into effective, agile practices that fit your unique environment. Lean thinking has a long history of generating dramatic improvements in fields as diverse as manufacturing, health care, and construction. Can it do the same for software development? One thing is clear: The field of software development has plenty of opportunity for improvement.

Jim Johnson, chairman of the Standish Group, told an attentive audience[1] the story of how Florida and Minnesota each developed its Statewide Automated Child Welfare Information System (SACWIS). In Florida, system development started in 1990 and was estimated to take 8 years and to cost $32 million. As Johnson spoke in 2002, Florida had spent $170 million and the system was estimated to be completed in 2005 at the cost of $230 million. Meanwhile, Minnesota began developing essentially the same system in 1999 and completed it in early 2000 at the cost of $1.1 million. That's a productivity difference of over 200:1. Johnson credited Minnesota's success to a standardized infrastructure, minimized requirements, and a team of eight capable people.

This is but one example of dramatic performance differences between organizations doing essentially the same thing. Such differences can be found not only in software development but in many other fields as well. Differences between companies are rooted in their organizational history and culture, their approach to the market, and their ability to capitalize on opportunities.

The difference between high-performance companies and their average competitors has been studied for a long time, and much is known about what makes some

1. Johnson, "ROI, It's Your Job."

companies more successful than others. Just as in software development, there is no magic formula, no silver bullet.[2] There are, however, some solid theories about which approaches foster high performance and which are likely to hinder it. Areas such as manufacturing, logistics, and new product development have developed a body of knowledge of how to provide the best environment for superior performance.

We observe that some methods still considered standard practice for developing software have long been abandoned by other disciplines. Meanwhile, approaches considered standard in product development, such as concurrent engineering, are not yet generally considered for software development.

Perhaps some of the reluctance to use approaches from product development comes from unfortunate uses of metaphors in the past. Software development has tried to model its practices after manufacturing and civil engineering, with decidedly mixed results. This has been due in part to a naive understanding of the true nature of these disciplines and a failure to recognize the limits of the metaphor.

While recognizing the hazards of misapplied metaphors, we believe that software development is similar to product development and that the software development industry can learn much from examining how changes in product development approaches have brought improvements to the product development process. Organizations that develop custom software will recognize that their work consists largely of development activities. Companies that develop software as a product or part of a product should find the lessons from product development particularly germane.

The story of the Florida and Minnesota SACWIS projects is reminiscent of the story of the General Motors GM-10 development, which began in 1982.[3] The first model, a Buick Regal, hit the streets seven years later, in 1989, two years late. Four years after the GM-10 program began, Honda started developing a new model Accord aimed at the same market. It was on the market by the end of 1989, about the same time the GM-10 Cutlass and Grand Prix appeared. What about quality? Our son was still driving our 1990 Accord 12 years and 175,000 mostly trouble-free miles later.

Studies[4] at the time showed that across multiple automotive companies, the product development approaches typical of Japanese automakers resulted in a 2:1 reduction in engineering effort and shortened development time by one-third when compared to traditional approaches. These results contradicted the conventional wisdom at the time, which held that the cost of change during final production was 1,000 times greater than the cost of a change made during design.[5] It was widely held

2. See Brooks, "No Silver Bullet."

3. Womack, Jones and Roos, *The Machine That Changed the World,* 110.

4. Ibid., 111.

that rapid development meant hasty decision making, so shortening the development cycle would result in many late changes, driving up development cost.

To protect against the exponentially increasing cost of change, traditional product development processes in U.S. automotive manufacturers were sequential, and relationships with suppliers were arm's length. The effect of this approach was to lengthen the development cycle significantly while making adaptation to current market trends impossible at the later stages of development. In contrast, companies such as Honda and Toyota put a premium on rapid, concurrent development and the ability to make changes late in the development cycle. Why weren't these companies paying the huge penalty for making changes later in development?

One way to avoid the large penalty for a change during final production is to make the right design decision in the first place and avoid the need to change later. That was the Detroit approach. Toyota and Honda had discovered a different way to avoid the penalty of incorrect design decisions: Don't make irreversible decisions in the first place; delay design decisions as long as possible, and when they are made, make them with the best available information to make them correctly. This thinking is very similar to the thinking behind just-in-time manufacturing, pioneered by Toyota: Don't decide what to manufacture until you have a customer order; then make it as fast as possible.

Delaying decisions is not the whole story; it is an example of how thinking differently can lead to a new paradigm for product development. There were many other differences between GM and Honda in the 1980s. GM tended to push critical decisions up to a few high-level authorities, while Honda's decision to design a new engine for the Accord emerged from detailed, engineering-level discussions over millimeters of hood slope and layout real estate. GM developed products using sequential processes, while Honda used concurrent processes, involving those making, testing, and maintaining the car in the design of the car. GM's designs were subject to modification by both marketing and strong functional managers, while Honda had a single leader who envisioned what the car should be and continually kept the vision in front of the engineers doing the work.[6]

The approach to product development exemplified by Honda and Toyota in the 1980s, typically called *lean development,* was adopted by many automobile companies in the 1990s. Today the product development performance gap among automakers has significantly narrowed.

---

5. Thomas Group, National Institute of Standards & Technology Institute for Defense Analyses.

6. Womack, Jones and Roos, *The Machine That Changed the World,* 104–110.

Lean development principles have been tried and proven in the automotive industry, which has a design environment arguably as complex as most software development environments. Moreover, the theory behind lean development borrows heavily from the theory of lean manufacturing, so lean principles in general are both understood and proven by managers in many disciplines outside of software development.

LEAN PRINCIPLES, THINKING TOOLS, AGILE PRACTICES

This book is about the application of lean principles to software development. Much is known about lean principles, and we caution that organizations have not been uniformly successful in applying them, because lean thinking requires a change in culture and organizational habits that is beyond the capability of some companies. On the other hand, companies that have understood and adopted the essence of lean thinking have realized significant, sustainable performance improvements.[7]

Principles are guiding ideas and insights about a discipline, while practices are what you actually do to carry out principles.[8] Principles are universal, but it is not always easy to see how they apply to particular environments. Practices, on the other hand, give specific guidance on what to do, but they need to be adapted to the domain. We believe that there is no such thing as a "best" practice; practices must take context into account. In fact, the problems that arise when applying metaphors from other disciplines to software development are often the result of trying to transfer the practices rather than the principles of the other discipline.

Software development is a broad discipline—it deals with Web design and with sending a satellite into orbit. Practices for one domain will not necessarily apply to other domains. Principles, however, are broadly applicable across domains as long as the guiding principles are translated into appropriate practices for each domain. This book focuses on the process of translating lean principles to agile practices tailored to individual software development domains.

At the core of this book are 22 thinking tools to aid software development leaders as they develop the agile practices that work best in their particular domain. This is not a cookbook of agile practices; it is a book for chefs who are setting out to design agile practices that will work in their domain.

There are two prerequisites for a new idea to take hold in an organization:

---

7. Chrysler, for example, adopted a lean approach to supplier management, which is credited with making significant contributions to its turnaround in the early 1990s. See Dyer, *Collaborative Advantage.*

8. Senge, *The Fifth Discipline,* 373.

- The idea must be proven to work operationally, and
- People who are considering adopting the change must understand why it works.[9]

Agile software development practices have been shown to work in some organizations, and in *Adaptive Software Development*[10] Jim Highsmith develops a theoretical basis for why these practices work. *Lean Development* further expands the theoretical foundations of agile software development by applying well-known and accepted lean principles to software development. But it goes further by providing thinking tools to help translate lean principles into agile practices that are appropriate for individual domains. It is our hope that this book will lead to wider acceptance of agile development approaches.[11]

GUIDED TOUR

This book contains seven chapters devoted to seven lean principles and thinking tools for translating each principle into agile practices. A brief introduction to the seven lean principles concludes this introduction.

1. **Eliminate waste.** Waste is anything that does not add value to a product, value as perceived by the customer. In lean thinking, the concept of waste is a high hurdle. If a component is sitting on a shelf gathering dust, that is waste. If a development cycle has collected requirements in a book gathering dust, that is waste. If a manufacturing plant makes more stuff than is immediately needed, that is waste. If developers code more features than are immediately needed, that is waste. In manufacturing, moving product around is waste. In product development, handing off development from one group to another is waste. The ideal is to find out what a customer wants, and then make or develop it and deliver exactly what they want, virtually immediately. Whatever gets in the way of rapidly satisfying a customer need is waste.
2. **Amplify learning.** Development is an exercise in discovery, while production is an

9. See Larpé and Van Wassenhove, "Learning Across Lines."

10. Highsmith, *Adaptive Software Development.*

11. Agile software development approaches include Adaptive Software Development, ASD (Highsmith, 2000); Crystal Methods (Cockburn, 2002); Dynamic Systems Development Method, DSDM (Stapleton, 2003); Feature-Driven Development, FDD (Palmer and Felsing, 2002); Scrum (Schwaber and Beedle, 2001); and Extreme Programming, XP (Beck, 2000). See Highsmith, *Agile Software Development Ecosystems* for an overview of agile approaches.

exercise in reducing variation, and for this reason, a lean approach to development results in practices that are quite different than lean production practices. Development is like creating a recipe, while production is like making the dish. Recipes are designed by experienced chefs who have developed an instinct for what works and the capability to adapt available ingredients to suit the occasion. Yet even great chefs produce several variations of a new dish as they iterate toward a recipe that will taste great and be easy to reproduce. Chefs are not expected to get a recipe perfect on the first attempt; they are expected to produce several variations on a theme as part of the learning process.[12] Software development is best conceived of as a similar learning process with the added challenge that development teams are large and the results are far more complex than a recipe. The best approach to improving a software development environment is to amplify learning.

3. **Decide as late as possible.** Development practices that provide for late decision making are effective in domains that involve uncertainty, because they provide an options-based approach. In the face of uncertainty, most economic markets develop options to provide a way for investors to avoid locking in decisions until the future is closer and easier to predict. Delaying decisions is valuable because better decisions can be made when they are based on fact, not speculation. In an evolving market, keeping design options open is more valuable than committing early. A key strategy for delaying commitments when developing a complex system is to build a capacity for change into the system.
4. **Deliver as fast as possible.** Until recently, rapid software development has not been valued; taking a careful, don't-make-any-mistakes approach has seemed to be more important. But it is time for "speed costs more" to join "quality costs more" on the list of debunked myths.[13] Rapid development has many advantages. Without speed, you cannot delay decisions. Without speed, you do not have reliable feedback. In development the discovery cycle is critical for learning: Design, implement, feedback, improve. The shorter these cycles are, the more can be learned. Speed assures that customers get what they need now, not what they needed yesterday. It also allows them to delay making up their minds about what they really want until they know more. Compressing the value stream as much as possible is a fundamental lean strategy for eliminating waste.
5. **Empower the team.** Top-notch execution lies in getting the details right, and no one understands the details better than the people who actually do the work. Involving developers in the details of technical decisions is fundamental to achiev-

12. See Ballard, "Positive vs. Negative Iteration in Design."
13. Womack, Jones and Roos, *The Machine That Changed the World,* 111.

ing excellence. The people on the front line combine the knowledge of the minute details with the power of many minds. When equipped with necessary expertise and guided by a leader, they will make better technical decisions and better process decisions than anyone can make for them. Because decisions are made late and execution is fast, it is not possible for a central authority to orchestrate activities of workers. Thus, lean practices use pull techniques to schedule work and contain local signaling mechanisms so workers can let each other know what needs to be done. In lean software development, the pull mechanism is an agreement to deliver increasingly refined versions of working software at regular intervals. Local signaling occurs through visible charts, daily meetings, frequent integration, and comprehensive testing.

6. **Build integrity in.** A system is perceived to have integrity when a user thinks, "Yes! That is exactly what I want. Somebody got inside my mind!" Market share is a rough measure of perceived integrity for products, because it measures customer perception over time.[14] Conceptual integrity means that the system's central concepts work together as a smooth, cohesive whole, and it is a critical factor in creating perceived integrity.[15] Software needs an additional level of integrity—it must maintain its usefulness over time. Software is usually expected to evolve gracefully as it adapts to the future. Software with integrity has a coherent architecture, scores high on usability and fitness for purpose, and is maintainable, adaptable, and extensible. Research has shown that integrity comes from wise leadership, relevant expertise, effective communication, and healthy discipline; processes, procedures, and measurements are not adequate substitutes.
7. **See the whole.** Integrity in complex systems requires a deep expertise in many diverse areas. One of the most intractable problems with product development is that experts in any area (e.g., database or GUI) have a tendency to maximize the performance of the part of the product representing their own specialty rather than focusing on overall system performance. Quite often, the common good suffers if people attend first to their own specialized interests. When individuals or organizations are measured on their specialized contribution rather than overall performance, suboptimization is likely to result. This problem is even more pronounced when two organizations contract with each other, because people will naturally want to maximize the performance of their own company. It is challenging to implement practices that avoid suboptimization in a large organization, and it is an order of magnitude more difficult when contracts are involved.

---

14. Clark and Fujimoto, "The Power of Product Integrity," 278.

15. Brooks, *The Mythical Man Month,* 255.

This book was written for software development managers, project managers, and technical leaders. It is organized around the seven principles of lean thinking. Each chapter discusses the lean principle and then provides thinking tools to assist in translating the lean principle to agile software development practices that match the needs of individual domains. At the end of each chapter are practical suggestions for implementing the lean principle in a software development organization. The last chapter is an instruction and warranty card for using the thinking tools in this toolkit.

Chapter 1

Eliminate Waste

THE ORIGINS OF LEAN THINKING

In the late 1940s, a small company named Toyota set out to manufacture cars for Japan, but it had a problem. Since people did not have much money, cars had to be cheap. Mass production was the cheapest way to make cars, but mass production meant making thousands of the same kind of car, and the Japanese market was simply not large enough to need all those cars. So the question was, how could Toyota make cars in small quantities but keep them as inexpensive as mass-produced cars?

From this dilemma, the Toyota Production System emerged to form the basis of a whole new way to think about manufacturing, logistics, and eventually product development. The mastermind behind this new way of thinking was Taiichi Ohno, known as the father of the Toyota Production System. At the heart of Ohno's thinking was the fundamental lean principle: *Eliminate waste.*

Waste seems like a reasonably clear-cut term, but Ohno gave new meaning to the word. In his mind, anything that does not create value for a customer is waste. A part that is sitting around waiting to be used is waste. Making something that is not immediately needed is waste. Motion is waste. Transportation is waste. Waiting is waste. Any extra processing steps are waste. And of course defects are waste.

Ohno was not trying to copy mass production, so he did not adopt mass production values. His ideal was to both make and deliver a product immediately after a customer placed an order. He believed that it is better to wait for an order than to build up inventory in anticipation of the order. Yet he also believed that the ideal is to deliver the product immediately.

Toyota transferred its concept of waste from manufacturing to product development. When a development project is started, the goal is to complete it as rapidly as possible, because all of the work that goes into development is not adding value until a car rolls off the production line. In a sense, ongoing development projects are just like inventory sitting around a factory. Designs and prototypes are not useful to customers; they receive value only when the new product is delivered.

If it seems strange that the intermediate steps of a development program might be considered waste, in the 1980s it seemed equally strange that inventory should be considered waste. After all, inventory was the thing that allowed immediate delivery once a customer order was placed, and inventory was the thing that allowed all machines to run at maximum capacity. How could inventory be waste?

Actually, inventory is a very big waste. Running all of those machines at maximum capacity produces piles of unneeded inventory that hide quality problems, grow obsolete, and clog distribution channels. A large backlog of product development suffers from the same drawbacks.

Eliminating waste is the most fundamental lean principle, the one from which all the other principles follow. Thus, the first step to implementing lean development is learning to see waste. The second step is to uncover the biggest sources of waste and eliminate them. The next step is to uncover the biggest remaining sources of waste and eliminate them. The next step is to do it again. After a while, even things that seem essential can be gradually eliminated.

The True Story of a Death March Project, Part 1: Eliminating Waste

I took over a troubled project[1] four and a half months before it had to go live. The first two months had been spent gathering requirements. The next two months had been spent trying to get the customers to sign off on the requirements, but they were reluctant to sign because they knew that if they made a mistake in interpreting the volumes of obtuse documents, they would be held accountable and may never get the functionality they really needed. Two weeks before I took over the project, the entire three-inch document was made obsolete by a management decision.

As I said, delivery had to be in four and a half months; the features of the new system were required by law. The contract called for a traditional waterfall approach, but in five and a half months there was nothing to show for that approach, so I set out with Gene,[2] the customer project manager, to eliminate all waste.

1. Edward Yourdon, in *Death March*, defines a death march project as "one whose 'project parameters' exceed the norm by at least 50%."

2. Not his real name.

The first thing I did was eliminate all features that were not required to meet the law. They could be implemented later, but they were not going to be implemented by the deadline. Resistance of senior managers was strong, but since they couldn't change reality, it was simply a matter of time before they came around to accepting the situation. We started a second project to put a Web front end on the parts of the system that could not be implemented immediately, so they would look new.

Then, we eliminated the change control system. Since the requirements documents were obsolete, there was nothing to control. Instead, we agreed upon a simple criterion to determine if any feature was in or out of scope. Since we were modifying software originally developed for another customer, we agreed that the scope was defined by the features developed for the original customer, adapted to meet local laws, and run in the local technical environment. Our "one-minute scope control" rule worked for almost every user request; we had to resort to a backup arbitration method for only a few features.

Next, we eliminated the finger pointing. We were late. The environment, which the customer was to supply, did not work. We all had problems. Gene and I agreed that we simply did not have any time to assess blame, and there was plenty enough for both sides. We worked together on every problem, trying mightily not to dump it in the other person's lap. We found that difficult problems got resolved easier with both of us working on them, and usually there was a problem on both sides anyway.

Finally, there were the design documents called for in the contract. We didn't have any, nor did we have anyone who knew what it meant to produce design documents. We were adapting existing software to a new environment, and we had no choice but to use the existing, undocumented design, such as it was. Adding gap design documents on top of no design documents did not make much sense. Even if it did, the analysts who understood the customer requirements were not capable of producing design documents suitable for the (remote) programming team.

Instead, I sent the analysts to the programming site to talk with the programmers and told them to come back with the first iteration of code. When they brought that first iteration back, we could not get it working in the customer environment, because it had not been tested there. The customer site was not replicated at the development site; security concerns did not allow remote access. So, I had some of the developers come to the customer site, where a delegation stayed for the remainder of the project. They communicated effectively with the remote development site for a while, but the entire effort eventually moved to the customer site.

The old system was shut down when the new law went into effect, and after three weeks of down time, the new system went live. At that point only half of the features were working, but the law was not broken and the remainder of the system was implemented with weekly iterations over the next few months.

—Mary

TOOL 1: SEEING WASTE

Learning to see waste is the first step in developing breakthroughs with lean thinking. If something does not directly add value as perceived by the customer, it is waste. If there is a way to do without it, it is waste. In 1970 Winston Royce wrote that the fundamental steps of all software development are analysis and coding. "[While] many additional development steps are required, none contribute as directly to the final product as analysis and coding, and all drive up the development costs."[3] With our definition of waste, we can interpret Royce's comment to indicate that *every step in the waterfall process except analysis and coding is waste.*

Agile software development practices seek to eliminate waste. To do this, it is first necessary to *see* the waste, and Royce suggests a good place to start looking. Good candidates include everything your organization does to develop software that is not analysis or coding. Do all of those processes *really* add value for customers?

Shigeo Shingo, one of the masterminds of the Toyota Production System, identified seven types of manufacturing waste.[4] His list has helped many manufacturing managers find waste where they never would have thought to look. To aid software development managers in their quest to find that elusive thing called waste, we translate the seven wastes of manufacturing into the seven wastes of software development in Table 1.1.

Table 1.1 *The Seven Wastes*

The Seven Wastes of Manufacturing	The Seven Wastes of Software Development
Inventory	Partially Done Work
Extra Processing	Extra Processes
Overproduction	Extra Features
Transportation	Task Switching
Waiting	Waiting
Motion	Motion
Defects	Defects

3. Royce, "Managing the Development of Large Software Systems." For a description of the waterfall approach, see Chapter 2, "Amplify Learning," especially Figure 2.5.

4. Shingo, *Study of "Toyota" Production System*, 287.

Partially Done Work

Partially done software development has a tendency to become obsolete, and it gets in the way of other development that might need to be done. But the big problem with partially done software is that you might have no idea whether or not it will eventually work. Sure, you have a stack of requirements and design documents. You may even have a pile of code, which may even be unit tested. But until the software is integrated into the rest of the environment, you don't really know what problems might be lurking, and until the software is actually in production, you don't really know if it will solve the business problem.

Partially done development ties up resources in investments that have yet to yield results. In software development these investments are sometimes capitalized, and depreciation starts when the software goes into production. What if the system never makes it into production? Then there is a big investment to write off. Partially done software development can carry huge financial risks. Minimizing partially done software development is a risk-reduction as well as a waste-reduction strategy.

Extra Processes

Do you ever ask, Is all that paperwork really necessary? Paperwork consumes resources. Paperwork slows down response time. Paperwork hides quality problems. Paperwork gets lost. Paperwork degrades and becomes obsolete. Paperwork that no one cares to read adds no value.

Many software development processes require paperwork for customer sign-off, or to provide traceability, or to get approval for a change. Does your customer really find this makes the product more valuable to them? Just because paperwork is a required deliverable does not mean that it adds value. If you must produce paperwork that adds little customer value, there are three rules to remember: Keep it short. Keep it high level. Do it off line.

Safety-critical systems are frequently regulated and are often required to have written requirements, traceable to code. In this case, formatting the requirements so they can be easily evaluated and checked for completeness may qualify as a value-adding activity. Look for a table-driven or template-driven format that reduces the requirements to a condensed format that both users and developers can rapidly understand and validate.

A good test of the value of paperwork is to see if there is someone waiting for what is being produced. If an analyst fills out templates, makes tables, or writes use cases that others are eager to use—for coding, testing, and writing training manuals—then these probably add value. Even so, there should be a constant search for the most efficient, effective means to transmit the information. Consider writing customer tests instead of requirements. In general, delay documenting the details of desired features until the iteration in which they are implemented.

Extra Features

It may seem like a good idea to put some extra features into a system just in case they are needed. Developers might like to add a new technical capability just to see how it works. This may seem harmless, but on the contrary, it is serious waste. Every bit of code in the system has to be tracked, compiled, integrated, and tested every time the code is touched, and then it has to be maintained for the life of the system. Every bit of code increases complexity and is a potential failure point. There is a great possibility that extra code will become obsolete before it's used; after all, there wasn't any real call for it in the first place. If code is not needed *now,* putting it into the system is a waste. Resist the temptation.

Task Switching

Assigning people to multiple projects is a source of waste. Every time software developers switch between tasks, a significant switching time is incurred as they get their thoughts gathered and get into the flow of the new task.[5] Belonging to multiple teams usually causes more interruptions and thus more task switching. This task switching time is waste.

The fastest way to complete two projects that use the same resources is to do them one at a time. Say you have two projects that should each take two weeks. If you start one of them, it should be done in two weeks. When it's done, you can start the second project, and it should be done in two weeks. What if you start both projects together and expect people to switch between them? First of all, neither one will be done in two weeks, but will they both be done in four weeks? When you add the switching time, they will probably take closer to five weeks.[6]

It is difficult to resist the temptation to start several projects at the same time, but releasing too much work into a software development organization creates a lot of waste, since it actually slows things down. Work moves much faster through a pipeline that is not filled to capacity, as we discuss in the section on queueing theory in Chapter 4, "Deliver as Fast as Possible."

5. DeMarco and Lister, *Peopleware*, 63.

6. See Goldratt, *Critical Chain*, 126.

Waiting

One of the biggest wastes in software development is usually waiting for things to happen. Delays in starting a project, delays in staffing, delays due to excessive requirements documentation, delays in reviews and approvals, delays in testing, and delays in deployment are waste. Delays are common in most software development processes, and it seems counterintuitive to think of these delays as a waste. It would seem that at worst, delays are neutral.

So what's wrong with waiting? Delay keeps the customer from realizing value as quickly as possible. When a critical customer need arrives in your development organization, the speed with which you can respond is directly related to the systemic delays in your development cycle.

For some environments, delay may not loom as large as other problems. However, if you are developing software for an evolving domain, delays in development are more serious. A fundamental lean principle is to delay decisions until the last possible moment so you can make the most informed decision possible. This is an options-based approach to software development, and it is the best way to deal with uncertainty, as we discuss in Chapter 3, "Decide as Late as Possible." You cannot delay decisions, however, if you cannot implement rapidly once a decision is made.

Motion

When a developer has a question, how much motion does it take to find out the answer? Are people at hand to help with a technical problem? Is the customer or customer representative readily accessible to answer a question about features? Can the developer find out the results of tests without walking down the hall? Development is an activity that requires great concentration, so walking down the hall takes a lot more time than you might think. It will probably take the developer several times as long to reestablish focus as it took to get the question answered. It is for this reason that agile software development practices generally recommend that a team work in a single workroom where everyone has access to developers, to testers, and to customers or customer representatives.

People aren't the only things that move—various artifacts move also. Requirements may move from analysts to designers, and then design documents move from designers to programmers, and then code moves from coders to testers, and so on. Each handoff of an artifact is fraught with opportunities for waste. The biggest waste of all in document handoffs is that documents don't—can't, really—contain all of the information that the next person in line needs to know. Great amounts of tacit knowledge remain with the creator of the document and never get handed off to the receiver. Moving artifacts from one group to another is a huge source of waste in software development.

Defects

The amount of waste caused by a defect is the product of the defect impact and the time it goes undetected. A critical defect that is detected in three minutes is not a big source of waste. A minor defect that is not discovered for weeks is a much bigger waste. The way to reduce the impact of defects is to find them as soon as they occur. Thus, the way to reduce the waste due to defects is to test immediately, integrate often, and release to production as soon as possible.

Management Activities

Management activities do not directly add value to a product, but they do have a big impact on waste in an organization. Consider, for example, a project prioritization process and work release system. Minimizing waste means keeping the amount of unfinished work in the pipeline at a minimum, and this is usually the result of the way work is prioritized and released. Unless the work release system is focused on keeping work flowing smoothly through the development pipeline, it is probably a big generator of waste.

Project tracking and control systems also do not add value, and further, they may be an indication of too much work in the system. In a just-in-time manufacturing system, work moves through the factory so quickly that sophisticated tracking is unnecessary. If work moved through a development organization in a just-in-time manner, it would not need a sophisticated tracking system either. If project tracking is complicated, there probably are a lot of other kinds of waste in the system. Before building a complicated tracking system, minimize the tracking problem by making sure that work flows rapidly through the system.

Authorization systems that are set up to review and approve changes to requirements often add significant delay as opposed to adding value for the customer. But authorization systems are symptoms of the larger waste associated with collecting large lists of requirements in the first place. The thing to do is to figure out how to make the authorization system unnecessary; we offer many ideas on this topic in chapters 2 and 3.

Learning to see waste is an ongoing process of changing the way you think about what is really necessary. One way to discover waste is to think about what you would jettison if you had to get rid of all the excess baggage on a troubled project. It's usually easier to see waste in a crisis.

TOOL 2: VALUE STREAM MAPPING

In the book *Lean Thinking*,[7] James Womack and Daniel Jones chronicle the journey of a cola can from raw material to consumption. It looks like Figure 1.1.

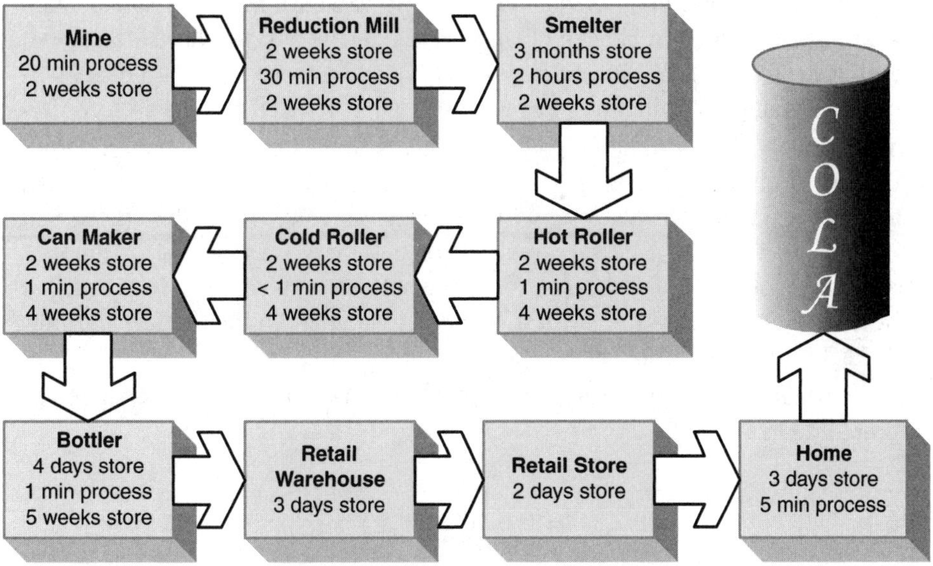

Figure 1.1 *Value stream for cola cans.*

The interesting thing about this value stream is that it takes a cola can an average of 319 days to move from the mine to consumption, while the processing time–the time that value is actually being added—is only 3 hours, or 0.04 percent of the total time. Aluminum cans have to be a very stable industry to be able to tolerate such a long value stream. Consider the opposite end of the spectrum: personal computers. Michael Dell considers inventory to be his biggest risk, because almost every component will become obsolete in a short time. That is why Dell Computer Corporation focuses aggressively on shortening its value stream.

Map Your Value Stream

Mapping your value stream is a good way to start discovering the waste in your software development process. In industry after industry, the process of mapping the value stream has invariably led to deeper insights about how internal processes

7. Data from Womack and Jones, *Lean Thinking*, 43. Used with permission.

work—or don't work—to meet customer needs. By mapping your value stream, you say to yourself and your organization, "First and foremost, our mission is to provide customer value."

Creating a value stream map is a paper and pencil exercise you can easily perform while walking around your organization. Pretend you are a customer request and imagine yourself going through each step of your process. Don't ask people what happens; walk around, look at the data, find out for yourself. Don't buy specialized computer software, and even though training might be useful, you don't need it to get started.

With a pencil and pad in hand, go to the place where a customer request comes into your organization. You goal is to draw a chart of the average customer request, from arrival to completion. Working with the people involved in each activity, you sketch all the process steps necessary to fill the request, as well as the average amount of time that a request spends in each step. At the bottom of the map, draw a timeline that shows how much time the request spends in value-adding activities, and how much time it spends in waiting states and non-value adding activities.

If your organization is using a traditional development process, your map might look something like Figure 1.2.

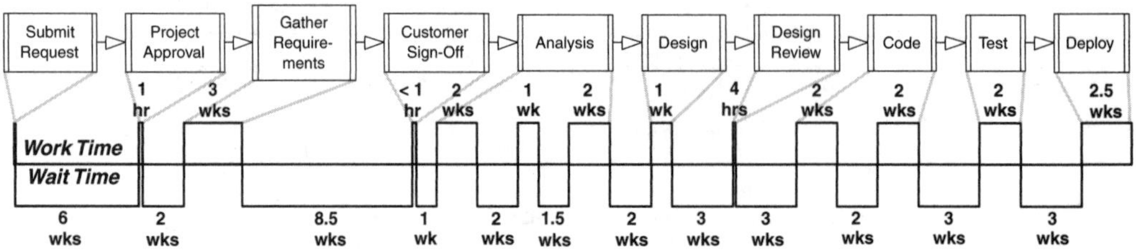

Figure 1.2 *Traditional value stream map.*

This map shows that an average project is ready to deploy in a year, with about a third of the time spent on value-adding activity. The management team reviews projects every 12 weeks, so projects wait an average of 6 weeks before starting. They must then compete for resources, which can be seen in wait times for analysis, design, coding, and testing. Customer sign-off is very slow, taking a couple of months on the average. This is probably because customers consider signing off a high risk, since, as this map indicates, they don't get another chance to influence what they need. Design reviews take 3 weeks to schedule, and coding doesn't begin for another 3 weeks, since developers are working on other projects. Testing times are short, indicating that few problems develop late in projects. However, it takes almost 6 weeks to deploy a tested system. This is a long time.

An Agile Value Stream Map

Let's assume that the organization depicted in the traditional value stream map has decided to move to agile practices. What will its future value stream map look like? The value stream map in Figure 1.2 might generate the following analysis:

> The as-is value stream map indicates that the approval process should be shortened, so the management team agrees to meet weekly to make yes/no decisions on new requests. The team has decided that its highest priority will be rapid response to customer requests, so the members agree to approve only requests that can be handled immediately and to either add staff or subcontract additional requests. Staff availability will be managed so that an early design team can be assigned to approved projects within a week, and all projects should be fully staffed within 3 weeks with dedicated analysts and developers.
>
> The initial value stream map indicates that customer sign-off might be a source of irritation as well as a delay. It shows design reviews should be moved inline with development, since they are currently a great source of delay. Finally, it indicates that planning for deployment should occur earlier in the process. Since the team has decided on agile development, it will solve these problems by moving to incremental development, gathering requirements as needed, integrating design reviews with coding, and planning early for regular deployments.

The agile value stream map from this analysis might look something like Figure 1.3. This map shows that with the changes being considered, a typical customer request should move through the organization in about three months, with most of that time spent actually adding value.

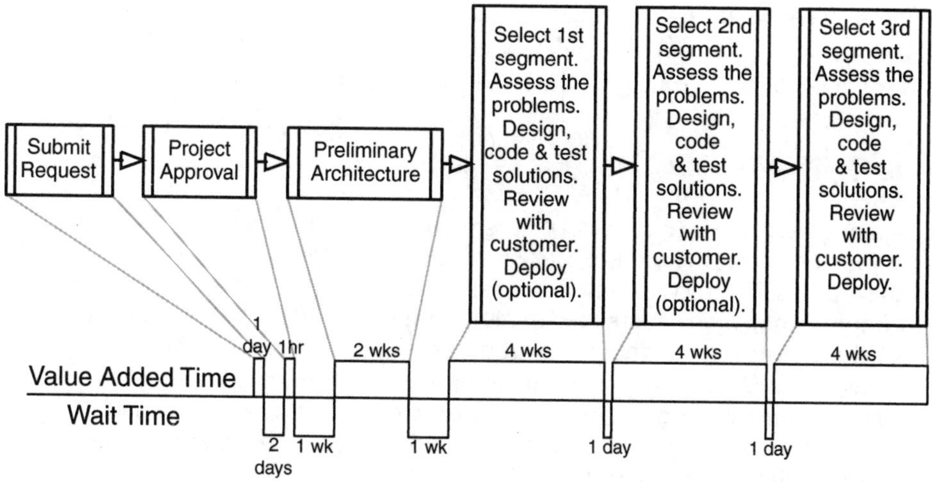

Figure 1.3 *Agile value stream map.*

Value Stream Maps

Value stream maps often show that nondevelopment activities are the biggest bottlenecks in a software development value stream. Figure 1.4 is an example of a value stream map that Kent Beck posted on the discussion group Software-in-Process. It shows that the biggest delays in this particular organization come after development and testing are complete.

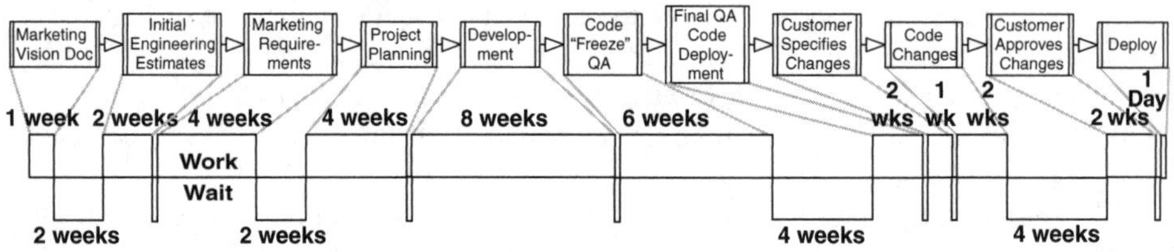

Figure 1.4 *Kent Beck's value stream map.*

"It took us about a half hour to come up with this (don't spend longer than that or you'll have too much detail)."

– from Kent Beck

A value stream map provides a starting point for evaluating and improving your software development process. Once you have a map, pick the biggest opportunities to increase flow and value-added time, and send your team after them. Then, update your value stream map, pick the next biggest opportunities, and repeat the process.

Once you have a value stream map of your organization, the next step is to extend it to your customers. If you can understand how your customers create value, you have a tremendous tool for helping them realize that value.

The Bicycle Factory

Our idea of a vacation is to take our tandem on a week's bicycle trip. One summer, as we biked across Wisconsin, our group of several hundred cyclists was invited to stop at a Trek bicycle factory for refreshments and a tour. Tom, an avid photographer, took many pictures with his digital camera during our tour. After the trip, the pictures joined thousands of others in our screen saver file.

One day, while Mary was writing this chapter, she returned from a break to see a value stream map, right there, filling her screen. On the tour Tom had snapped a picture of a big chart on the wall, and sure enough, it was a value stream map of the bicycle factory.

—Tom and Mary

Many companies have discovered the power of value stream mapping. It helps organizations step back and get an overall view of their processes. It is a tool for uncovering and eliminating wasteful activities and grouping activities that truly create value into a rapid flow that responds to customer demand. The reason value stream mapping is so effective is that it focuses attention on products and their value to customers rather than on organizations, assets, technologies, processes and career paths. It helps managers to step back and rethink their entire development process from a value-creation point of view.

TRY THIS

1. Make a list of the 10 or 15 most important activities in your organization. Put yourself in the shoes of a customer and rate each item from 1 to 5, with 1 meaning customers probably don't care about the activity and 5 meaning customers value it highly. Think of the low-scoring activities as waste. Take the two lowest scoring items and develop a plan to cut the time on these activities in half.
2. At your next seven team meetings, take some time to discuss each of the seven wastes of software development, one at a time:

    - Partially done work
    - Extra processes
    - Extra features
    - Task switching
    - Waiting
    - Motion
    - Defects

    For each waste, ask the questions

    - Do you agree that this "waste" is really a waste? Why or why not?
    - Whether or not you agree that the item is a waste, estimate how much time it consumes in an average week.
    - What can or should be done to reduce that time?

3. Develop a value stream map for your organization. Start with an incoming request and map a timeline of its progress to providing customer value. Find out how much of the time is spent adding value and how much is spent waiting. Take the biggest cause of delay and develop a plan to cut it in half.

Chapter 2

Amplify Learning

THE NATURE OF SOFTWARE DEVELOPMENT

The origins of lean thinking lie in production, but lean *principles* are broadly applicable to other disciplines. However, lean production *practices*—specific guidelines on what to do—cannot be transplanted directly from a manufacturing plant to software development. Many attempts to apply lean production practices to software development have been unsuccessful because generating good software is not a production process; it is a development process.

Development is quite different than production. Think of development as creating a recipe and production as following the recipe. These are very different activities, and they should be carried out with different approaches. Developing a recipe is a learning process involving trial and error. You would not expect an expert chef's first attempt at a new dish to be the last attempt. In fact, the whole idea of developing a recipe is to try many variations on a theme and discover the best dish.

Once a chef has developed a recipe, preparing the dish means following the recipe. This is equivalent to manufacturing, where the objective is to faithfully and repeatedly reproduce a "recipe" with a minimum of variation. The difference between development and production is outlined in Table 2.1.[1]

1. See Ballard, "Positive vs. Negative Iteration in Design."

Table 2.1 Development versus Production

Development	Production
Designs the Recipe	*Produces the Dish*
• Quality is fitness for use	• Quality is conformance to requirements
• Variable results are good	• Variable results are bad
• Iteration generates value	• Iteration generates waste (called rework)

Perspectives on Quality

In production, quality is defined as conformance to requirements specified in the design or "recipe." In the service industry, a different perspective on quality has emerged.

The Service View of Quality

Walt Disney designed Disneyland as a giant stage where several hundred actors make it their job to be sure every guest has a wonderful time. One guest's requirements for having a wonderful time are quite different from the next, and the actors are supposed to figure out exactly what each guest thinks a quality experience should be and make sure he or she has it.

Quality at Disneyland

At Disneyland, even the tram drivers are actors. A friend told me the story of a tram driver who noticed a small girl crying on her way back to the Disneyland hotel. He asked her why she was crying and found out that the crowd around Mickey Mouse was too large, so the girl had not been able to talk to Mickey. The driver called ahead, and when the tram arrived at the hotel, there was Mickey Mouse, waiting to meet it. The girl was thrilled, and the driver had done his job of making sure she had a quality experience.

—*Mary*

The service view of quality takes into account that every customer has a different idea of what constitutes a quality experience. In a service economy, quality does not mean conformance to a script; it means adapting to meet the changing expectations of many different customers.[2]

Quality in Software Development

Quality in software development results in a system with ***both perceived*** integrity and ***conceptual integrity. Perceived integrity*** means that the totality of the product achieves a balance of function, usability, reliability, and economy that delights customers.[3] ***Conceptual integrity***[4] means that the system's central concepts work together as a smooth, cohesive whole. We devote Chapter 6, "Build Integrity In," to the important topic of software integrity.

Customers of a software system will perceive integrity in a system if it solves their problem in an easy-to-use and cost-effective manner. It does not matter whether the problem is poorly understood, changes over time, or is dependent on outside factors; a system with perceived integrity is one that continues to solve the problem in an effective manner. Thus, quality in design means *realization of purpose* or *fitness for use* rather than *conformance to requirements.*

Variability

When you think of quality in a service business such as Disney World, the one thing you can count on is that each customer will have different expectations. True, most people expect the theme park to be clean and the rides to work, but if you provided only one experience to all customers, your theme park would not be widely popular. The difference between providing a service and manufacturing a product is that in service, dynamically shifting customer expectations require variation, while in manufacturing, variation is the enemy. Manufacturing assumes a homogeneous, unchanging set of customer expectations, so the objective is to make a product the same way every time.

Somehow, the idea that variation is bad has found its way into software development, where people have tried to develop standardized processes to reduce variation and achieve repeatable results every time. But development is not intended to produce repeatable results; development produces appropriate solutions to unique customer problems.

---

2. See Prahalad and Krishnan, "The New Meaning of Quality in the Information Age," and Prahalad and Krishnan, "The Dynamic Synchronization of Strategy and Information Technology."

3. The definition of perceived and conceptual integrity is adapted from Clark and Fujimoto, *Product Development Performance*, 30.

4. A term found in Brooks, *The Mythical Man Month*, 42.

Design Cycles

It was once thought that good programmers develop software though a structured, top-down approach.[5] In 1990, Raymonde Guindon evaluated the paradigm that top-down decomposition is the best approach to software design. She reported on research in which experienced designers were asked to design an elevator control system and to describe each step of their thought process to researchers. She found that when experienced designers are presented with ill-defined problems, their design activities are not at all top-down. They move repeatedly between scenario examination, requirements elucidation, high-level solution segmentation, and low-level design of difficult elements. (See Figure 2.1.)

Shifts in design activities and levels of abstraction of Designer 2. Plus signs indicate newly inferred or added requirements. Light bulbs indicate sudden discovery of partial solutions or requirements. The region marked by *R* indicates the period of solution review.

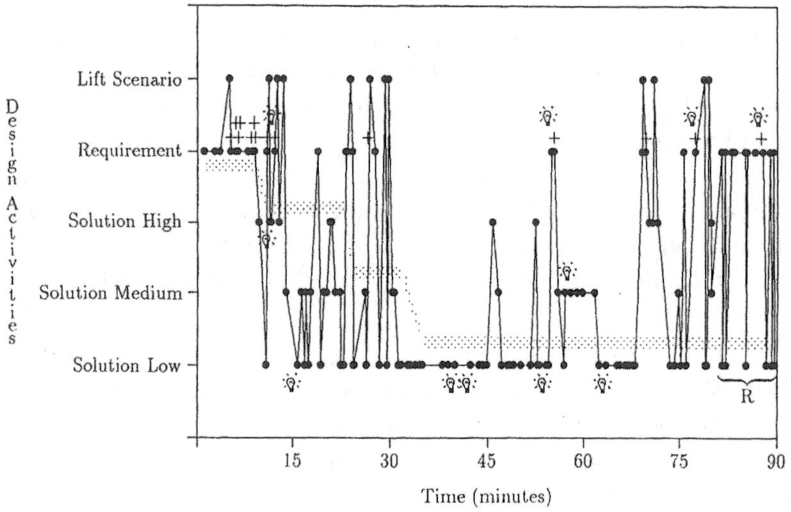

Figure 2.1 *Design activity.*[6]

Guindon found that cycling between high-level design and detailed solution was typical of good designers when dealing with ill-structured problems, that is, problems

5. See Yourdon, *Classics in Software Engineering,* particularly the articles "Structured Programming" by Dijkstra and "On the Composition of Well-Structured Programs" by Niklaus Wirth. See also Brooks, *The Mythical Man Month,* 143.

6. Guindon, "Designing the Design Process," 320, Figure 4. Used with permission.

that do not have a single right answer or a best way to arrive at a solution. She theorized that this unstructured approach is necessary to understand and ultimately give structure to such problems.[7]

The bulk of the work of software development is a problem-solving activity similar to that investigated by Guindon. Software problems are solved at many levels, by all members of the development team. Software architects are clearly involved in a design activity, but so are developers who write the code. The process of writing code involves deep problem understanding, recognition of patterns from experience, experimentation with various approaches, testing the results, and determination of the best approach.

Today it is widely accepted that design is a problem-solving process that involves discovering solutions through short, repeated cycles of investigation, experimentation, and checking the results. Software development, like all design, is most naturally done through such learning cycles.

Do It Right the First Time?

In order to solve problems that have not been solved before, it is necessary to generate information. For complex problems, the preferred approach to a solution is to use the scientific method: observe, create a hypothesis, devise an experiment to test the hypothesis, run the experiment, and see if the results are consistent with the hypothesis. One of the interesting features of the scientific method is that if your hypothesis is always correct, you are not going to learn very much. The maximum amount of information is generated when the probability of failure is 50 percent, not when the hypotheses are always correct. It is necessary to have a reasonable failure rate in order to generate a reasonable amount of new information.[8]

There are two schools of thought in developing software. One is to encourage developers to be sure that each design and each segment of code is perfect the first time. The second school of thought holds that it is better to have small, rapid *try-it, test-it, fix-it* cycles than it is to make sure the design and code are perfect the first time. The first school of thought leaves little room for knowledge generation through experimentation; instead, it believes that knowledge generation should happen through deliberation and review. The *right the first time* approach may work for well-structured

7. Ibid.

8. Reinertsen, *Managing the Design Factory*, 71.

problems,[9] but the *try-it, test-it, fix-it* approach is usually the better approach for ill-structured problems.

If the *right the first time* approach is preferred in your organization, you might ask yourself why this is a value. As Yourdon points out, "A piece of program logic often needs to be rewritten three or four times before it can be considered an elegant, professional piece of work." Why, he asks, do we object to revising programming logic when we are quite happy to rewrite prose three or four times to achieve a professional result?[10]

Your objective should be to balance experimentation with deliberation and review. In order to do this, consider how you can generate the most knowledge at the least cost in your circumstances. For instance, if the cost of testing is very high, you will want more knowledge to be generated through deliberation and review. If experimentation is relatively inexpensive and yields better knowledge faster, then it is the least expensive, most effective approach. Usually, some combination of experimentation, peer review, and iteration will yield the best results.

Learning Cycles

Quite often, the problem to be solved is understood best by the people in the business with the problem, so it is usually necessary to have business people—or representatives such as focus groups—in the knowledge-generation loop. In this case, it is important to speak to the businesspeople with a representation they readily grasp, or the knowledge generation will be inefficient. There are many ways to represent the system, from models to prototypes, to incremental deliveries, but the important thing is to select the representation that gathers the most knowledge. Most users relate better to seeing working screens than to a requirements document, so working software tends to generate better knowledge faster.

Iterations with refactoring—improving the design as the system develops—have been found to be one of the most effective ways to generate knowledge, find answers early, and generate a system with integrity, because this approach generates knowledge most effectively for ill-defined problems. The important question in development is, *How can I learn most effectively?* The answer is often to have many short learning cycles. If you ask instead, *How can I minimize the number of learning cycles?* you are likely to get long cycles, large batches, long feedback loops, and as a result, ineffective learning.

---

9. Well-structured problems have a single right solution and a preferred approach to arriving at the solution. For example, most problems children encounter in elementary school are well-structured problems.

10. Yourdon, *Classics in Software Engineering*, 151.

The True Story of a Death March Project, Part 2: Weekly Iterations

As the first installment of this drama drew to a close in Chapter 1, we had just released a very shaky system to production in a mission-critical area. Only half of the features worked, but the law required the new logic, so against our better judgment, we went live. The customer agreed to work around missing features manually, while we agreed to release new capabilities to the system every week.

We made a list of missing features and known defects, which we called a punch list. Every week, we had the customer review and prioritize the list. On Friday, the developers selected from the top of the punch list those features that they thought they could complete in a week. Users ran a lengthy, manual regression test on the new release the following Thursday, and usually we had to rebuild and retest on Friday. We did not allow new features into the build after the first regression test, so we usually could release the build to production after the second regression test. If not, we tested over the weekend. Almost every Monday morning for three months, a new release went into production. Generally, scripts were run on the database as part of the release, so once production started, there was no going back to the previous release.

Releasing a new version of a mission-critical system to 100 users every week, with no fallback, seems like a high-risk approach. But we never had a disaster, and the weekly releases caused remarkably few problems. The discipline of the regression testing coupled with the small increments of functionality worked like magic. Development and testing was done at the customer site, so if there were questions or problems, feedback was immediate.

Once most of the features were delivered, the customers no longer wanted the hassle of weekly regression tests, so the iterations stretched to two or three weeks. We found that it was devilishly difficult to pass regression testing with the longer increments. As release intervals stretched out, it became tempting to add just one last feature to a release even after its first or second regression test. This was invariably a mistake, making another build and more testing necessary, causing the interval to stretch out, making it more tempting to add more features to the current release. Stretching out intervals was a vicious circle.

Things never went so well as during that heady time when things were so bad that weekly production releases seemed to be the only option. As the urgency faded and we lengthened the feedback cycle, it got more and more difficult for a new release to pass the regression tests. We never were able to automate the regression tests, but were we to do this over again, that would be the first step.

—Mary

TOOL 3: FEEDBACK

It's two in the morning and you are driving home. The traffic light is red, and there's not another car in sight. But the traffic light is red, so you stop. And wait. And wait. Finally, the light changes, after allowing time for lots of nonexistent cross-traffic. You think to yourself, *It's going to be a long drive home*. And sure enough, the next light is also red. But as you approach the light, it turns green. *Ah ha!* you think, *An automatic sensor. That light is smart enough to know I'm here and there's no one else around. I hope the rest of the lights are like that!*

The difference between the two lights is feedback. The first light was preprogrammed based on the assumption that there will be three times as much traffic on the main road as on the side road, so you sat through a long light. The second light had sensors buried throughout the intersection and was programmed to adjust its cycle based on traffic patterns as they vary throughout the day and night.

Figure 2.2 shows how the first traffic signals works.

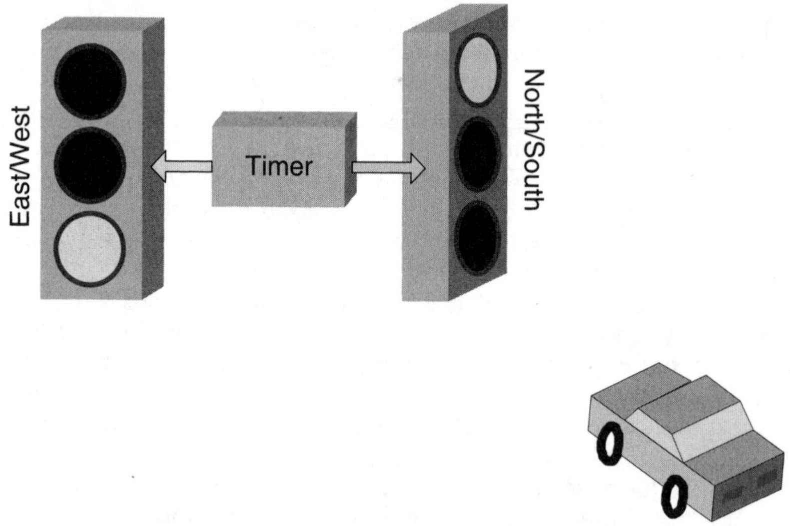

Figure 2.2 *Timed traffic light.*

Figure 2.3 shows how the second traffic signal works.

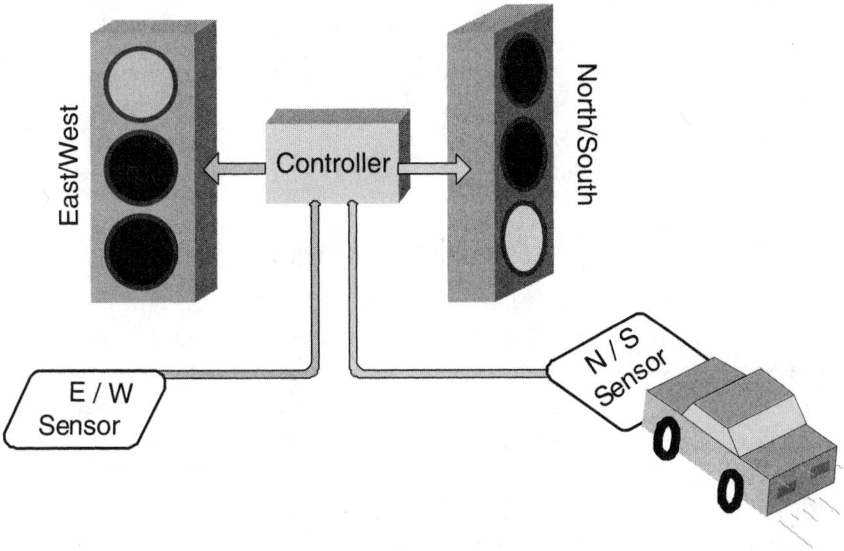

Figure 2.3 *Traffic signal with sensors.*

Notice that the second set of traffic signals have more components, more logic, and more things to go wrong. But traffic lights with feedback are desirable despite their increased complexity. Feedback adds considerable value, and thus it is very common. Your home heater and air conditioner are controlled with a feedback loop, as is your oven. Figure 2.4 shows a feedback loop for an oven:

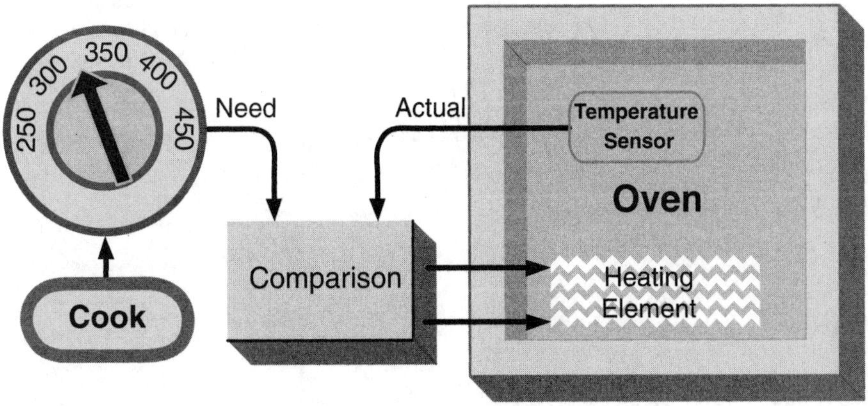

Figure 2.4 *Oven.*

In a steel mill or a tape manufacturing plant, there are many variables to control: speed, pressure, heat, thickness. The formula for making tape or steel includes a setpoint for each variable. Operators or computers dial in the setpoint, and then a feedback loop provides the control for each variable. It is rare to find control without feedback, because feedback gives much better control and predictability than attempting to control complicated processes with predefined algorithms.

Software Development Feedback Loops

There are many unforeseeable events in developing software, so why would anyone think that software systems should be developed without feedback loops? In 1970, Winston Royce proposed a sequential software design process that closely resembled the sequential product development processes of the time. He advocated creating detailed documentation at each step but also pointed out that waiting until the end to test the system was not practical, because the feedback provided by testing was needed early in the development process. Therefore, he suggested that an early prototype be built to provide feedback.[11] See Figure 2.5.

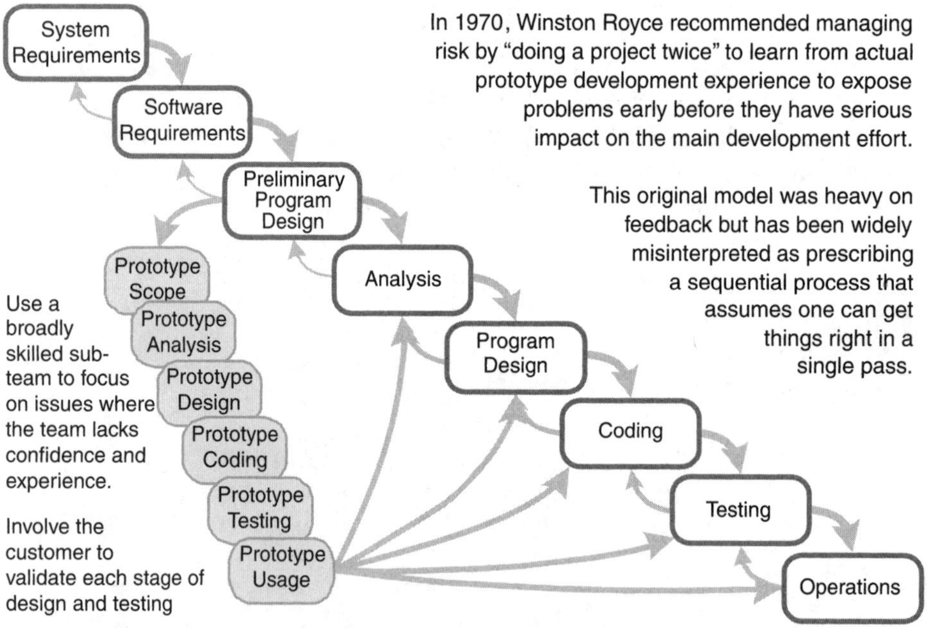

Figure 2.5 *Original Royce "waterfall" recommendation.*

11. See Royce, "Managing the Development of Large Software Systems," Figure 7.

In 1975, Fred Brooks wrote, "Plan to throw one away; you will anyhow."[12] Brooks retracted this in 1995, saying, "Don't build one to throw away—the waterfall model is wrong."[13] He notes that his original quote implicitly assumed a sequential development process, while it has become clear that an incremental model with progressive refinement is the proper approach.[14]

As actually implemented, the sequential, or waterfall, development model does not usually provide for much feedback; it is generally thought of as a single-pass model. This can be called a deterministic model because it assumes that the details of a project are determined at the beginning. A deterministic model is favored by project management disciplines that have their origins in contract administration. The contract-inspired model of project management generally favors a sequential development process with specifications fixed at the start of the project, customer sign-off on the specifications, and a change authorization process intended to minimize changes. There is a perception that these processes give greater control and predictability, although sequential development processes with low feedback have a dismal record in this regard.[15]

Traditional project management approaches often consider feedback loops to be threatening because there is concern that the learning involved in feedback might modify the predetermined plan. The conventional wisdom in project management values managing scope, cost, and schedule to the original plan. Sometimes this is done at the expense of receiving and acting on feedback that might change the plan; sometimes it is done at the expense of achieving the overall business goal. This mental model is so entrenched in project management thinking that its underlying assumptions are rarely questioned. This might explain why the waterfall model of software development is so difficult to abandon.

Imagine Deterministic Cruise Control

You are driving along the highway. You get up to the speed you want to go, turn on the cruise control, and push *set*. The car has a control loop, which operates every few seconds, checking the actual speed of the car against the speed you set (the *setpoint*). If the car speed is less than the setpoint, the cruise control de-

12. Brooks, *The Mythical Man Month.*

13. Ibid., 264.

14. Ibid., 267.

15. Johnson, "ROI, It's Your Job."

presses the accelerator a bit. If the speed is higher than the setpoint, the cruise control lets up on the accelerator.

Imagine driving a car in which the position of the accelerator was preprogrammed at the factory. If you want to go 60 mph, it moves the accelerator to position A; if you want to go 65 mph, it moves the accelerator to position B, and so on. This might work on flat terrain, but when it got to a steep hill, the car would slow to a crawl. Upon reaching the top, the car would careen dangerously fast down the other side.

Deterministic control simply does not work when there is variability in the terrain.

When an organization has software development challenges, there is a tendency to impose a more disciplined process on the organization. The prevailing concept of a more disciplined software process is one with more rigorous sequential processing: Requirements are documented more completely, all agreements with the customer are written, changes are controlled more carefully, and each requirement must be traced to code. This amounts to imposing additional deterministic controls on a dynamic environment, lengthening the feedback loop. Just as control theory predicts, this generally makes a bad situation worse.

In most cases, increasing feedback, not decreasing it, is the single most effective way to deal with troubled software development projects and environments.

- Instead of letting defects accumulate, run tests as soon as the code is written.
- Instead of adding more documentation or detailed planning, try checking out ideas by writing code.
- Instead of gathering more requirements from users, show them an assortment of potential user screens and get their input.
- Instead of studying more carefully which tool to use, bring the top three candidates inhouse and test them.
- Instead of trying to figure out how to convert an entire system in a single massive effort, create a Web front end to the legacy system and try the new idea out.

Whenever people do work, they should be doing it for an *immediate customer*; that is, someone, somewhere, should be eager to make use of the results of their work. Developers should know their immediate customers and have ways for those customers to provide regular feedback. When a problem develops, the first thing to do is to make sure the feedback loops are all in place; that is, make sure everyone knows who his or her immediate customer is. The next thing to do is to increase the frequency of the feedback loops in the problem areas.

The True Story of a Death March Project, Part 3: Amplifying Feedback

When I took over the project, it was stuck. The design was supposed to be done, but there were no designers on the team. No one could agree on what constituted an appropriate design format. The analysts did not know what to do, and the programmers did not find the existing documents detailed enough to work from. Wheels were spinning, but nothing was happening.

I was new, so I could change things. I asked the analysts to choose a small part of the system and take a day to write use cases, then sit down with the developers and see if the use cases were useful. Working together, the analysts and developers were to discover the level of detail needed in a use case that was possible for the analysts to provide and sufficient for programming to proceed. Then, the developers were to write code for the small part of the system and have analysts test it to see if it was what they had in mind.

After two weeks, the log jam was broken and code started flowing. The analysts developed a style of writing use cases that the developers found useful, and the developers started holding regular meetings with the analysts so they could ask questions that were not covered in the use cases. It was a start.

—*Mary*

TOOL 4: ITERATIONS

If a manufacturer wants to start applying lean production principles, there is one starting point that always works—use just-in-time inventory flow. The simple act of working to fill customer orders rather than working to meet a schedule drives a host of other improvements. One reason just-in-time flow is so effective is that it requires significantly improved worker-to-worker communication and surfaces quality problems as soon as they occur.

In concurrent product development, which we discuss in Chapter 3, "Decide as Late as Possible," there is an equivalent universal starting point that always works—drive the effort with prototypes at closely placed milestones. A prototype synchronizes efforts toward a well-understood short-term goal without the need for detailed scheduling. Regular prototype milestones make concurrent product development possible because they provide a focal point around which crossfunctional communication can and must occur. Prototypes also provide early feedback on design problems and customer preferences.

There is an equivalent universal starting point for all agile software development approaches: iterations. An iteration is a useful increment of software that is designed, programmed, tested, integrated, and delivered during a short, fixed timeframe. It is very similar to a prototype in product development except that an iteration produces a working portion of the final product. This software will be improved in future iterations, but it is working, tested, integrated code from the beginning. Iterations provide a dramatic increase in feedback over sequential software development, thus providing much broader communication between customers/users and developers, and among various people who have an interest in the system. Testers are involved from the first iteration; hardware and software environments are considered early. Design problems are exposed early, and as changes occur, change-tolerance is built into the system.

There are three fundamental principles at work here. First, as we will see in Chapter 4, "Queuing Theory," small batches moving rapidly through a system lead to all manner of good things. Small batches enforce quality and worker-level communication while allowing for greater resource utilization. They provide short feedback loops, which enhances control. For this reason, short, complete iterations are as fundamental to lean development as small batches are to lean manufacturing.

Second, short iterations are an options-based approach to software development. They allow the system to respond to facts rather than forecasts. There are few endeavors in which it is more important to keep options open than in software development. In Chapter 3, "Decide as Late as Possible," we see that options-based approaches are fundamentally risk-reduction strategies, and as counterintuitive as it may sound, you actually reduce your risk by keeping options open rather than freezing design early.[16]

Finally, iterations are points of synchronization across individual and multiple teams and with the customer. Iterations are the points when feature sets are completed and the system is brought as close as possible to a releasable or shippable state—even if it will not actually be released. Thus, iterations force decisions to be made. Frequent points of synchronization allow teams to work independently yet never stray far from the work of other teams or the interests of customers and users.

---

16. See Thimbleby, "Delaying Commitment," 78–86.

Iteration Planning[17]

What work should be done in each iteration? The idea is to implement a coherent set of features in each iteration. A feature is something that delivers meaningful business value to the customer but is small enough that the team can confidently estimate the effort required to deliver it. If a feature cannot be done in a single iteration, it should be broken down into smaller features. Features come from customers or customer representatives in the form of use cases, stories, or backlog items.[18]

At the beginning of each iteration, a planning session occurs at which the development team estimates the level of difficulty of the features under consideration and the customers or customer representatives decide which features are most important, given their estimated cost. The highest priority features should be developed first in order to deliver the highest business value first. High-risk items should be addressed earlier rather than later.

An iteration should have a fixed time-box. Some people suggest keeping all iterations to the same length to establish a rhythm. Others vary the iteration length based on local circumstances. How long should the iteration time-box be? It should be long enough to support a meaningful design-build-test cycle and short enough to provide frequent feedback from customers that the system is on track. Some people feel a one-month time-box is ideal. Others suggest time-boxes of a couple of weeks. Some companies use 6-week to 10-week time-boxes, but these are coupled with daily builds and extensive weekly testing.

The development team must be free to accept only the amount of work for an iteration that team members believe they can complete within the time-box. Customers will probably want to load iterations with lots of features, but it is important to resist the temptation to be accommodating at the expense of setting unreasonable expectations. If iterations are short and delivery is reliable, customers should be content to wait for the next iteration. If a development team overcommits—which often happens to inexperienced teams—it is best to deliver some of the features on time rather than all of them late.

---

17. See Schwaber and Beedle, *Agile Software Development with Scrum*, 47–50, for a discussion of planning a sprint in Scrum. In Beck, *Extreme Programming Explained*, chapters 17 and 18 discuss iteration planning in extreme programming.

18. The best reference on use cases is Cockburn, *Writing Effective Use Cases*. Stories are used in extreme programming. See Beck, *Extreme Programming Explained*. A backlog list is used in Scrum. See Schwaber and Beedle, *Agile Software Development with Scrum*.

Team Commitment

A project team can evaluate a list of features and, with a little bit of investigation, come up with a good idea of what it can do in a few weeks or a month. If you ask a team to choose items from the top of a list that the members believe they can do in a short time-box, the team will probably choose and commit to a reasonable set of features. Once the team members have committed to a set of features that they think they can complete, they will probably figure out how to get those features done within the time-box.

A team should not be expected to set and meet time-box goals without organizational support.[19]

- The team must be small and staffed with the necessary expertise. Some team members must be experienced in the domain and some in each critical technology.
- The team must have enough information about requested features to be able to decide what is feasible to accomplish in the time-box.
- The team must be assured of getting the resources it needs.
- Team members must have the freedom, support, and skill to figure out how to meet its commitments.
- The team must have or create the basic environment for good programming:
  - Automated build process
  - Automated testing
  - Coding standards
  - Version Control Tool
  - Etc.

Good iteration planning gives customers a way to ask for features that are important to them and creates a motivating environment for the development team. The best part about these benefits is that they feed upon success. As customers see the features they regard as highest priority actually implemented in code, they start to believe the system is going to be real and begin to envision what it can do for them. They become comfortable that features scheduled for future iterations will actually be delivered. At the same time, developers gain a sense of accomplishment, and as customers begin to appreciate their work, they are even more motivated to satisfy the customers.

19. See Schwaber and Beedle, *Agile Software Development with Scrum.*

Convergence

Iterations sound like a good idea, yet there is a significant reluctance to use them. The reason behind this can often be traced to a fear that the software development effort will not converge. There is a concern that the project will continue indefinitely if it does not have a predefined stopping point.[20] This is a valid concern; how can you be sure that any system with a feedback loop will converge on a solution? In fact, books on control theory have more pages on convergence than on any other topic. It is not a concern to be taken lightly.

A fluid business situation might send unpredictable and constantly changing signals to the software development process. It is not unusual for a situation called *thrashing* to develop; that is, the feedback changes so fast that the system doesn't have time to complete one response before being told to go in the opposite direction.

Consider a thermostat. It does not turn on the furnace the moment the room temperature falls below the setpoint, and then turn it off the moment the temperature rises to the setpoint. If this happened, the furnace would cycle on and off constantly, something that is not good for furnaces. Instead, the thermostat turns on heat when the temperature falls a couple of degrees below the setpoint and leaves the furnace on until the temperature is a degree or two above the setpoint.

An iterative software development process achieves this same effect by limiting customer requests for feature changes to the beginning of each iteration. During the iteration, the team concentrates on delivering the features it committed to at the beginning of the iteration. If the iterations are short—2 to 4 weeks—the feedback loop is still quite short.

Delaying response to feedback must be handled with care; long delays in feedback tend to cause system oscillation. Convergence requires small, frequent adjustments. For example, a cruise control adjusts the accelerator only slightly when the car falls below the desired speed. Similarly, if software is delivered in small, frequent increments, the customer can see business value increasing with each increment and make adjustments on a regular basis. Delivering large increments on an infrequent basis is far more likely to produce oscillations than is accepting frequent feedback.

There is an optimal window for feedback—it should be as short as possible without being so short as to create thrashing. The optimal size of this window depends on the dynamics of the situation, but in general, environments that are more dynamic require more rapid feedback. Some have found that larger teams do better with more frequent feedback, because if a large team gets off track, it is more difficult to reverse direction.

20. Highsmith, *Adaptive Software Development*, 87.

Negotiable Scope

A good strategy for achieving convergence is to work on top priority items first, leaving the low priority items to fall off the to-do list. By delivering high priority features first, it is likely that you will deliver most of the business value long before the customer's wish list is completed. Here comes the tricky part. If you are working under the expectation that development is not complete until a fixed, detailed scope is achieved, then the system may indeed not converge. It is therefore best to avoid this expectation, either by stating at the front that scope is negotiable or by defining scope at a high level so it is negotiable in detail. With negotiable scope, iterative development will generally converge.

Why should a customer accept the idea of negotiable scope? In the introduction to this book, we told the story of how Florida and Minnesota each set out to develop a SACWIS (Statewide Automated Child Welfare Information System). The systems are quite similar, but the Florida system will take about 15 years and cost about $230 million, while the Minnesota system was completed in 2 years at the cost of $1.1 million. This vast difference in time and cost for developing essentially the same system is credited to two factors: Minnesota used a standardized infrastructure and minimized requirements. [21]

A Standish Group study found that 45 percent of features in a typical system are never used and 19 percent are rarely used.[22] Since customers often don't know exactly what they want at the beginning of a project, they tend to ask for everything they think they might need, especially if they think they will get only one shot at it. This is one of the best ways we know to increase the scope of a project well beyond what is necessary to accomplish the project's overall mission.

If you let customers ask for only their highest priority features, deliver them quickly, then ask for the next highest priority, you are more likely to get short lists of what is important. Moreover, you can respond to their changing circumstances. Therefore, it is usually a good idea to work down a prioritized feature list from the top. In general, this strategy will accomplish the overall mission by the time the allocated resources are up.

This approach to project management may seem to lead to unpredictable results, but quite the opposite is true. Once a track record of delivering working software is established, it is easy to project how much work will be done in each iteration as the project proceeds. By tracking the team *velocity,* you can forecast from past work how much work will probably be done in the future. Velocity measurements are signifi-

---

21. Johnson, "ROI, It's Your Job."

22. Ibid.

cantly more accurate tools than scope-based controls because they measure how much time it actually took to deliver complete, tested, releasable code at the end of each iteration. You know exactly where things stand after only a few iterations, which provides highly reliable early predictions of project performance.

It is a good idea to make progress visible to both the development team and the customer. One way to do this is with burn-down charts.[23] Let's assume that you develop a high-level list of features to be delivered and make a preliminary estimate of the development time of each feature. You add all the estimated times and get a time-to-complete number, say 500 staff days. Assume for simplicity that your iterations are one month long. After the first iteration, the customer may have added more items, and the team will have completed some items. You add up the time to complete and notice that it is actually larger than the month before, say 620 staff days. After 4 months, your graph might look like the left-hand burn-down chart in Figure 2.6, which shows that the system is not converging very quickly.

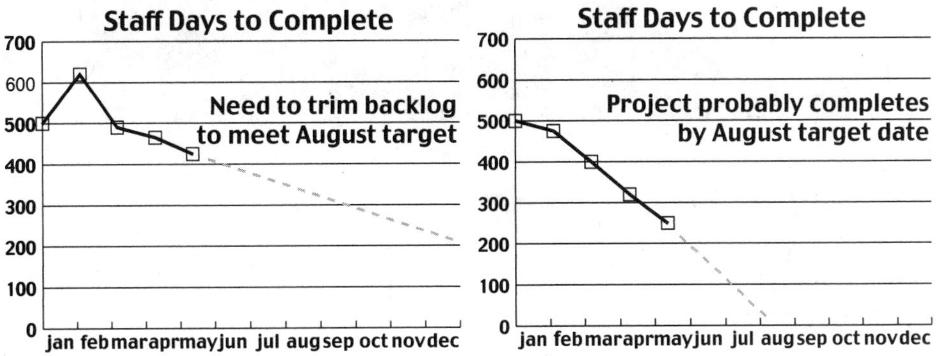

Figure 2.6 *Burn-down charts.*

If you expect the system to be done in 9 months, you should be seeing convergence more like that in the right-hand burn-down chart in Figure 2.6. Since that is not what is happening, you know after a couple of months that action is necessary. If the customer is adding new features as fast as the team is completing others, it is time to consider deleting features from the list. If the team is bogging down, it is time to get them help. In any case, this kind of burn-down chart gives actionable data to all parties so that convergence—or lack thereof—is visible early in the project.

23. More detail on using burn-down charts can be found in Schwaber and Beedle, *Agile Software Development with Scrum*, 63–68.

Another chart commonly used to show convergence in agile software development is a chart showing the rate at which acceptance tests—and thus features—are being added to the system and the rate at which these tests have passed. For an example, see Figure 2.7.[24]

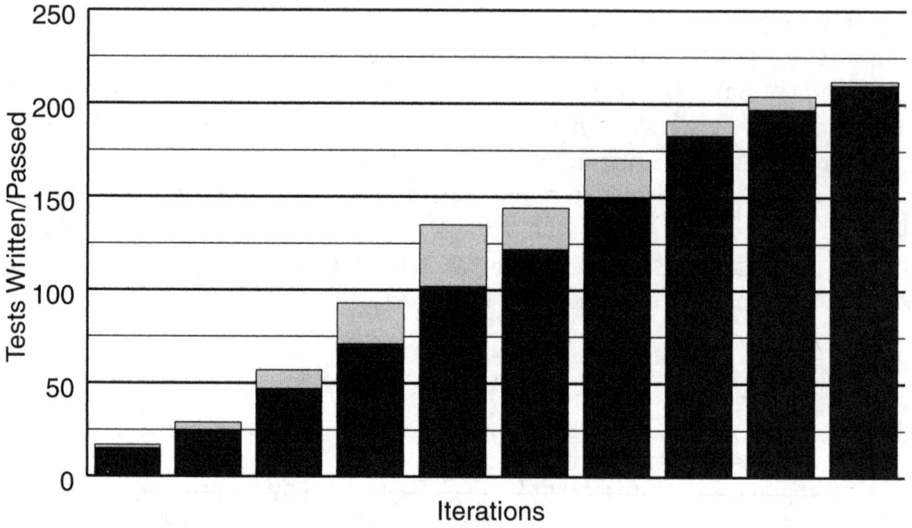

Figure 2.7 *Acceptance tests written and passed.*

TOOL 5: SYNCHRONIZATION

Iterations are planned by selecting features that are important to customers, and if multiple teams are involved, they generally divide the work by feature. One of the problems with a feature-based approach to software development is that a feature will most likely involve several different areas of the code. Traditionally, the integrity of a module was ensured by having only one developer, who understood it clearly, assigned to work on it. Most agile approaches recommend common ownership of code, although Feature-Driven Development (FDD) maintains individual ownership of modules, or classes.[25] Since individual features require several different classes to be modified, FDD forms feature teams consisting of the relevant class owners.

Whenever several individuals are working on the same thing, a need for synchronization occurs. So in FDD, synchronizing the several people working on a feature is

24. See Jeffries, Anderson and Hendrickson, *Extreme Programming Installed*, 139.

25. Palmer and Felsing, *A Practical Guide to Feature-Driven Development*, 42–44.

necessary, while common code ownership requires that several people working on the same piece of code must be synchronized. The need for synchronization is fundamental to any complex development process.

The same problem occurs in automobile design. A slight change in hood slope for better aerodynamics might have an impact on the shape of the front fenders or the layout of components under the hood. When things get complicated in automotive design, there is no substitute for building a mock-up to see how things actually fit together. Toyota builds far more prototypes than most other automakers because they are such an effective way to rapidly synchronize the efforts of many people.

Synch and Stabilize[26]

In a software development environment with collective code ownership, the idea is to build the system every day, after a very small batch of work has been done by each of the developers. In the morning, developers check out source code from a configuration management system, make changes, test their changes in a "private build," check to see if anyone else has made change to the same code, and if so, check for conflicts, then check in the new code. At the end of the day, a build takes place, followed by a set of automated tests. If the build works and the tests pass, the developers have been synchronized. This technique is often called the *daily build and smoke test.*

There are many variations on this theme: A build might occur every few days, or it might run every time new code is checked in. More frequent builds are better; they provide much more rapid feedback. Builds and build tests should be automated. If they are not, the build process itself will introduce errors, and the amount of manual work will prohibit sufficiently frequent builds.

Sometimes the build is of the whole system; sometimes only subsets of the system are built, because the whole system is too large. Sometimes an entire suite of tests is run, and sometimes, especially when tests are manual, only some tests are run. The general principle is that if builds and test suites take too long, they will not be used, so invest in making them fast. This provides a bias toward more frequent builds with less comprehensive tests, but it is still important to run all the tests overnight or every weekend.

A standard approach to keeping automated tests reasonable in size is to stub-out or simulate slow layers to keep up the speed. For example, you probably want to stub-out database access and the user interface. If you are designing software to control a device, you will want to simulate the hardware performance as you develop the system. The *span* of a build and test operation is an important development decision.

26. See Cusumano, "How Microsoft Makes Large Teams Work Like Small Teams."

If the entire system is not spanned in the daily build and smoke test, full system tests should be run as frequently as possible. Remember the rule of small batches: If you integrate changes in small batches, it will be infinitely easier to detect and fix problems. Keep it simple by doing it as often as possible. The goal should be to have workable code at the end of every day.

Spanning Application[27]

Another way to synchronize the work of several teams is to start by having a small advance team develop a simple spanning application through the system. For example, suppose you are converting an insurance system to a new environment. You might begin by choosing a simple policy type, preferably one with low volume. The advance team develops a spanning application for that type of policy all the way through the system. This includes establishing a new policy, renewing the policy, handling a claim, and terminating the policy. If possible, the spanning application should go into production when it's done.

Once the spanning application is developed, you have in effect driven a nail through the system, sort of like a carpenter positioning a piece of wood. When the spanning application is proven in production, you know you have a workable approach. At this point, multiple teams can use the same approach and drive in many nails at the same time.

A spanning application works well to test various commercial components. Say you have three possible vendors for middleware, and you are not quite sure which one will really work in your environment. By having a small team build a simple spanning application, you can get a real understanding of the strengths and weaknesses of each possibility before you commit to any single solution.

Matrix

A more traditional approach to synchronizing multiple teams is to sketch out an overall architecture and then have teams develop separate components or subsystems. This approach is particularly appropriate when the different teams are not located in the same place, because it allows them to go about their work with a mini-

27. There are several different names used for a spanning application. The description here is modeled after the *thread* described in Simons, "Big and Agile?" Hunt and Thomas, *The Pragmatic Programmer*, 48–52, call the same concept a *tracer bullet*. Cockburn uses the term *walking skeleton*, and Hohmann, in *Beyond Software Architecture*, calls it a *spike*. In Jeffries, Anderson and Hendrickson, *Extreme Programming Installed*, a *spike* is an experiment to validate an estimate.

mum of communication with other teams. The problem, of course, comes at the interfaces. When the various teams' components have to work together, high bandwidth communication is usually necessary to resolve the many detailed design issues involved. Moreover, if the teams have already developed their subsystems, they are not going to be eager to change what they have done.

Therefore, the matrix approach starts by developing the interfaces and then the subsystems. All points of cross-team interaction should be laid out at the beginning; teams should be assigned to each of these interaction points. The interface should be developed first, stubbing out the components to allow the cross-component software to be demonstrated. After the interfaces are working, the component teams can work reasonably independently to develop their subsystems, but they should integrate their code into the full system regularly to be sure that the interface continues to work.

This approach was used by Motorola to design a new communication system.[28] Teams from around the world were involved, and each team was responsible for developing the software in a single piece of hardware. Before the teams got started with their subsystem designs, they assembled in a single place to study the overall architecture and define the interactions among the devices. Each link between devices, called a *strata,* was identified, and a team consisting of people from the two device teams in question was assigned to each strata. This is illustrated in Figure 2.8, which shows the strata among devices A, B, C, D, and E.

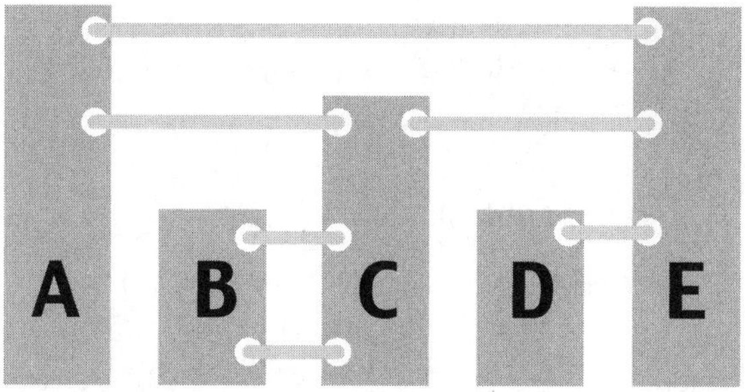

Figure 2.8 *Implement interfaces first.*

Each strata was developed and validated independently, focusing principally on the interactions across devices. They did this by stubbing out the interaction of the strata with the individual devices and focusing on the cross-device communication first. As the various strata reached some level of maturity, they were integrated into

28. See Battin, Crocker, Kreidler, and Subramanian, "Leveraging Resources in Global Software Development." The *cluster* concept in that paper has been renamed *strata*. This is more fully described in Crocker, *Large Scale Agile Software Development*.

the devices. This "internal" integration was the easy part, since each device team was collocated in a particular country, and members were used to working together.

The beauty of this approach is that the highest risk areas likely to cause the biggest delays and create the biggest communications problems were the interteam interactions; these were resolved at the beginning of the project, when there was plenty of time and there was no prior code to change. The easier part, the device integration, was saved for later in the project. This technique provided superior synchronization throughout the project, because a team could integrate into the overall structure regularly, making sure that whatever it did from within did not compromise the overall system.

TOOL 6: SET-BASED DEVELOPMENT

Set-Based Versus Point-Based

Let's say you want to set up a meeting. There are two ways to go about it, you can use a point-based or a set-based approach. Figure 2.9 illustrates the point-based approach: First you choose a meeting time, and then you refine it until it works. Unfortunately, it may take several iterations to find an acceptable meeting time, and the process may never converge. Figure 2.10 illustrates the set-based approach: You start by defining everyone's constraints and then select a meeting time that fits within those constraints. This approach involves considerably less communication, yet it quickly converges on an acceptable meeting time.

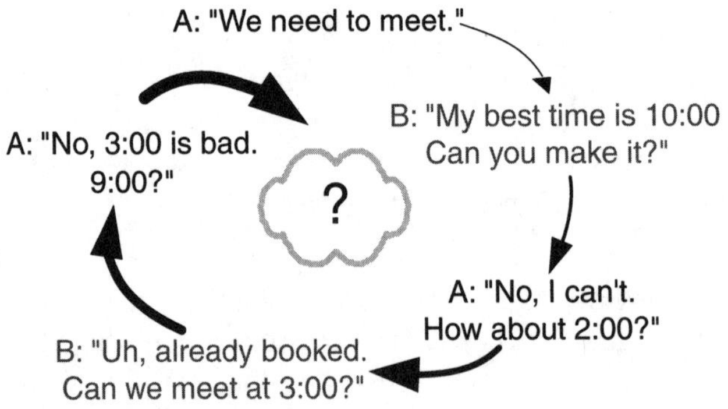

Figure 2.9 *Point-based scheduling.*[29]

29. Diagram adapted from Durward Sobek. Used with permission.

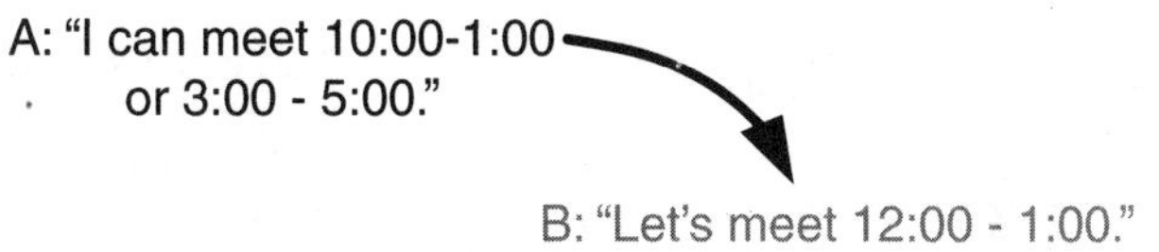

Figure 2.10 *Set-based scheduling.*[30]

In set-based development, communication is about constraints, not choices. This turns out to be a very powerful form of communication, requiring significantly less data to convey far more information. In addition, talking about constraints instead of choices defers making choices until they have to be made, that is, until the *last responsible moment,* which we discuss in Chapter 3.

Let's consider how constraint-based communication can speed up large-scale product development. Durward Sobek studied Toyota and Chrysler product development approaches for his 1997 dissertation at the University of Michigan.[31] He found that a primary engineering discipline at Toyota is to maintain and refer to *checklists,* which record known tradeoffs and constraints.

For example, a styling engineer might want a rear fender section with a dramatic new look. However, the manufacturing engineer might suspect that the new design is going to be difficult to manufacture. Instead of expressing a vague doubt, the manufacturing engineer would send the styling engineer a checklist showing the time it takes to stamp body panels with certain characteristics and detailing the limits of those characteristics. The checklist isn't necessarily a list; it is often a graph of the boundary conditions, similar to Figure 2.11. The styling engineer would examine the checklist along with many similar checklists and come up with two or three designs that take all of the constraints into consideration.

---

30. Ibid. Used with permission.

31. Sobek, *Principles That Shape Product Development Systems: A Toyota-Chrysler Comparison*.

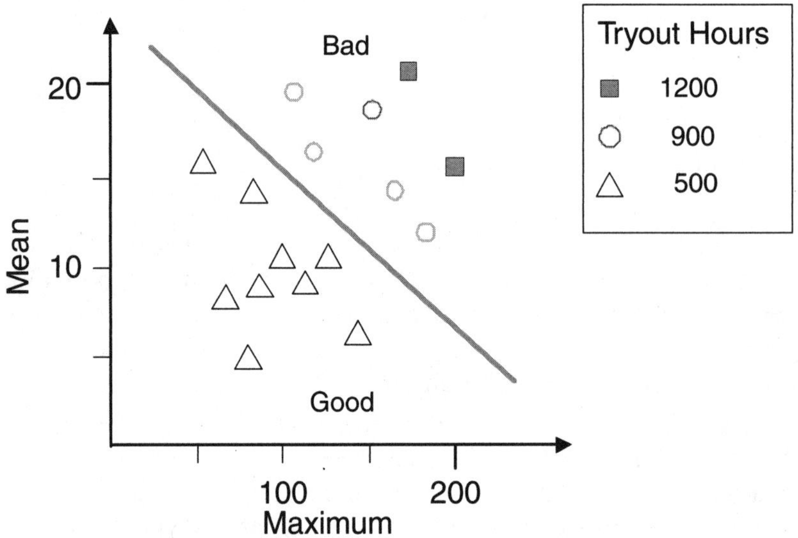

Figure 2.11 *Checklist: Rear quarter panel cross-section deformity ratio.*[32]

If you were a manufacturing engineer at Chrysler, it is more likely that the styling engineers would send you one or two possible styles and ask for comments. You would respond that you think the panel is going to be difficult to manufacture. At the same time, many other engineers would have problems with the proposed style, so meetings would be called to resolve the issues. However, once you get a style you think you can manufacture, perhaps the design of the gas cap will be difficult, or maybe there is not enough room left for all of the targeted wheel sizes. More meetings are needed to iron out these problems, which will no doubt lead to more problems. A never-ending game ensues, reminiscent of point-based meeting scheduling.

Figures 2.12 and 2.13 show how the two approaches work.

32. Diagram from Durward Sobek. Used with permission.

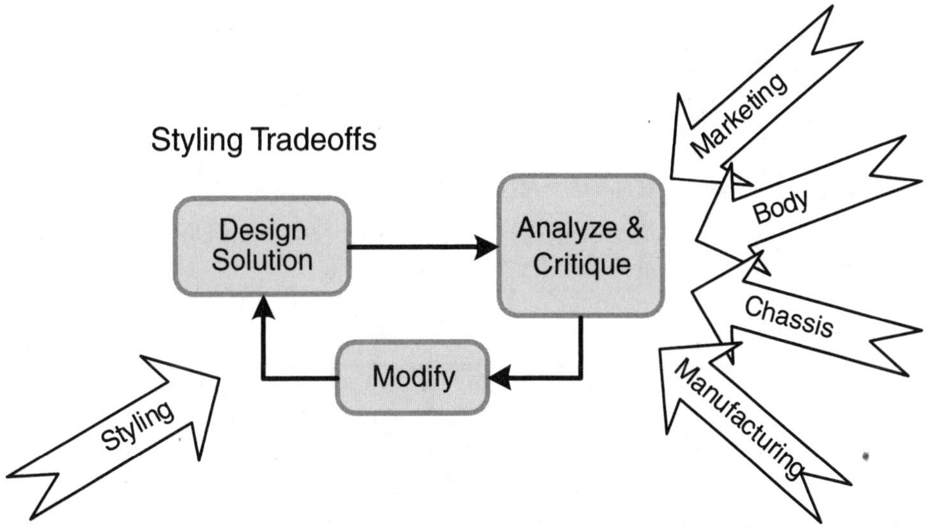

Figure 2.12 *Point-based development.*[33]

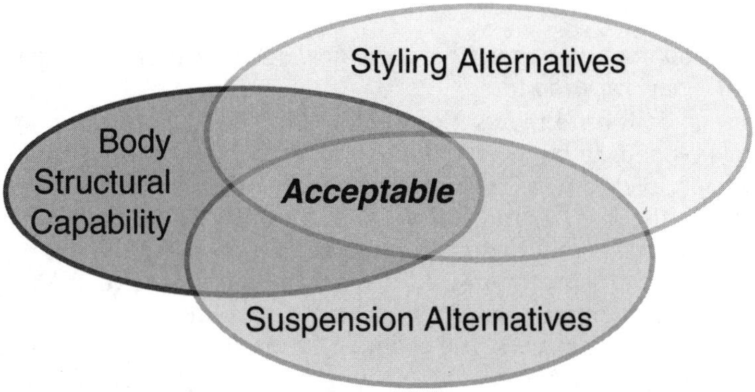

Figure 2.13 *Set-based development.*[34]

Toyota explores a large number of concepts at the beginning of a vehicle program, expending significantly more resources than other automakers. It maintains a large number of options throughout the development process and produces an extraordinary number of prototypes of subsystems and clay models of vehicles. Final

33. Ibid. Used with permission.

34. Ibid. Used with permission.

body dimensions are fixed far later in the development process than is common among other automakers, and final specifications are released to suppliers very late in the development process. The quality, popularity, and profitability of the cars it produces indicate that Toyota's development process is highly effective.[35]

Set-Based Software Development

So how do you apply set-based development to software? You develop multiple options, communicate constraints, and let solutions emerge.

Develop Multiple Options

When you have a difficult problem, try this: Develop a set of alternative solutions to a problem, see how well they actually work, and then merge the best features of the solutions or choose one of the alternatives. It might seem wasteful to develop multiple solutions to the same problem, but set-based development can lead to better solutions faster, as the examples in the sidebars illustrate.

Set-Based Embedded Software Development

A software development manager from a medical device company described to us how he runs a new program:

The first thing I do is have the user champion describe to a group of developers what problem needs to be solved. Now, I don't think anyone can put into words what they really want, so I set a team to working on maybe a half dozen possibilities. This is the first iteration, and it lasts a month. Then I have the developers show the champion their work, and we can narrow down what is really needed to a couple of the prototypes. At this point, I reduce the team size and have some developers continue developing the most promising options for the next iteration. Based on this work, the champion can usually let the developers know exactly what is needed, and by that time, the work is better than half done. The champion is always happy, and we get results very fast.

35. Ward, Liker, Cristaino, and Sobek, "The Second Toyota Paradox: How Delaying Decisions Can Make Better Cars Faster."

Set-Based Technology Selection

A friend from a company that does enterprise applications told us how he made a critical decision:

We had to choose a technical platform for a system. However, it was not clear which of the three available options was going to be the winner, let alone meet our needs. So we started developing on all three. This required the underlying development to be a bit more general than otherwise, but it turned out to be quite robust because of that. It was really not necessary to decide on a platform until quite near to the end of the project, and by that time, the correct choice was pretty obvious, but it was not the one we would have made in the beginning.

Set-Based Web Site Design

A colleague from a company that does Web designs for many customers told us how she answers difficult usability questions:

When we can't agree on how to structure the Web site, what we do is create two or three versions, with different paths and page layouts. We then do usability testing with several target users. It turns out that there is never one design that stands out above the others. Instead, we find that some features from each design are good, and some are rather poor. We put together the best features of all the options and retest. Invariably we get a far better usability score with the combination. We're thinking that we should design all of our sites this way.

Set-based development does not replace iterative development—it adds a new dimension. During early iterations, multiple choices are developed for key features; in later iterations, they are merged or narrowed to a single choice.

Communicate Constraints

Set-based development means that you communicate constraints, not solutions. On the surface, this might seem to be the opposite of using an iterative approach. Since you are supposed to produce working, deployable code with each iteration, an iteration might seem like a point-based solution, the opposite of set-based development.

Thinking of an iteration as a point-based solution is a misinterpretation of iterative development. In an iteration, you implement only the minimum amount of functionality necessary to demonstrate the core concepts of that iteration. For example, you do not start with an entire database design in the first iteration; you use a simple persistence layer to deal with the current subset of features. The design will evolve, and in that sense, the early iteration is a prototype of a piece of the overall design.

In Chapter 6 we discuss refactoring, that is, restructuring the code as the design evolves. Aggressive refactoring is the key to making sure that iterative development converges on a solution. When an iteration implements "frozen" code that is not available for refactoring, then it is a point-based solution and can lead to the same circular iterations we saw in point-based meeting scheduling. When an iteration implements a design that is available for refactoring, then the design is an instance of a range of options that can be refined later in development, similar to a prototype in set-based development.

An iteration should be considered a demonstration of a possible solution; it should not be considered the only solution. Early iterations should leave wide latitude for implementing the rest of the system in many possible ways. As iterations progress and more choices are made, the design space should be gradually narrowed.

Let the Solution Emerge

Communicating constraints is very useful when tackling a particularly difficult problem, because it helps assure that the solution is worked out by all concerned. As the group grapples with the problem, resist the temptation to jump to a solution; keep the constraints of the problem visible so that the team can discover the intersection of the design space that will work for all concerned.

The True Story of a Death March Project, Part 4: A Solution Emerges

The team had a disagreement on how to translate the data from the old database to the new database. It was necessary to use a new database key, but when customers sent in changes for legacy data, the new key would not be available to the data entry clerk. There was a raging debate between the people who understood the legacy database structure, those designing the new database, the people designing the new GUI, and the managers of the data entry clerks.

I had all of the interested parties list the range of options (as opposed to their preferred solution) that could work in their area. We had a series of meetings in which each group presented their constraints rather than their solutions. At each meeting, we tossed out any ideas that were completely unworkable, and then allowed a couple of days for each group to reevaluate their options. At first, the options expanded rather than contracted, because each group found that ideas from other groups expanded their idea of what might work. Every few days, the groups met again and repeated the process.

The solution that emerged was novel and very well thought out. It wasn't something that anyone would have thought of at the beginning, but it was probably about the only thing that would have worked. Once everyone agreed on the approach at a fine level of detail, the development team mounted a massive effort to implement it quickly. Despite the many changes involved, this was one area of the code that worked from the first day it was released.

—Mary

TRY THIS

1. Take your most difficult problem and devise a way to increase feedback.
   a. Increase the feedback of development teams to management by asking each team at the end of each iteration the following questions:
      i. Was the team properly staffed for this iteration?
      ii. Were there any needed resources that were not forthcoming?
      iii. How can things be changed to make things go better and faster?
      iv. What is getting in the way?
   b. Increase the feedback of customers to development teams by holding a customer focus group at the end of each iteration. Ask questions such as the following:
      i. How well does this section solve the problem it was meant to solve?
      ii. How could it be improved?
      iii. How does this iteration affect your view of what you need?
      iv. What do you need to put this part of the system into production?
   c. Increase the feedback of the product to the development team in the following ways:
      i. Have developers write and run developer tests as they write the code.
      ii. Have analysts, customers, or testers write and run customer tests as the developers work on the code. Have developers help with the customer tests if that's what it takes to get them automated.
      iii. Have developers observe usability tests of each feature as it nears completion, so they can see how users react to their implementation.
   d. Increase the feedback within the team in the following ways:
      i. Make testers an integral part of the development team.
      ii. Involve operations people at the beginning of the project.
      iii. Establish the policy that the development team maintains the product.
2. Start iterations with a negotiation session between customers and developers. Customers should indicate which features are the highest priority, and develop-

ers should select and commit to only those features from the top of the priority list which they can realistically expect to complete in the iteration time-box.

3. Post a progress chart for your current project in a common area so the team can see what needs to be done and everyone can see how the project is converging.
4. If you divide a system across multiple teams, make every effort to have a divisible architecture that allows teams to work on their own areas as independently as possible. Find ways for multiple teams to synchronize as often as possible by integrating their code and running automated tests.
5. If strata teams work for machine interfaces, consider them for user interfaces also. If you have several teams working on different components of a system, consider forming strata teams focused on user interfaces that cross components.
6. Find your toughest outstanding development problem and have the development team come up with three options on how to solve it. Instead of choosing one of the solutions, have the team explore all three options at the same time.

Chapter 3

Decide as Late as Possible

CONCURRENT DEVELOPMENT[1]

When sheet metal is formed into a car body, a massive stamping machine presses the metal into shape. The stamping machine has a huge metal die, which makes contact with the sheet metal and presses it into the shape of a fender, door, or another body panel. Designing and cutting the dies to the proper shape accounts for half of the capital investment of a new car development program and drives the critical path. If a mistake ruins a die, the entire development program suffers a huge setback. If there is one thing that automakers want to do right, it is the die design and cutting.

The problem is, as the car development progresses, engineers keep making changes to the car, and these find their way to the die design. No matter how hard the engineers try to freeze the design, they are not able to do so. In Detroit in the 1980s the cost of changes to the design was 30 to 50 percent of the total die cost, while in Japan it was 10 to 20 percent. These numbers seem to indicate the Japanese companies must have been much better at preventing change after the die specs were released to the tool and die shop. But such was not the case.

The U.S. strategy for making a die was to wait until the design specs were frozen, and then send the final design to the tool and die maker, which triggered the process of ordering the block of steel and cutting it. Any changes went through an arduous change approval process. It took about two years from ordering the steel to the time the die would be used in production. In Japan, however, the tool and die makers order

1. Information drawn from Womack, Jones and Roos, *The Machine That Changed the World*, 116–119, and Clark and Fujimoto, *Product Development Performance*, 187, 236–237.

up the steel blocks and start rough cutting at the same time the car design is starting. This is called concurrent development. How can it possibly work?

The die engineers in Japan are expected to know a lot about what a die for a front door panel will involve, and they are in constant communication with the body engineer.[2] They anticipate the final solution, and they are also skilled in techniques to make minor changes late in development, such as leaving more material where changes are likely. Most of the time die engineers are able to accommodate the engineering design as it evolves. In the rare case of a mistake, a new die can be cut much faster because the whole process is streamlined.

Japanese automakers do not freeze design points until late in the development process, allowing most changes to occur while the window for change is still open. When compared to the early design freeze practices in the United States in the 1980s, Japanese die makers spent perhaps a third as much money on changes and produced better die designs. Japanese dies tended to require fewer stamping cycles per part, creating significant production savings.[3]

The impressive difference in time-to-market and increasing market success of Japanese automakers prompted U.S. automotive companies to adopt concurrent development practices in the 1990s, and today the product development performance gap has narrowed significantly.

Concurrent Software Development

Programming is a lot like die cutting. The stakes are often high, and mistakes can be costly, so sequential development, that is, establishing requirements before development begins, is commonly thought of as a way to protect against serious errors. The problem with sequential development is that it forces designers to take a depth-first rather than a breadth-first approach to design. Depth-first forces making low-level dependent decisions before experiencing the consequences of the high-level decisions. The most costly mistakes are made by forgetting to consider something important at the beginning. The easiest way to make such a big mistake is to drill down to detail too fast. Once you set down the detailed path, you can't back up and are un-

2. The close collaboration between Japanese die engineer and designer occurs even though the die engineer is an external supplier. Changes are anticipated in the contract and are done on a worker-to-worker basis without the delay of a change approval process. We discuss contracts that allow for such close collaboration in Chapter 7, "See the Whole."

3. Typical Japanese stamping in 1990 took five shots per panel, compared to seven in the United States (Clark and Fujimoto, *Product Development Performance*, 186).

likely to realize that you should. When big mistakes may be made, it is best to survey the landscape and delay the detailed decisions.

Concurrent development of software usually takes the form of iterative development. It is the preferred approach when the stakes are high and the understanding of the problem is evolving. Concurrent development allows you to take a breadth-first approach and discover those big, costly problems before it's too late. Moving from sequential development to concurrent development means you start programming the highest value features as soon as a high-level conceptual design is determined, even while detailed requirements are being investigated. This may sound counterintuitive, but think of it as an exploratory approach that permits you to learn by trying a variety of options before you lock in on a direction that constrains implementation of less important features.

In addition to providing insurance against costly mistakes, concurrent development is the best way to deal with changing requirements, because not only are the big decisions deferred while you consider all the options, but the little decisions are deferred as well. When change is inevitable, concurrent development reduces delivery time and overall cost while improving the performance of the final product.

If this sounds like magic—or hacking—it would be if nothing else changed. Just starting programming earlier, without the associated expertise and collaboration found in Japanese die cutting, is unlikely to lead to improved results. There are some critical skills that must be in place in order for concurrent development to work.

Under sequential development, U.S. automakers considered die engineers to be quite remote from the automotive engineers, and so too, programmers in a sequential development process often have little contact with the customers and users who have requirements and the analysts who collect requirements. Concurrent development in die cutting required U.S. automakers to make two critical changes—the die engineer needed the expertise to anticipate what the emerging design would need in the cut steel and had to collaborate closely with the body engineer.

Similarly, concurrent software development requires developers with enough expertise in the domain to anticipate where the emerging design is likely to lead and close collaboration with the customers and analysts who are designing how the system will solve the business problem at hand.

Cost Escalation

Software is different from most products in that software systems are expected to be upgraded on a regular basis. On the average, more than half of the development work that occurs in a software system occurs after it is first sold or placed into production.[4] In addition to internal changes, software systems are subject to a changing environment—a new operating system, a change in the underlying database, a change in the client used by the GUI, a new application using the same database, and so on. Most software is expected to change regularly over its lifetime, and in fact once upgrades are stopped, software is often nearing the end of its useful life. This presents us with a new category of waste: waste caused by software that is difficult to change.

In 1987 Barry Boehm wrote, "Finding and fixing a software problem after delivery costs 100 times more than finding and fixing the problem in early design phases."[5] This observation became the rationale behind thorough upfront requirements analysis and design, even though Boehm himself encouraged incremental development over "single-shot, full product development."[6] In 2001 Boehm noted that for small systems the escalation factor can be more like 5:1 than 100:1; and even on large systems, good architectural practices can significantly reduce the cost of change by confining features that are likely to change to small, well-encapsulated areas.[7]

There used to be a similar, but more dramatic, cost escalation factor for product development. It was once estimated that a change after production began could cost 1,000 times more than if the change had been made in the original design.[8] The belief that the cost of change escalates as development proceeds contributed greatly to standardizing the sequential development process in the United States. No one seemed to recognize that the sequential process could actually be the ***cause*** of the high escalation ratio. However, as concurrent development replaced sequential development in the United States in the 1990s, the cost escalation discussion was forever altered. It was no longer how much a change might cost later in development; the discussion centered on how to reduce the need for change through concurrent engineering.

Not all change is equal. There are a few basic architectural decisions that you need to get right at the beginning of development, because they fix the constraints of the system for its life. Examples of these may be choice of language, architectural layering decisions, or the choice to interact with an existing database also used by other applications. These kinds of decisions might have the 100:1 cost escalation ratio. Because these decisions are so crucial, you should focus on minimizing the number of

4. The percentage of software lifecycle cost attributed to maintenance ranges between 40 and 90 percent. See Kajko-Mattsson et al., "Taxonomy of Problem Management Activities."

5. Boehm, "Industrial Software Metrics Top 10 List."

6. Boehm and Papaccio, "Understanding and Controlling Software Costs," 1465–1466.

7. Boehm and Basili, "Software Defect Reduction List."

8. Concurrent engineering has been credited with reducing product development time by 30 to 70 percent, engineering changes by 65 to 90 percent, and time to market by 20 to 90 percent, while improving quality by 200 to 600 percent and productivity by 20 to 110 percent (Thomas Group, 1990).

these high-stakes constraints. You also want to take a breadth-first approach to these high-stakes decisions.

The bulk of the change in a system does not have to have a high-cost escalation factor; it is the sequential approach that causes the cost of most changes to escalate exponentially as you move through development. Sequential development emphasizes getting all the decisions made as early as possible, so the cost of all changes is the same—very high. Concurrent design defers decisions as late as possible. This has four effects:

- Reduces the number of high-stake constraints.
- Gives a breadth-first approach to high-stakes decisions, making it more likely that they will be made correctly.
- Defers the bulk of the decisions, significantly reducing the need for change.
- Dramatically decreases the cost escalation factor for most changes.

A single cost escalation factor or curve is misleading.[9] Instead of a chart showing a single trend for all changes, a more appropriate graph has at least two cost escalation curves, as shown in Figure 3.1. The agile development objective is to move as many changes as possible from the top curve to the bottom curve.

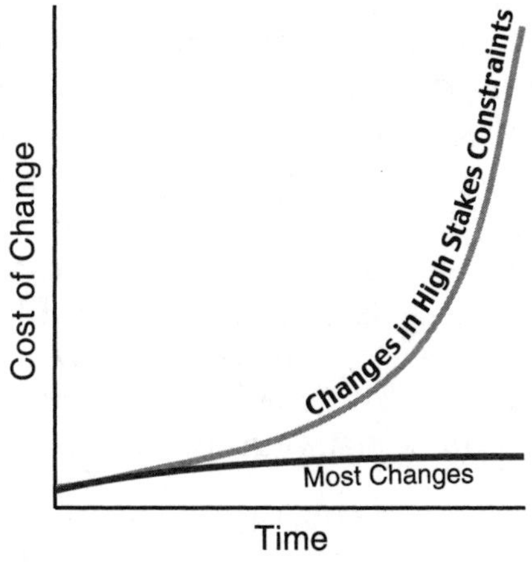

Figure 3.1 *Two cost escalation curves.*

9. The cost escalation number of 100:1 in Boehm and Papaccio, "Understanding and Controlling Software Costs," refers to the cost of fixing or reworking software. In Beck, *Extreme Programming Explained,* the cost escalation curve on page 23 refers to all change, not just fixing or rework.

Returning for a moment to the die cutting example, the die engineer sees the conceptual design of the car and knows roughly the necessary door panel size. With that information, a big enough steel block can be ordered. If the concept of the car changes from a small, sporty car to a mid-size family car, the block of steel may be too small, and that would be a costly mistake. But the die engineer knows that once the overall concept is approved, it won't change, so the steel can be safely ordered long before the details of the door emerge. Concurrent design is a robust design process because the die adapts to whatever design emerges.

Lean software development delays freezing all design decisions as long as possible, because it is easier to change a decision that hasn't been made. Lean software development emphasizes developing a robust, change-tolerant design, one that accepts the inevitability of change and structures the system so that it can be readily adapted to the most likely kinds of changes.

The main reason software changes throughout its lifecycle is that the business process in which it is used evolves over time. Some domains evolve faster than others, and some domains may be essentially stable. It is not possible to build in flexibility to accommodate arbitrary changes cheaply. The idea is to build tolerance for change into the system along domain dimensions that are likely to change. Observing where the changes occur during iterative development gives a good indication of where the system is likely to need flexibility in the future.[10] If changes of certain types are frequent during development, you can expect that these types of changes will not end when the product is released. The secret is to know enough about the domain to maintain flexibility, yet avoid making things any more complex than they must be.

If a system is developed by allowing the design to emerge through iterations, the design will be robust, adapting more readily to the types of changes that occur during development. More importantly, the ability to adapt will be built in to the system so that as more changes occur after its release, they can be readily incorporated. On the other hand, if systems are built with a focus on getting everything right at the beginning in order to reduce the cost of later changes, their design is likely to be brittle and not accept changes readily. Worse, the chance of making a major mistake in the key structural decisions is increased with a depth-first rather than a breadth-first approach.

TOOL 7: OPTIONS THINKING

"Satisfaction Guaranteed or Your Money Back." Sears. Target. L.L. Bean. Land's End. Amazon.com. What store doesn't guarantee satisfaction? On the other hand, it's

10. See the discussion on developing a sense of how to absorb changes in "Tool 8: The Last Responsible Moment" later in this chapter.

somewhat scary to think about offering a satisfaction guarantee for software. Usually, the message is, After you open the shrink wrap—or after you sign off the requirements—it's yours. Software rarely comes with a warranty.

Let's step to the other side of this transaction and consider why *satisfaction guaranteed* warranties are so attractive. The underlying dynamic is that people find it difficult to make irrevocable decisions when there is uncertainty present. For example, if you are buying a gift and aren't certain about the recipient's size or color preference, a satisfaction guarantee lets you purchase before you get the answers. You are not being asked to make an irrevocable decision until the uncertainty is resolved. You have the right to return the product, usually in new condition in a set timeframe, so if it doesn't work out, you don't lose any more than the time and effort required to evaluate and return it.

It would be nice if business transactions came with a *satisfaction guaranteed* clause, but they rarely do. Most business decisions are irrevocable; we usually don't have the option to change our mind. Interestingly enough, even though we would like to be able to change our mind, we usually don't give our customers the option to change their minds. And yet, almost everyone resists making irrevocable decisions in the face of uncertainty. It would be nice if we could find a way to delay making decisions and a way to provide the same benefit for our customers.

Delaying Decisions

Hewlett-Packard discovered a way to increase profits by delaying decisions. HP sells a lot of printers around the world, and in many countries, the electrical connection must be tailored to the local electrical outlets. You would think that HP could accurately forecast how many printers it would sell in each country, but the forecasts are always just a bit off. HP always had some excess printers for one country and not enough for another. Then the company hit upon the idea of doing final electrical configuration in the warehouse after the printer was ordered. It costs more to configure a printer in a warehouse than in the factory, but overall, the cost of the option to customize was more than offset by the benefit of always having the right product. Even though unit costs rose, HP saved $3 million a month by more effectively matching supply to demand.[11]

As a keynote speaker at a software conference,[12] Enrico Zaninotto, an Italian economist, pointed out that the underlying economic mechanism for controlling complexity in just-in-time systems is minimizing irreversible actions. What does this

11. Coy, "Exploring Uncertainty."

12. Zaninotto, "From X Programming to the X Organization."

mean? In HP's case, there was a huge amount of complexity involved in getting the right electrical connection on printers going to different countries. The approach used to control this complexity was delaying the decision about what electrical connection to install until after an order was received in the warehouse. Voila! The system was no longer so complex.

Zaninotto contrasted just-in-time systems with Fordist mass production systems, which manage complexity by limiting the number of options—"You can have any color as long as it's black." For example, a mass production system for printers would use only the most common type of plug and make differences in plug styles the customers' problem; they can buy an add-on converter at their local electronic shop.

Zaninotto suggested that when a system that prespecifies options is confronted by a system that keeps options open, the second system wins out in a complex dynamic market. Thus, once HP started customizing power options on printers, the market expected all the other manufacturers to do the same.

Delaying irreversible decisions until uncertainty is reduced has economic value. It leads to better decisions, it limits risk, it helps manage complexity, it reduces waste, and it makes customers happy. On the other hand, delaying decisions usually comes at a cost. In HP's case, the unit cost of adding a cord in the warehouse was higher than the cost of adding the cord in the factory. Still, the overall system was more profitable, because delaying decisions allowed the correct decision to be made every time.

Options

The financial and commodities markets have developed a mechanism—called *options*—to allow decisions to be delayed. An option is the right, but not the obligation, to do something in the future. It's like a *satisfaction guaranteed* warranty—if things work out the way you expect them to, you can exercise the option (equivalent to keeping the product). If things don't work out, you can ignore the option (equivalent to returning the product), and all you lose is whatever the option cost you in the first place.

Uncertainty can move in two directions—unexpected good things can happen just as easily as unexpected bad things. No one knows this better than farmers, who have to deal with rising and falling commodity prices. Starting in 1985, the Chicago Board of Trade started selling options contracts, which provide farmers with commodity price insurance. Farmers can now buy options that guarantee a minimum price for their crop and still be free to sell it at a higher price if the market goes up.

A hotel reservation is an option on a hotel room in the future. The price of the option is the cost to make the reservation, which may include a reservation fee. If you exercise the option—if you show up at the hotel—you pay the price negotiated at the time the reservation was made. If you cancel the trip all you lose is the reservation fee.

Stock options are a way to give employees an opportunity to profit if the company does well in the future while limiting their risk if the company does poorly.[13] In general, financial options give the buyer an opportunity to capitalize on positive events in the future while limiting exposure to negative events. Options provide opportunities to make decisions down the road, while providing insurance against things going wrong.

Microsoft Strategy, circa 1988

In 1999 Eric Beinhocker[14] reminisced about the 1988 Comdex trade show. All the big players were there with big booths: Apple was at the peak of its powers; IBM, Hewlett-Packard, DEC, Apollo, and Sun Microsystems were all touting their latest strategies. And then there was Microsoft, with a modest booth that "was more like a Middle Eastern bazaar than a trade-show booth." Microsoft showed its then current strength, DOS, along with an early version of Windows, OS/2 for IBM machines, a version of UNIX, and new releases of Word and Excel, which were a far distant second to Lotus and WordPerfect in the DOS environment but led the applications on Apple platforms. Beinhocker notes: "Along with confused customers, the press was also grumbling. Columnists claimed that Microsoft was adrift and Gates had no strategy."

In 1988 it was not at all clear which platform would win, and Gates did have a strategy—to cover all the bases. He wanted Windows to win but hedged his bets with DOS, OS/2, and even a version of UNIX. If Apple won the war, he would lose the operating system but win as the dominant application provider on that platform. In any case, he would develop expertise in both operating systems and applications. He played the options game and let the market emerge.

Microsoft was not the only company to invest in options. IBM's strategy was to offer multiple options in hardware, thus the introduction of the PC in 1981. IBM did not fully realize that it was the software business, not the hardware business, that would become the economic driver of the future, so it had allowed Microsoft to hold most of the options in the software market. This made sense at the time, since all options come at a price, but IBM chose the wrong options.

In the 1990s Cisco Systems acquired companies with relevant technologies rather than maintaining a large research and development effort. This allowed Cisco to delay selecting technologies until both the market and the technology emerged, considerably reducing its risk. The cost of this options-based approach was the premium paid for the companies that had born the initial risk.

---

13. This assumes that the options are in addition to a reasonable salary.

14. Beinhocker, "Robust Adaptive Strategies," 95–96.

Options Thinking in Software Development

One of the hot debates in software development concerns the tradeoff between predictive processes and adaptive processes. The prevailing paradigm has been a predictive process: Software development should be specified in detail prior to implementation, because if you don't get the requirements nailed down and the design right, it will surely cost a lot to make changes later. This paradigm may work in a highly predictable world. However, if there is uncertainty about what customers really need, whether their situation will change, or where technology is moving, then an adaptive approach is a better bet. Options limit downside risk by limiting the cost and time allocated to resolving uncertainty. They maximize upside reward by delaying decisions until more knowledge is available. Economists and manufacturing managers alike understand that the adaptive paradigm of delaying decisions until uncertainty is reduced usually produces better results than a predictive approach.

Agile software development processes can be thought of as creating options that allow decisions to be delayed until the customer needs are more clearly understood and evolving technologies have had time to mature. This is not to say that agile approaches are unplanned. Plans help clarify confusing situations, allow consideration of tradeoffs, and establish patterns that allow rapid action. So, plans tend to enhance the flexibility to respond to change. However, *a plan should not prespecify detailed actions based on speculation.* Agile software development follows speculation with experiments and learning to reduce uncertainty and adapt the plan to reality.[15]

Conventional wisdom in software development tends to generate detailed decisions early in the process—like freezing the customer requirements and specifying the technical framework. In this approach, what is taken for planning is usually a process of predicting the future and making early decisions based on those predictions without any data or validation. Plans and predictions are not bad, but making irrevocable decisions based on speculation is to be avoided.

In 1988 Harold Thimbleby published a paper in *IEEE Software* titled "Delaying Commitment." He notes that when faced with a new situation, experts will delay firm decisions while they investigate the situation, because they know that delaying commitments often leads to new insights. Amateurs, on the other hand, want to get everything completely right, so they tend to make early decisions, quite often the wrong ones. Once these early decisions are made, other decisions are built on them, making them devilishly difficult to change. Thimbleby notes that premature design commitment is a design failure mode that restricts learning, exacerbates the impact of defects, limits the usefulness of the product, and increases the cost of change.

---

15. See Highsmith, *Adaptive Software Development*, 41–48.

Options thinking is an important tool in software development as long as it is accompanied by recognition that options are not free and it takes expertise to know which options to keep open. Options do not guarantee success; they set the stage for success if the uncertain future moves in a favorable direction. Options allow fact-based decisions based on learning rather than speculation.

TOOL 8: THE LAST RESPONSIBLE MOMENT

Concurrent software development means starting developing when only partial requirements are known and developing in short iterations that provide the feedback that causes the system to emerge. Concurrent development makes it possible to delay commitment until the *last responsible moment*,[16] that is, the moment at which failing to make a decision eliminates an important alternative. If commitments are delayed beyond the last responsible moment, then decisions are made by default, which is generally not a good approach to making decisions.

Procrastinating is not the same as making decisions at the last responsible moment; in fact, delaying decisions is hard work. Here are some tactics for making decisions at the last responsible moment:

Share partially complete design information. The notion that a design must be complete before it is released is the biggest enemy of concurrent development. Requiring complete information before releasing a design increases the length of the feedback loop in the design process and causes irreversible decisions to be made far sooner than necessary. Good design is a discovery process, done through short, repeated exploratory cycles.

Organize for direct, worker-to-worker collaboration. Early release of incomplete information means that the design will be refined as development proceeds. This requires that people who understand the details of what the system must do to provide value must communicate directly with people who understand the details of how the code works.

Develop a sense of how to absorb changes. In "Delaying Commitment" Harold Thimbleby observes that the difference between amateurs and experts is that experts know how to delay commitments and how to conceal their errors for as long as possible. Experts repair their errors before they cause problems. Amateurs try to get everything right the first time and so overload their problem-

16. The Lean Construction Institute coined the term *last responsible moment*. See *www.leanconstruction.org*.

solving capacity that they end up committing early to wrong decisions. Thimbleby recommends some tactics for delaying commitment in software development, which could be summarized as an endorsement of object-oriented design and component-based development:

- **Use modules:** Information hiding, or more generally behavior hiding, is the foundation of object-oriented approaches. Delay commitment to the internal design of the module until the requirements of the clients on the interfaces stabilize.
- **Use interfaces:** Separate interfaces from implementations. Clients should not depend on implementation decisions.
- **Use parameters:** Make magic numbers—constants that have meaning—into parameters. Make magic capabilities like databases and third-party middleware into parameters. By passing capabilities into modules wrapped in simple interfaces, your dependence on specific implementations is eliminated and testing becomes much easier.
- **Use abstractions:** Abstraction and commitment are inverse processes. Defer commitment to specific representations as long as the abstract will serve immediate design needs.
- **Avoid sequential programming:** Use declarative programming rather than procedural programming, trading off performance for flexibility. Define algorithms in a way that does not depend on a particular order of execution.
- **Beware of custom tool building:** Investment in frameworks and other tooling frequently requires committing too early to implementation details that end up adding needless complexity and seldom pay back. Frameworks should be extracted from a collection of successful implementations, not built on speculation.

Additional tactics for delaying commitment include

- **Avoid repetition:** This is variously known as the Don't Repeat Yourself (DRY)[17] or Once And Only Once (OAOO)[18] principle. If every capability is expressed in only one place in the code, there will be only one place to change when that capability needs to evolve, and there will be no inconsistencies.
- **Separate concerns:** Each module should have a single, well-defined responsibility. This means that a class will have only one reason to change.[19]

---

17. Hunt and Thomas, *The Pragmatic Programmer*, 27.

18. Beck, *Extreme Programming Explained*, 109.

19. Martin, *Agile Software Development Principles, Patterns, and Practices*, Chapter 8, calls this the Single Responsibility Principle.

- **Encapsulate variation:** What is likely to change should be inside; the interfaces should be stable. Changes should not cascade to other modules. This strategy, of course, depends on a deep understanding of the domain to know which aspects will be stable and which variable. By application of appropriate patterns, it should be possible to extend the encapsulated behavior without modifying the code itself.[20]
- **Defer implementation of future capabilities:** Implement only the simplest code that will satisfy immediate needs rather than putting in capabilities you "know" you will need in the future.[21] You will know better in the future what you really need then, and simple code will be easier to extend if necessary.
- **Avoid extra features:** If you defer adding features you "know" you will need, then you certainly want to avoid adding extra features "just-in-case" they are needed. Extra features add an extra burden of code to be tested, maintained, and understood. Extra features add complexity, not flexibility.

Much has been written on these delaying tactics,[22] so they are not covered in detail in this book.

Develop a sense of what is critically important in the domain. Forgetting some critical feature of the system until too late is the fear that drives sequential development. If security, or response time, or failsafe operation are critically important in the domain, these issues need to be considered from the start; if they are ignored until too late, it will indeed be costly. However, the assumption that sequential development is the best way to discover these critical features is flawed. In practice, early commitments are more likely to overlook such critical elements than late commitments, because early commitments rapidly narrow the field of view.

Develop a sense of when decisions must be made. You do not want to make decisions by default, or you have not delayed them. Certain architectural concepts such as usability design, layering, and component packaging are best made early so as to facilitate emergence in the rest of the design. A bias toward late commitment must not degenerate into a bias toward no commitment. You need to develop a keen sense of timing and a mechanism to cause decisions to be made when their time has come.

---

20. Ibid. Chapter 9 describes how to do this in the Open Closed Principle implemented via the Strategy or Template pattern.

21. Beck, *Extreme Programming Explained,* Chapter 17, uses the acronym YAGNI (You Aren't Going to Need It) for this practice and explains its rationale.

22. See Fowler, Patterns of *Enterprise Application Architecture*; Larman, *Applying UML and Patterns*; as well as the works cited above.

Develop a quick response capability. The slower you respond, the earlier you have to make decisions. Dell, for instance, can assemble computers in less than a week, so it can decide what to make less than a week before shipping. Most other computer manufacturers take a lot longer to assemble computers, so they have to decide what to make much sooner. If you can change your software quickly, you can wait to make a change until customers know what they want.

TOOL 9: MAKING DECISIONS

Depth-First Versus Breadth-First Problem Solving

There are two strategies for problem solving: breadth-first and depth-first. Breadth-first problem solving might be thought of as funnel, while depth-first problem solving is more like a tunnel. Breadth-first involves delaying commitments, while depth-first involves making early commitments. Some people prefer the breadth-first approach, while others prefer the depth-first approach. However, most people prefer to use depth-first when approaching new problems, because this approach tends to quickly reduce the complexity of the problem to be solved.[23] Since design is, by definition, the consideration of a new problem, most novice designers are biased toward the depth-first approach.

The risk of depth-first problem solving is that the field under consideration will be narrowed too soon, especially if those making the early commitments are not experts in the domain. If a change of course is necessary, the work done in exploring the details will be lost, so this approach has a large cost of change.

Notice that both breadth-first and depth-first approaches require expertise in the domain. A depth-first approach will work only if there was a correct selection of the area to zero in on. Getting this selection right requires two things: someone with the expertise to make the early decisions correctly and assurance that there will not be any changes that render these decisions obsolete. Lacking these two conditions, a breadth-first approach will lead to better results.

A breadth-first approach requires someone with the expertise to understand how the details will most likely emerge and the savvy to know when the time to make commitments has arrived. However, the breadth-first approach does not need a stable domain; it is the approach of choice when the business domain is expected to evolve. It is also an effective approach when the domain is stable.

23. See Thimbleby, "Delaying Commitment," 84.

Personality Types

We, the authors, exemplify the breadth-first and depth-first personality types.[24] Tom has a strong bias toward delaying commitment, so he enjoys the process of evaluating options, sometimes at the expense of getting things done. Mary, on the other hand, in her eagerness to make things happen, quite often sets off down the wrong path. Since we have complementary strengths and weaknesses, we have learned how to combine them to get the best of both worlds.

When a decision must be made, it falls naturally to the person whose style is most appropriate. For example, Tom evaluates available computer networking approaches, while Mary decides when and what to buy. Tom mulls over the best approach for a new Web site, while Mary oversees getting the Web site developed and deployed.

Mary has learned that for important decisions, the results are always better if she delays commitment until Tom does the breadth-first search. Tom finds that Mary has developed a better sense of when decisions have to be made and is more likely to make things happen. However, when it comes to implementation, both know that pair troubleshooting resolves network issues and Web site problems much faster than working alone.

—Mary and Tom

Intuitive Decision Making

Gary Klein studied decision making of emergency responders, military personnel, airline pilots, critical-care nurses, and others, to see how they make life-and-death decisions. He expected to find that these people make rational decisions in life-threatening situations; that is, they survey a range of options and weigh the benefits and risks of each option, then choose the best one from the analysis. When he started the study, he was amazed to discover that fire commanders felt they rarely, if ever, made decisions. Fire commanders were very experienced, or they would not have their jobs. They claimed that they just *knew* what to do based on their experience; there was no decision making involved. We call this *intuitive* decision making.[25]

When experienced people use pattern matching and mental simulation to make decisions, they are employing a very powerful tool that has an unquestioned track record of success. To make even better decisions, emergency responders, pilots, and military commanders engage in situational training that establishes correct pat-

24. Thimbleby, "Delaying Commitment," 84, sidebar.

25. Klein, *Sources of Power*, Chapter 3.

terns and enables better mental simulations. With the proper training and experience, intuitive decision making is highly successful the vast majority of the time.

Klein found that firefighter commanders resort to rational decision making only when experience is inadequate. Deliberating about options is a good idea for novices who have to think their way through decisions. However, intuitive decision making is the more mature approach to decisions, and it usually leads to better decisions as well.[26]

Rational decision making involves decomposing a problem, removing the context, applying analytical techniques, and exposing the process and results for discussion. This kind of decision making has a place in making incremental improvements, but it suffers from tunnel vision, intentionally ignoring the instincts of experienced people. It helps clarify complicated situations but contains significant ambiguity. Even though rational analysis gives specific answers, these are based on fuzzy assumptions and it is difficult to know exactly when and how to apply the rules.[27]

It would be nice if rational analysis could be counted on to point out when there is an inconsistency, when there is a key factor that everyone is overlooking. However, rational analysis is less useful than intuition in this regard, because rational analysis tends to remove context from analysis. Thus, rational decision making is unlikely to detect high-stakes mistakes; intuitive decision making is better in this regard.

Sometimes it seems that there are not enough experienced people available to allow intuitive decision making, and therefore rational decision making is the better approach. We strongly disagree. It is much more important to develop people with the expertise to make wise decisions than it is to develop decision-making processes that purportedly think for people. We are also convinced that it is quite possible to develop many people who are able to make wise intuitive decisions. Consider the Marines.

The Marines

The U.S. Marine Corps doesn't have any real need to exist; the army, navy, and air force are equipped to handle any job the Marines tackle. However, the Marines specialize in chaos. "Everything about the Marines…is geared toward high-speed, high-complexity environments," writes David Freedman in *Corps Business*.[28] "The Marine Corps is one of the most open-minded, innovative, knowledge-oriented…organizations in the world."

26. Ibid., 23, 28–29. Note that intuitive decision making can yield incorrect results if the underlying assumptions are incorrect or the constraints are not understood.

27. Ibid., Chapter 15.

28. Freedman, *Corps Business*, xix.

Freedman outlines 30 management principles that the Marines use to enable young recruits to deal with extremely challenging combat missions as well as tricky, ill-defined humanitarian missions. If you want to know how to deal with complexity, the Marines have a few good ideas.

Marines plan, but they do not predict. A mission plan is both rapid and thorough, but it is not a scenario of how the mission will unfold. Instead, the planning process focuses on understanding the essence of the situation and the strengths and weaknesses of both sides; finding simplifying assumptions, boundary conditions, and alternate approaches; settling on an approach with a 70 percent chance of success; searching for what is being overlooked; and inviting dissent. These issues are covered rapidly in the hours immediately preceding the mission, and the Marines have a plan.

Once engaged in a mission, the organizational structure collapses, and those on the front lines, who have access to the most current information, are expected to make decisions. They also are expected to make mistakes. The theory is that they will make fewer, less serious mistakes than will distant officers. Mistakes are not penalized; they are considered necessary to learn the boundaries of what works and what doesn't.

Extreme training is used to be sure Marines don't encounter situations on the job more challenging than those faced in training. They develop skills and learn patterns that they are expected to adapt to new and changing situations. Training is done with stories and analogies, but Marines are not told how to do a job. Instead, the Marines "manage by end state and intent. [They] tell people what needs to be accomplished and why, and leave the details to them."[29]

The Marines focus attention and resources on small teams at the lowest levels of the organization. There is no personnel department; hiring, training, and assigning people are required and prized rotational assignments for every senior officer. They look for leaders who can motivate people, and they clearly distinguish management tasks—getting the maximum value from the dollar—from leadership tasks—helping people to excel. Marines are taught to be comfortable with paradox and value opposing traits. Thus, they learn to balance discipline and creativity, empowerment and hierarchy, plans and improvisation, rapid action and careful analysis.

Organizations that deal successfully with complexity, as do the Marines, understand that complex problems can be dealt with only on the front line. Thus, they focus on enabling intelligent, self-organizing, mission-focused behavior at the lowest levels of the organization. Marine leaders are trained how to clearly communicate command intent so that frontline people understand the mission and know how to make intuitive decisions.

---

29. Ibid., 208.

A clear statement of intent is the key to enabling emergent behavior on the front line. In business, the communicating intent is generally done through a small set of well chosen, simple rules.

Simple Rules

Termites build amazing mounds and bees build complex hives. Birds migrate in flocks and fish swim in schools. These are not extraordinarily intelligent animals, yet as a group they exhibit extraordinarily sophisticated behavior. How do they know how to do it?

In the article "Swarm Intelligence" Eric Bonabeau and Christopher Meyer describe how ants find food efficiently by following two simple rules: (1) Lay down a chemical as you forage for food, and (2) follow the trail with the most chemical. If two ants go out looking for food, the one returning first will have laid down a double layer of chemical, so other ants will follow that trail, adding more chemical. The ants converge on the food very efficiently.

It turns out that these same two routing rules are equally effective in routing telephone traffic on a network. In this scheme, digital "ants" roam through a network, laying down "digital chemicals" in places of low congestion. Phone calls follow and reinforce the "digital trails." If congestion develops, the digital chemicals decay and are not reinforced, so calls are no longer attracted to that route.

Simple rules can lead to surprising results. Southwest Airlines had a rule that freight was to be loaded onto the first plane going in the right direction. The result was severe bottlenecks in the system even though very little of the overall capacity was being used. Then Southwest changed this one rule to ant forging rules: Find and use uncontested paths, just like the telecommunications industry. This meant that some cargo might actually start out moving away from its destination or taking a longer route than seemed necessary, which seemed very counterintuitive. However, the result was an 80 percent reduction in transfer rates at the busiest terminals, a 20 percent decrease in workload for cargo handlers, less need for cargo storage, and spare room on flights available for new business. Southwest estimated an annual gain of more than $10 million.[30]

Social insects act without supervision, self-organizing based on a set of simple rules. Their collective behavior results in efficient solutions to difficult problems. Bonabeau and Meyer call this *swarm intelligence* and list its advantages:

30. Bonabeau and Meyer, "Swarm Intelligence," 108.

- **Flexibility**—the group can quickly adapt to a changing environment.
- **Robustness**—even when one or more individuals fail, the group can still perform its tasks.
- **Self-organization**—the group needs relatively little supervision or top-down control.

Simple rules are very efficient at fostering flexibility, robustness, and self-organization in business environments. In the article "Strategy as Simple Rules," Kathleen Eisenhardt and Donald Sull note that managers have three choices when deciding how to compete. First they can "build a fortress and defend it." Second, they can count on unique resources to maintain a competitive advantage. Third, they can place their organizations in a position to rapidly pursue fleeting opportunities by choosing "a small number of strategically significant processes and [crafting] a few simple rules to guide them."[31]

The interesting thing about simple rules is that they enable decision making at the lowest levels of an organization. People do not have to wonder what to do in a situation or get permission to act. If they follow the simple rules, they know how to make decisions, and they know their decisions will be supported. Eisenhardt and Sull suggest that a simple-rules strategy gives a company a strong competitive advantage in high-velocity markets because they allow an entire organization to act uniformly and quickly with little supervision.

This is the key to simple rules: They allow everyone in an organization to act quickly, synchronously, in a coordinated manner, without the necessity of waiting for instructions from above. In a complex and changing environment, long decision chains slow decision making down and separate decision making from execution. Simple rules allow decisions to be made on the spot, when and where they need to be made, taking current information into account. Thus, simple rules are a key mechanism to enable people to *decide as late as possible.*

Simple Rules for Software Development

Simple rules for knowledge workers are a bit different than simple rules for moving freight or switching packets through networks. Simple rules give people a framework for making decisions; they are not instructions telling people exactly what to do. Thus, simple rules are principles that will be applied differently in different domains; they are used by experienced people as guidance when making intuitive decisions.

31. Eisenhardt and Sull, "Strategy as Simple Rules."

People have a limit to the number of things they can consider when making a decision, so the list of simple rules should be short. George A. Miller's law suggests that somewhere around seven would be a good number.[32] Simple rules should be limited to the few key principles that really must be considered when making a decision. Quite often, simple rules are used to reinforce a paradigm shift, so they often focus on the counterintuitive elements of decision making.

We offer seven simple rules, or principles, for software development along with the tools to help you translate the principles to agile practices that are appropriate for your particular environment:

1. **Eliminate waste:** Spend time only on what adds real customer value.
2. **Amplify learning:** When you have tough problems, increase feedback.
3. **Decide as late as possible:** Keep your options open as long as practical, but no longer.
4. **Deliver as fast as possible:** Deliver value to customers as soon as they ask for it.
5. **Empower the team:** Let the people who add value use their full potential.
6. **Build integrity in:** Don't try to tack on integrity after the fact—build it in.
7. **See the whole:** Beware of the temptation to optimize parts at the expense of the whole.

A set of simple rules are guideposts; their purpose is to allow the people on the ground to make quick decisions about how to proceed, knowing that their decisions will not be second-guessed because they are making the same decision their managers would make given the same circumstances. It is the power that simple rules give to the people who add value that makes them so valuable. It is not so important that the rules give detailed guidance; it is important that people know that these rules are guidelines, which gives them the freedom to make their own decisions.

32. Miller, "The Magical Number Seven, Plus or Minus Two: Some Limits on Our Capacity for Processing Information."

TRY THIS

1. Think of examples in your life when you have used options to delay decisions. For example, have you ever paid extra to lock in a low interest rate as you negotiated a mortgage? How effective has this been for you? Fill in the following table:

Example of keeping options open	Very favorable result	No gain; lost the cost of the option	Very unfavorable result
Mortgage Negotiation	X		
Example 2		X	
Example 3	X		

   We think you will find most examples fall into either the favorable or no-gain category, but few fall into the unfavorable category.

2. At a team or department meeting, ask people to list decisions that are about to be made. Group the list of decisions into two categories—tough to make and easy to make. Then discuss what information you would need to turn each tough decision into an easy decision. Pick three tough decisions and apply the delaying tactics under "Tool 8: The Last Responsible Moment" to delay those decisions as long as possible.
3. Evaluate your personality—are you inclined toward breadth-first or depth-first problem solving? Find someone who has the opposite inclination, and pair with him or her as you decide how to approach your next development project.
4. Select a few critical processes and develop simple rules for them so that people understand intent and can make independent decisions.

Chapter 4

Deliver as Fast as Possible

"Haste Makes Waste"

In the late 1990s there was a rush for Internet real estate reminiscent of the Oklahoma Land Rush of the 1890s. At high noon the bugles went off and the race for land was on. By sunset it was all over, with tens of thousands of people camped on plots of land. The problem was, in their rush to get land, few had slowed themselves down with provisions. People made a fortune selling food and water, but it would be a long time before those who claimed the land would prosper. First they needed seed, tools, and time for a crop to mature. Top real estate was soon selling at bargain prices as people left in droves. The racers had discovered that to make any money, you had to be able to farm.[1]

When we say *deliver as fast as possible,* we are not talking about rushing at breakneck speed to claim real estate. We are recommending a good farming practice. Rapid delivery is an operational practice that provides a strong competitive advantage. Customers like rapid delivery so much that once a company in an industry learns how to deliver quickly, its competitors are generally expected to follow suit.

The idea of delivering packages overnight was novel when Federal Express was started in 1971, but today even the U.S. Postal Service offers overnight delivery. The concept of shipping products the same day they are ordered was a breakthrough concept when L.L. Bean upgraded its distribution system in the late 1980s. The Sears Catalog, which started mail-order business in 1892, was unable to respond in kind and closed operations after 100 years. In 1983 LensCrafters changed the basis of competition in the eyeglasses industry by manufacturing prescription glasses in an hour.

1. Howard, "The Rush to Oklahoma."

In the late 1980s Japanese companies took an average of 46 months, 485 workers, and 1.7 million hours of labor to bring a new car to market. U.S. automakers took an average of 60 months, 903 workers, and 3.1 million hours of labor.[2] Commenting on these numbers, James Womack said, "We suggest that 'faster is dearer' will now join 'quality costs more' on the junk heap of ideas left over from the age of mass production."[3]

WHY DELIVER FAST?

Customers like rapid delivery. That is why immediate shipping and rapid delivery is standard for online and mail-order catalogs and why while-you-wait services are popular. Rapid delivery allows some customers to delay decisions, and for others rapid delivery means quicker gratification. For customers of software development, rapid delivery often translates to increased business flexibility.

Even as its customers are realizing the benefits of rapid delivery, savvy businesses are saving money. Rapid delivery means companies can deliver faster than customers can change their minds. It means that companies have fewer resources tied up in work-in-process, whether inventory or partially done development. When work-in-process represents risk, rapid delivery reduces risk.

For example, Dell Computer believes that inventory obsolescence is its biggest risk, so Dell waits until it receives an order and then makes and ships the computer in less than a week. Thus, when a faster video card or bigger disk drive becomes available, Dell can offer the improved part sooner than its competitors can. Once the more desirable part is offered in Dell machines, its competitors often find they have to offer the new part also, writing off a significant amount of inventory.

A big pile of in-process work holds additional risks besides obsolescence. Problems and defects, both large and small, often lurk in piles of partially done work. When developers create a lot of code without testing, defects pile up. When code is developed but not integrated, the high risk part of the effort usually remains. When a system is complete but not in production, risks remain. All of these risks can be significantly reduced by shortening the value stream.

Finally, the principle *deliver as fast as possible* complements *decide as late as possible*. The faster you can deliver, the longer you can delay decisions. For example, if you can make a software change in a week, then you do not have to decide exactly what you are going to do until a week before the change is needed. On the other hand, if it takes you a month to make the change, then you have to decide on the details of

2. Womack, Jones and Roos, *The Machine That Changed the World*, 118.

3. Ibid., 111.

the change a whole month before it is due. Rapid delivery is an options-friendly approach to software development. It lets you keep your options open until you have reduced uncertainty and can make more informed, fact-based decisions.

TOOL 10: PULL SYSTEMS

Rapid delivery does not happen by accident. When people show up for work, they have to figure out how to spend their time. It must be clear to every person, at all times, what she or he should do to make the most effective contribution to the business. When people do not know what to do, time is lost, productivity suffers, and rapid delivery is not possible.

There are two ways to assure that workers make the most effective use of their time. You can either tell them what to do or set things up so they can figure it out for themselves. In a fast-moving environment, only the second option works. People who routinely deal with fluid situations, such as emergency workers and military personnel, do not depend on a remote commander to tell them how to respond to the latest development. They figure out how to respond to events with the other people who are on the scene.

When things are happening quickly, there is not enough time for information to travel up the chain of command and then come back down as directives. Therefore, methods for local signaling and commitment must be developed to coordinate work. One of the keys ways to do this is to let customers' needs *pull* the work rather than have a schedule *push* the work.

Manufacturing Schedules

In complex manufacturing plants, one of the larger challenges is to figure out just what each machine and each person should be doing at any time so as to maximize the performance of the plant. In the 1980s, there was a concerted attempt to use MRP (material requirements planning) software to schedule the shop floor. MRP is basically a scheduling tool, so the thought was, in addition to scheduling materials, why not schedule production as well?

Already mediocre at scheduling materials, MRP systems were a disaster when used for scheduling the shop floor. Why? Because they were *nervous*. That means, whenever the slightest change was introduced—say the red boxes did not come in or the drill press was acting up—the new plan for dealing with the problem was completely different from the last plan. After a re-plan, every area in the plant would be scheduled to stop what it had been doing and do something else. The old schedule had been the optimal schedule based on the old assumptions. The new schedule was optimized based on the new assumptions. The fact that this changed what every person and machine in the plant was doing made no difference to the computer.

The simple mathematical fact working here is that variation is always amplified as it moves down a chain of connected events. A little variation in step one introduces a huge variation five steps later. Quite often, production workers were blamed for not doing exactly what was scheduled, but that was hardly the problem. The problem was that when even the smallest glitch arose, the schedule became invalid, and from then on, following the schedule just made things worse.

Just-in-time changed all of this by bringing the concept of pull scheduling to manufacturing. Pull systems use a mechanism called *kanban,* which was originally patterned after restocking grocery store shelves.[4] *Kanban* means *sign* or *placard* in Japanese.[5] Here is how a *kanban* system works:

> When an order is received in a *kanban* system, it is immediately sent to a shipping workstation. The shipping workers go to their supply shelves to get the parts they need to fill the order. Each part has an identifying *kanban* card attached, which is removed and left on the shelf. Someone brings the *kanban* card over to a supplier workstation which makes that kind of part. The people at the supplier workstation make the part identified on the *kanban* card, attach the card, and restock the empty spot on the shipping shelf. They in turn get their parts from their own shelves, and they have suppliers who keep their shelves stocked. This cascades through the plant, with all work scheduled by *kanban* cards or perhaps by empty spots on the shelves of a downstream customer workstation.
>
> When people show up at work, they look at their pile of *kanban* cards and know exactly what to do next. If they have more than one *kanban* card, they have simple rules which tell them which customer to restock first. If they have no *kanban* cards, they clean up their workstation and perhaps help the people at a customer workstation so as to generate some *kanban* cards to work on. They do not make anything until one of their customer workstations needs restocking.

Kanban is the enabling mechanism of just-in-time. It is the thing that tells people and machines what to do from hour to hour in order to achieve optimum plant output. Unlike other scheduling mechanisms, pull systems take variability into account at the end of the line, so there is very little nervousness.

Without pull scheduling and *kanban* cards, there would have to be some other way for people to figure out what to do next. In fact, in pre-lean days, people were told what to do by managers who modified the MRP schedule based on their personal knowledge and decided what each workstation should do. You can imagine that this

4. Ohno, *The Toyota Production System*, 25.

5. Ibid., 27.

was a hit-and-miss affair in a complex plant. The interesting thing about pull scheduling is that it takes the manager out of the loop of having to tell workers what to do. The work is self-directing. The managers spend their time coaching the team.[6]

Lean Construction

The construction industry has the same problem with master schedules as the manufacturing has with MRP systems. Every building site has a master schedule, but bad weather or shortage of building material or delays of previous crews means that the master schedule never really matches what's actually going on. A master schedule really isn't very useful for scheduling construction on a day-to-day basis, because it doesn't start with an accurate representation of reality. Trying to update the master schedule usually makes things worse, just as it did with the nervous MRP system.

Still, the basic problem remains. People show up for work in the morning, and someone has to tell them what to do. Crews have a supervisor or crew chief who is supposed to give them instructions, but how does that person know what to tell them? Site managers and project managers can do little more than the plant managers of old—look at the master schedule, add some personal knowledge, and guess what everyone should be doing. The problem is, with various crew chiefs working for different companies and trying to maximize their companies' profits, there is little incentive for the crew chiefs to send signals and make commitments to each other.

The Lean Construction Institute[7] recommends a weekly planning meeting of crew chiefs at which they commit to each other what they will accomplish in the next week. They base their commitment on not only what should be done according to the master schedule but also what *can* be done based on actual site status and other crew chief commitments. After adopting this and a few other simple mechanisms for local signaling and commitment, work invariably proceeds more efficiently—a 10 to 30 percent increase in productivity at a construction site is not unusual.

---

6. Ibid. Page 8 describes managers as coaches of a baseball team. Ohno notes that a skilled baseball team can respond to any event without a coach telling it what to do; the coaches help the team members improve their skills and teamwork.

7. *www.leanconstruction.org*

Software Development Schedules

In the world of complex software development, the same basic problem exists: How do you make sure that when people come in to work, they know how to spend their time in the most effective manner to achieve the goal at hand? Lacking any better method for developers to figure this out for themselves, project managers often look at the project schedule, perhaps modify it based on their personal knowledge, and tell developers what to do.

But the problem is, a project schedule will be just as unreliable as an MRP schedule or a construction master schedule if it is used for fine-grained planning in an environment that experiences even a small amount of variability. Furthermore, telling developers what to do does not generate much motivation.[8]

We often hear complaints about micromanagement in software development. We understand why managers may feel the need to provide detailed direction to developers if the work is not organized to be self-directing and there are no local signaling and commitment mechanisms in place. If a system is complex, resources are scarce, and deadlines loom, then everybody must be productive all the time. How are people going to know how to best use their time unless someone tells them what to do?

No schedule can make effective fine-grained work assignments in a complex environment with even modest variability. Depending on a computerized schedule to make work assignments and telling developers what to do are not the best ways to handle complex or changing situations. A more effective approach is to use a pull system that creates appropriate signaling and commitment mechanisms, so that team members can figure out for themselves the most productive way to spend their time.

Software Pull Systems

The starting point for a pull system in software development is short iterations based on customer input at the beginning of each iteration.[9] Let's assume that at the beginning of the iteration, the customers or customer representatives write down descriptions of features they need on index cards.[10] There are many other ways to document

8. See Chapter 5, "Empower the Team."

9. See Chapter 2, "Tool 4: Iterations."

10. A story card is an index card with the name of a feature written on it and some indication of what the feature means. The story card is not the specification of the feature, merely a signal to the team to work on that feature. The feature should be small enough that it can be done in a few days. Story cards are used in Extreme Programming and other agile methods to represent features that may be implemented. See Jeffries, Anderson, and Henderson, *Extreme Programming Installed*, Chapter 4.

what the customers want, but index cards are a lot like *kanban* cards, so for now we will assume index cards.

As described in Chapter 2, "Amplify Learning," the developers estimate how much time each card will take to implement, and the customers prioritize the cards. At the end of the planning meeting, the work for the iteration is contained on the cards selected for implementation. These cards now become *kanban* cards; they basically tell the development team what work needs to be done for the length of the iteration.

Remember that the idea here is to make the work self-directing. Therefore, cards are not assigned to developers; the developers choose the cards they want to work on. Cards might be posted on a board in a *To Do* area, where developers go to figure out what to do. Developers working on cards move them to a *Checked Out* area with their name attached. Once a story passes its tests, the card is moved to the *Tests Passed* area. See Figure 4.1. The scheme is not as important as the effect: The *kanban* cards tell developers what to do. The work becomes self-directing, pulled from customer-selected features. Status is visible at a glance to anyone who cares to check the board.

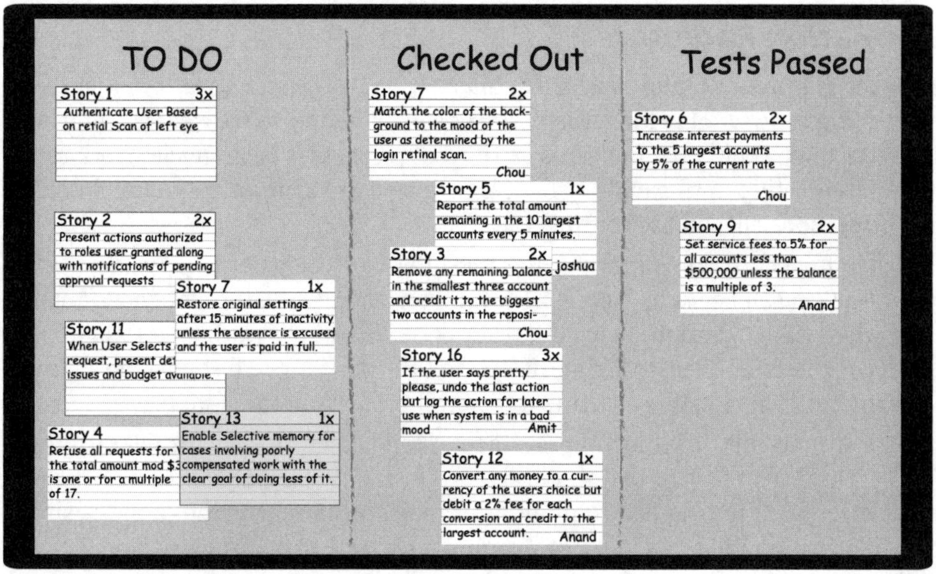

Figure 4.1 *A software kanban system.*

Cards alone are not enough for developers to know exactly what to do. A regular brief meeting, preferably daily, is also a good idea to help make work of the iteration self-directing. The daily team meeting should be no more than 15 minutes, and it should truly be a team meeting. Everyone on the team should be there—even if that means phoning in—and active participation should generally be limited to team members.

At the daily meeting, team members give a summary of what they did yesterday, what they plan to do today, and where they need help. If some issues generate more detailed discussion, these are deferred to later meetings of the interested parties. The job of the leader, or coach, is to run interference for the team. For example, if a developer needs more information from customers, the leader's job is to make sure the developer has access to customers or customer representatives to answer the questions.[11]

A pull system in software development requires short time-boxes—a month or less—otherwise, it can degenerate into a push system. If the iteration is too long, there will be too many cards or else the cards will not be detailed enough to effectively pull work. Pull systems work from customer orders—prioritized features—and use multiple signaling and commitment mechanisms to organize the work so that it is self-directing.

Information Radiators

One of the features of a pull system is *visual control,* or *management by sight.*[12] If work is going to be self-directing, then everyone must be able to see what is going on, what needs to be done, what problems exist, what progress is being made. Work cannot be self-directing until simple visual controls that are appropriate to the domain are in place, updated, and used to direct work.

Alistair Cockburn calls visual controls for software development *information radiators.*[13] The *kanban* board in Figure 4.1 is an information radiator that shows many things: what needs to be done, what is already done, and who is working on what. The burn-down charts in Chapter 2, Figure 2.6, and the acceptance test chart in Figure 2.7 are information radiators charting the overall progress of the system.

Lists of problems, ideas for improvements, candidates for refactoring, business impact of the system to date, daily build status, glossaries of the ubiquitous language, database test beds, testing backlog—all are candidates for entry onto a big, visible chart. Information radiators make problems visible, telegraph progress, and are an enabling mechanism for self-directing work.

---

11. The pivotal importance of a daily meeting is described in Schwaber and Beedle, *Agile Software Development with Scrum*, 40–46.

12. See Ohno, *The Toyota Production System*, 129.

13. See Cockburn, *Agile Software Development*, 84–88.

TOOL 11: QUEUING THEORY

We have often heard the lament "My biggest problem is the testing department." Now, testing people are very nice people: dedicated, hard working, and very important to the development effort. But there never seems to be enough of them to go around. And although the developers might write their own unit tests, testers frequently do acceptance testing.[14] So, without enough testers, the whole development process bogs down.

Your bottleneck might not be testers; it might be analysts. Or you might have trouble getting information from customers. Perhaps there is only one person alive who understands the legacy database. Whatever your bottleneck is, a brief look at queuing theory might give you some ammunition for addressing the problem.

Reducing Cycle Time

You spend a lot of time in queues. You get stuck in traffic jams, stand in lines at stores, get put on hold on the phone, and wait for a tax refund to come in the mail. Queuing theory concerns itself with making your wait as short as possible. Queuing theory has prompted banks to use a single line feeding multiple tellers; it has led to express lanes—10 items or less—at grocery stores, to low weekend phone rates, and to entrance ramp metering on freeways. It is probably used to calculate the number of servers you should have in your computer room.

The fundamental measurement of a queue is *cycle time*—that is, the average time it takes something to get from one end of a process to the other. The cycle time clock starts when something enters a queue and keeps on ticking away while it waits in the queue, while it gets service, while it waits in the next queue, gets the next service, and so on, until it pops out at the other end of the process.[15] For example, consider the process of getting from the entrance of an airport to the gate. Door-to-gate cycle time would include the time spent in line waiting to check luggage, the time it takes to check the luggage and get a boarding pass, the time spent in the security line, the time it takes to get through security, and the time it takes to walk to the gate.

---

14. Unit tests in this context are also called developer tests and are aimed at verifying design intent. Acceptance testing is also called customer testing and is aimed at verifying customer intent. See the section "Tool 20: Testing," in Chapter 6, "Build Integrity In."

15. The use of the term cycle time to denote the average *duration* of a process is common in product development and supply chain management. When the term cycle time is used in reference to load balancing a manufacturing line, it has a different meaning; it refers to the average *rate* at which the line produces product.

Notice that when you are in a queue, you always want cycle time to be as short as possible. After all, you joined the queue to accomplish something. The only reason you can't accomplish your goal immediately is that the resources necessary to achieve the goal are limited, so a queue has formed. The time spent waiting in the queue is wasted time.

Steady Rate of Arrival

There are two ways to reduce cycle time; one is to look at the way work arrives and the other is to look at the way work is processed. In some systems, it is not possible to influence the rate of arrival of work, but in others, policies can be established to even out incoming demand. Pricing policies are often used for this purpose. A phone company that offers very low night and weekend rates is doing this to even out peak demand. A restaurant with early bird specials is also using pricing to spread out demand. Airlines use variable pricing to fill flights. Doctor's offices use reservation systems to assure that patients arrive at regular intervals. When arrival of demand is spread out to match the capacity of the system, queues, and therefore cycle times, will be shortened.

One way to control the rate of work arrival is to release small packages of work. If you have to wait for a large batch of work to arrive before you can start processing it, then the queue will be at least as long as the whole batch. If the same work is released in small batches, the queue can be much smaller.

Consider the testing department bottleneck. Is there any way to even out the arrival of work? You really want someone to be running acceptance tests for a project every day rather than a suite of tests once a month. Can you negotiate the same amount of hours spread evenly over the month and assure that there is a steady rate of testing work to be done?

Software development organizations often control the arrival of work with a review process that sets priorities and selects projects. If this is an annual event tied to the budgeting process, then a year's worth of work arrives all at once. This makes for very long queues. Even with a quarterly project approval process, the queues are still quite large. Many managers still believe that it is good to group projects into a single priority-setting process to have more projects to compare at one time. Queuing theory suggests that they would probably be better off releasing projects more frequently—monthly or even weekly—to even out the arrival of work in the development area.

Steady Rate of Service

Once variability has been removed from the work arriving in a queue, the next step is to remove the variability in the processing time. Small work packages are a real help in removing variability from processing time, because a small package has fewer things that can go wrong. However, even with small work packages, it may be difficult to determine how much time each work package will take. The easiest way to solve this problem is to increase the number of servers that process work in a single queue. Banks and airport ticket counters don't have an easy way to determine which customers will take a lot of time, so they reduce the variability by having a single queue feed multiple stations. A few of the stations may become stalled with customers who take a long time, but the main line can still be served at a steady pace by the remaining stations.

Again, we see the importance of small work packages. Not only will small work packages *flow* much more easily through your system, they will also allow parallel processing of the small jobs by multiple teams so that if one is stalled by a problem, the rest of the project can proceed without delay.

If you have a process that involves several steps, then the processing time at the earlier steps will affect the rate at which work arrives at the later stations. If you have big processing variations in upstream workstations, these cascade throughout the system. Thus, it is a good idea to try to move any variability downstream.

The serious impact of upstream variation becomes very important to understand when you use iterative development. Let's say you have a bottleneck at acceptance testing. If acceptance testing is the last thing that happens before deployment, this bottleneck will not appreciably slow down earlier work. But when you are doing iterations, acceptance testing is no longer the last step; it is a vital part of every iteration and must be done before proceeding with the next iteration. If you skip this vital step, you will not get the feedback, which is a key purpose of the iteration in the first place. With iterative development, acceptance testing moves far upstream, and any delays there will be amplified in subsequent iterations. Thus, with iterative development, it is critically important that you do not have a bottleneck at testing.

Slack

The most obvious way to reduce cycle time is to have plenty of capacity to process the work. Short cycle times are not possible if resources are overloaded. You know that traffic slows to a crawl when a highway reaches its capacity. Computer operations managers know that as servers approach full utilization, the cycle time for processing requests to that server lengthens dramatically.

Consider the testing department that has become a bottleneck. Unable to make a case that more testers are needed, the manager tries to makes the best use of the available testers by making sure that a good-sized batch of work is always waiting in the queue so the testers are always busy. Developers keep coding while waiting for testing services, because their manager also wants them to keep busy. Even though it is cheaper to fix a bug immediately after it is coded than a week or two later, this system encourages developers to create ever larger batches of code to be tested. The testing queue grows and testing slows to a crawl. Testers start to test less thoroughly, errors are released, and still the queue grows. The cost to the company of fully utilized testing capability can be significant. This is a case where managers who do not understand queuing theory have created policies that actually have the opposite effect than they intended.

Another self-defeating policy is to delay acceptance testing until all of the coding is finished and unit tested. Again, this policy assures that work arrives at the testing department in large batches. Figure 4.2 puts some numbers on the impact of the large batches.

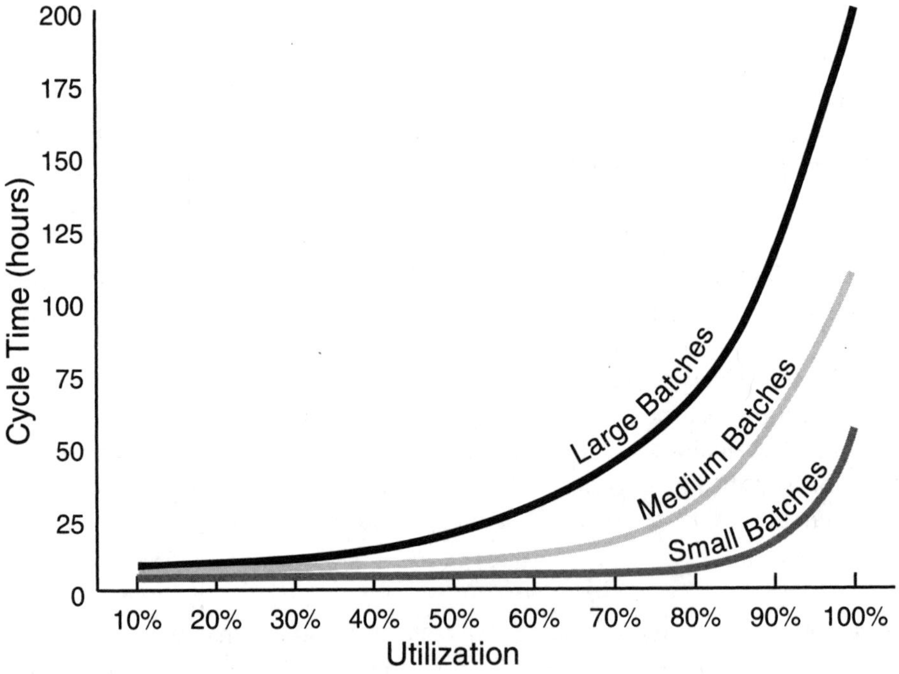

Figure 4.2 *Effect of utilization and batch size on cycle time.*[16]

16. Note: This graph assumes that variability (in both arrival and processing time) is proportional to batch size. It is the higher variability that causes lower utilization rates.

Assume that each large batch can be tested in 7 hours if nothing else were in the queue. The chart in Figure 4.2 says that when the testing department is run at 50 percent capacity, the time for a large job to get through testing will be about 25 hours, and at 85 percent capacity, the cycle time is up to 100 hours and increasing rapidly. This works just like a traffic jam at rush hour; go above 85 percent capacity and gridlock is inevitable.

Now let's assume that the testing department can be persuaded that moving tests through the department quickly is a better approach, so it removes the "complete systems only" policy and accepts features for testing as soon as they are coded.

Assume that the small batches can move through the department in 4 hours at low levels of utilization. Because batches are small, the department should be able to maintain a 5 hour turnaround time up to about 70 percent capacity, and things do not start getting slow until about 90 percent capacity, at which point small jobs move through the department eight times faster than large jobs. The bottom line of small batches? The department moves jobs through much faster while running at a higher capacity.

Many consulting firms use *applied ratio* as a key management measurement, one that they feel should be maximized, since utilization directly affects profits. Similar measures have found their way into internal software organizations, where their tie to profitability is more tenuous. It is difficult for those who think this way to understand that full utilization provides no value to the overall value stream; in fact, it usually does more harm than good. We would never run the servers in our computer rooms at full utilization—why haven't we learned that lesson in software development?

In his book *Slack,* Tom DeMarco makes the point that having slack in an organization gives it the capacity to change, to reinvent itself, and to marshal resources for growth. Actually, queuing theory would suggest that slack serves an even more basic purpose. Just as a highway cannot provide acceptable service without some slack in capacity, so you probably are not providing your customers with the highest level of service if you have no slack in your organization.

The Theory of Constraints

According to the theory of constraints,[17] the best way to optimize an organization is to focus on the throughput of the organization, because this is the key to generating profitable revenue. The way to increase throughput is to look for the current bottleneck that is slowing things down and fix it. Once that is done, find the next bottleneck and fix it. Keep this up and you will have a fast moving value stream.

Note that it doesn't do any good to increase the utilization of non-bottleneck areas. It doesn't matter how fast you develop software if you can't test it at the same rate. It doesn't matter how fast you develop a system if you don't have the people to deploy it. So, move people to the bottleneck; don't keep piling up work that can't be used immediately.

How Queues Work

Queuing theory is a well-known discipline that applies whenever something flows through a constrained resource. Here is a quick summary of how queues work:

1. Measuring the amount of work waiting to be done (let's call this *work-in-queue*) is equivalent to measuring the cycle time of a system.[18]
2. As variability (in arrival time or processing time) increases, cycle time and work-in-queue will increase.
3. As batch size increases, variability in arrival and processing time increases, and therefore cycle time and work-in-queue will increase.
4. As utilization increases, cycle time will increase nonlinearly.
5. As variability increases, the nonlinear increase in cycle time happens at ever-lower levels of utilization.
6. Continuous flow requires a reduction in variability.
7. Variability may be reduced by an even arrival of demand, small batches, an even rate of processing, and parallel processing.
8. Decreasing variability early in the process has larger impact than decreasing variability late in the process.

---

17. Goldratt, *Theory of Constraints*, and Goldratt, *The Goal.*

18. This is Little's law. For details, see Reinertsen, *Managing the Design Factory*, 63.

Software development managers tend to ignore cycle time, perhaps because they feel that they are already getting things done as fast as they can. In fact, reducing batch sizes and addressing capacity bottlenecks can reduce cycle time quite a bit, even in organizations that consider themselves efficient already.

TOOL 12: COST OF DELAY

A dollar saved is a dollar earned.[19]

Your developers bring you a request for a new development tool that they feel will speed up development. You estimate how much of their time the tool will save and find that the saved hours are worth less than the tool will cost. Can you justify buying the tool?

Conventional wisdom in product development says that there is a roughly even tradeoff between development cost and the cost of development time, and under this wisdom, you would turn down the request. However, in the book *Developing Products in Half the Time*, Preston Smith and Donald Reinertsen suggest that the benefits of rapid development are usually larger than you might expect. So, before you turn down the tool request, you should put a price tag on time.

This is done by creating a simple economic model of a new product for the next few years, basically a profit and loss statement (P&L). Then, a delay is added to the model and the difference in total profit is calculated, giving a good idea of the impact of the delay. The important thing is to get a good estimate from marketing about what delay will do to sales volumes and market share. The model shows what the difference in revenue and market share will do to profits. The result is often dramatic. If delay means loss of early high pricing or long-term loss of market share, the cost of delay can be very high. With just a month or two of delay, products can lose much of the overall profit of the program.

Smith and Reinertsen show how to create economic models for changes in development costs, fewer features, higher support costs, and so on. The result is a price tag on four key leverage points for product development: development cost, unit cost, performance, and introduction date. They found that an early introduction date was the dominant factor in long term profitability for many, but not all, products. To find out what *deliver as fast as possible* might mean to you, create an economic model of your business and use it to drive development decisions.

---

19. Inflated form of Ben Franklin's maxim "A penny saved is a penny earned."

An Accountant for Every Team

Every new product program at 3M has an accountant on the team. Every time the team makes a presentation to management, the accountant presents a product P&L. The team has worked with the accountant to project a unit cost, potential selling price, and volume over three years. Young scientists at 3M learn how to read a P&L and use it to guide their development decisions.

My team worked with products that used optical-grade plastics, which are very expensive. As we worked with the accountant, we found that the unit cost was likely to be too high to give good margins, based on the projected selling price of the product. We didn't think the product could be sold for more, so we knew we had to reduce the amount of the expensive plastic in the product.

We developed three P&Ls, showing a 30-percent, 60-percent, and 90-percent reduction. These showed us that the 90-percent reduction gave us a dynamite product, but at a 30-percent reduction, the product wasn't economically viable and at 60 percent it was marginal.

So, we started a research program to figure out how to make the expensive plastic very thin. The scientists knew what they needed to do and why, and within a few months, they had the breakthrough we needed to make the product economically viable.

—Mary

Software development is a discovery process in which technical people make continual tradeoff decisions in order to reach what they consider an optimal result. Of course, technical people bring their own unique perspectives to their work, so their decisions will be influenced by their background and experience. One of the biggest challenges for software development leaders is to assure that the constant tradeoff decisions being made by everyone on the team produce an optimal result.

All too often, a software development team is told that it must meet cost, feature, and introduction date objectives simultaneously; there can be no tradeoffs. This sends two messages to the development team:

- Support costs aren't important because they weren't mentioned.
- When something has to give, make your own tradeoffs.

Since various team members are likely to have different perceptions of what is important, the tradeoffs made by some will probably offset tradeoffs made by others—with the result that all objectives will be compromised.

Give the team an economic model, and you have empowered the members to figure out for themselves what is important for the business. You have given everyone the same frame of reference so they can all work from the same assumptions. Finally, the team is more likely to come up with an economic success, since the members now know what economic success means.

Product Model

Let's look at an economic model for a software product. The first step is to develop a simple baseline product P&L. The basic rule is to keep the model simple; after all, the numbers start out as guesses—and increased precision is not going to make the numbers more accurate. It is important to make sure everyone understands and buys into the economic model, because then they are more likely to buy into any decisions based on the model. In fact, to make your job easier and increase buy-in, we recommend that you get help from your accountants in preparing this P&L. A simple baseline P&L for a software product might look something like Table 4.1.

Table 4.1 *Baseline Software P&L*

	Assumptions	Year 0	Year 1	Year 2	Year 3	Year 4	Year 5
Revenue							
Average Selling Price	Decreases 10%/yr	$1,000	$900	$810	$729	$656	$590
Total Market Units		10,000	20,000	40,000	60,000	40,000	20,000
Market Share		30%	40%	50%	50%	50%	50%
Units Sold		3,000	8,000	20,000	30,000	20,000	10,000
Total Revenue		$3,000,000	$7,200,000	$16,200,000	$21,870,000	$13,122,000	$5,904,900
Expense							
Unit Mfg & Distribution Cost	Decreases 5%/yr	$200	$190	$181	$171	$163	$155
Unit Warranty & Support Cost	Decreases 10%/yr	$200	$180	$162	$146	$131	$118
Total Unit Cost		$400	$370	$343	$317	$294	$273
Manufacturing/ Support Cost		$1,200,000	$2,960,000	$6,850,000	$9,518,250	$5,882,425	$2,728,542
Gross Margin $		$1,800,000	$4,240,000	$9,350,000	$12,351,750	$7,239,575	$3,176,358
Gross Margin %		60%	59%	58%	56%	55%	54%
Development	$4,000,000 launch	$1,500,000	$750,000	$750,000	$500,000	$500,000	$500,000
Marketing	15% of sales	$450,000	$1,080,000	$2,430,000	$3,280,500	$1,968,300	$885,735

Table 4.1 *Baseline Software P&L (Continued)*

	Assumptions	Year 0	Year 1	Year 2	Year 3	Year 4	Year 5
G&A	5% of sales	$150,000	$360,000	$810,000	$1,093,500	$656,100	$295,245
Total Expense		$3,300,000	$5,150,000	$10,840,000	$14,392,250	$9,006,825	$4,409,522
Profit (Loss)		$(300,000)	$2,050,000	$5,360,000	$7,477,750	$4,115,175	$1,495,378
% of Revenue		–10%	28%	33%	34%	31%	25%
Cumulative Revenue		$3,000,000	$10,200,000	$26,400,000	$48,270,000	$61,392,000	$67,296,900
Cumulative Expense	$4,000,000 launch	$7,300,000	$12,450,000	$23,290,000	$37,682,250	$46,689,075	$51,098,597
Cumulative Profit	($4,000,000) launch	$(4,300,000)	$(2,250,000)	$3,110,000	$10,587,750	$14,702,925	$16,198,303
Cumulative Profit % of Revenue		–143%	–22%	12%	22%	24%	24%

This P&L shows that the year the product is introduced, the overall market opportunity is 10,000 units, growing to 20,000 the next year, 40,000 the following year, and so on. With the currently planned introduction date, marketing estimates an initial market share of 30 percent, increasing to 50 percent in two years. The product will sell for $1,000 each, decreasing at 10 percent per year. Manufacturing, distribution, warranty, and support costs start at $400 per unit and decrease each year. The cumulative 5-year profit is about $16,000,000.

This model can be varied in several ways. For instance, you might rerun the P&L with a 25 percent development cost overrun to see what that would do to the cumulative profit. Or you might want to see how an additional 15 percent unit or warranty cost overrun would affect cumulative profit. If you are considering eliminating features, your marketing department might speculate that without these features they would sell 5 percent fewer units. By changing the baseline P&L, you can see how that would affect cumulative profit.

The highest leverage point in this kind of economic model is frequently the cost of delay. Your marketing department might suggest that a 6-month delay would decrease market share from 30 percent to 10 percent the first year (customers are not going to wait), from 40 percent to 30 percent the second year, and from 50 percent to 40 percent in subsequent years (your competitor will have a lead). Table 4.2 shows the resulting P&L.

Table 4.2 *P&L: 6-Month Delay*

	Assumptions	Year 0	Year 1	Year 2	Year 3	Year 4	Year 5
Revenue							
Average Selling Price	Decreases 10%/yr	$1,000	$900	$810	$729	$656	$590
Total Market Units		10,000	20,000	40,000	60,000	40,000	20,000
Market Share		10%	30%	40%	40%	40%	40%
Units Sold		1,000	6,000	16,000	24,000	16,000	8,000
Total Revenue		$1,000,000	$5,400,000	$12,960,000	$17,496,000	$10,497,600	$4,723,920
Expense							
Unit Mfg & Distribution Cost	Decreases 5%/yr	$200	$190	$181	$171	$163	$155
Unit Warranty & Support Cost	Decreases 10%/yr	$200	$180	$162	$146	$131	$118
Total Unit Cost		$400	$370	$343	$317	$294	$273
Manufacturing/ Support Cost		$400,000	$2,220,000	$5,480,000	$7,614,600	$4,705,940	$2,182,834
Gross Margin $		$600,000	$3,180,000	$7,480,000	$9,881,400	$5,791,660	$2,541,087
Gross Margin %		60%	59%	58%	56%	55%	54%
Development	$4,000,000 launch	$1,500,000	$750,000	$750,000	$500,000	$500,000	$500,000
Marketing	15% of sales	$150,000	$810,000	$1,944,000	$2,624,400	$1,574,640	$708,588
G&A	5% of sales	$50,000	$270,000	$648,000	$874,800	$524,880	$236,196
Total Expense	$4,000,000 launch	$2,100,000	$4,050,000	$8,822,000	$11,613,800	$7,305,460	$3,627,618
Profit (Loss)		$(1,100,000)	$1,350,000	$4,138,000	$5,882,200	$3,192,140	$1,096,303
% of Revenue		–110%	25%	32%	34%	30%	23%
Cumulative Revenue		$1,000,000	$6,400,000	$19,360,000	$36,856,000	$47,353,600	$52,077,520
Cumulative Expense	$4,000,000 launch	$6,100,000	$10,150,000	$18,972,000	$30,585,800	$37,891,260	$41,518,878
Cumulative Profit	($4,000,000) launch	$(5,100,000)	$(3,750,000)	$388,000	$6,270,200	$9,462,340	$10,558,643
Cumulative Profit % of Revenue		-510%	-59%	2%	17%	20%	20%

The 6-month delay is projected to decrease cumulative profit approximately $5.6 million. This translates to cost of over $31,000 per week of delay ($5.6 million ÷ 180 weeks). A decision to spend $100,000 extra to speed up development by three months looks like a good investment in this economic model.

Typically, P&L models are used for making *go/no-go* decisions about the investments rather than for making tradeoff decisions as advocated here. Often, models used to make investment decisions include a net present value or discounted cash flow calculation. For product models used to make project-level tradeoff decisions rather than investment decisions, we don't see a need for net present value, but the best approach is to use whatever model your finance department favors. Just keep it simple.

Application Model

If your software development organization is not involved in product development, it is useful to develop an economic model of each application from the customer point of view. This is a simplified way of evaluating how different design decisions will affect the business value received by the customer and is further discussed in Donald Reinertsen's book *Managing the Design Factory* (see Chapter 2). In the same way that a simple P&L helps a team make product tradeoff decisions, a simple look at the customer's economic model helps the team make application tradeoff decisions.

The first step in developing an application model is to identify your customer's economic drivers related to the application. If you are working with a company that can't supply you with detailed financial numbers, even some rough estimates would be useful. Just as with a product model, an accountant is your best friend when doing this exercise.

Assume, for instance, that you are providing customer support call center software. You gather a small team and spend some time at your customer's site to understand the company's economic drivers. You find that the underlying drivers are call handling time, staffing levels, system support, and customer satisfaction.

The second step is to translate the drivers to economic terms. You find that your customer produces a monthly status report that looks something like Table 4.3.

Table 4.3 *Monthly Report for Call Center*

		Assumptions	
calls per day	10,000		
avg. minutes per call	0.53		
total time (hours) per day	88		
peak call rate	8.2		
staff utilization	75%		

Table 4.3 *Monthly Report for Call Center (Continued)*

required staffing level	14		
average hourly pay	$7.50		
regular hours in month	176		
total regular monthly pay	$18,480		
% overtime	19%		
$ overtime	$1,980		
total base pay	$20,460		
supervision	$2,455	12% base pay	
benefits	$7,161	35% base pay	
turnover	2		
training	$840	7 days	
total salary and benefits	$30,916		
system admin	$10,000		
content maintenance	$5,000		
hardware	$6,500		
facilities	$2,960		
total monthly cost	$55,376		
revenue	$60,000		
profit	$4,624		
margin	8%		
customer satisfaction	92%		
first call resolution	58%		
abandoned calls	3.60%		
downtime hours	3.5		

Your goal is to translate this information into an economic model that helps the development team make tradeoffs. You find that your customer has four goals:

1. The biggest justification of this particular project is to reduce hardware and system administration costs by moving to a new operating system.
2. The second goal is to lower the time per call. A 10 percent lower time per call would allow the center to operate with two less people, but this would not cause layoffs because there is a turnover of two people per month.

3. The third goal is to get more business. Your customer speculates that a 5 percent increase in external customer satisfaction would help to secure a new contract worth $10,000, which would generate an additional 2,000 calls per month.
4. Your customer also wants the system to be very easy to learn, because everyone will have to be trained initially and two people a month will have to be trained on an ongoing basis.

From this information, you put together the economic model in Table 4.4. You model each goal separately in its own column and compare each one to the base.

Table 4.4 *Monthly Economic Impact of Desirable System Features*

	Baseline	Goal 1: New operating system	Goal 2: $10,000 in new business	Goal 3: 10% lower time per call	Goal 4: 50% less training required	One time savings for 50% reduction in training
Revenue	$60,000	$60,000	$70,000	$60,000	$60,000	
Cost						
Call Center Staffing	$30,916	$30,916	$36,737	$26,615	$30,496	
Support Staffing	$15,000	$10,000	$15,000	$15,000	$15,000	
Hardware & Facilities	$9,460	$8,000	$9,460	$9,460	$9,460	
Total	$55,376	$48,916	$61,197	$51,495	$54,956	
Profit	$4,624	$11,084	$8,803	$8,505	$5,044	
Profit Margin	7.7%	18.5%	12.6%	14.2%	8.4%	
Monthly Benefit		$6,460	$4,179	$3,881	$420	
One Time Benefit						$2,940

Looking at each goal in turn, you see the following:

1. The customer stands to gain $6,460 per month in hardware and support staff costs as soon as the system is installed.
2. If new features lower call time by 10 percent, $3,881 will be realized monthly.

3. If the end customer satisfaction is increased by 5 percent and your customer can actually get the $10,000 in new business, there would be a resulting monthly benefit of $4,179.

4. Features that allow faster training will generate a one-time savings of $2,940, and $420 per month thereafter.

Thus, the projected customer benefit is $14,520 per month, so each week of delay will cost the customer over $3,000. (It's best not to make this number too precise and to underestimate it rather than overestimate it.) The model also tells the team that speeding up training provides a one-time benefit of $2,940 and a monthly benefit of $420 after that, so they shouldn't spend a large amount of time adding features to speed up training.

Tradeoff Decisions

Tradeoffs are easiest to make if they are expressed in the same units. How can a developer decide if it is better to save a week, save $10,000, or add new features? If all of these decisions are expressed in dollars—or Euros, or yen—the decision will be more straightforward. Thus, the reason to develop simple economic models of a development project is to provide the development team with guidance in making tradeoffs.

Economic models have long been used when deciding what projects to fund, but their use in making decisions during development has been limited. We suggest that basing development decisions on economic models helps the development team make good tradeoff decisions. Providing intelligent people with guidelines for making tradeoffs leads to more effective decisions, to developers who feel empowered, and to an organization that is most likely to be able to respond to and thrive in a competitive environment.

Finally, economic models may help you justify the cost of reducing cycle time, eliminating bottlenecks, and purchasing tools that will allow you to deliver as fast as possible.

TRY THIS

1. Create a single place where everyone who is interested in a project can come to see:
   a. The goal of the current iteration, and
      i. what has already been done
      ii. what is being done
      iii. what has yet to be done
   b. The mission of the overall project, and
      i. what has already been done to meet the project mission
      ii. what has yet to be done to meet the project mission
2. At the end of the next iteration, review your process with an eye for understanding how everyone knows what to do. Ask the team to focus on the way they decide how to spend their time. What would help them make faster and better decisions about what is important? Pick the best two ideas and implement them for the next iteration.
3. Find the three longest queues in your area and chart the cycle time for each job as it goes through each queue. It might look something like Figure 4.3. Look for patterns: Is variability high or low? Is there an upward or downward trend?

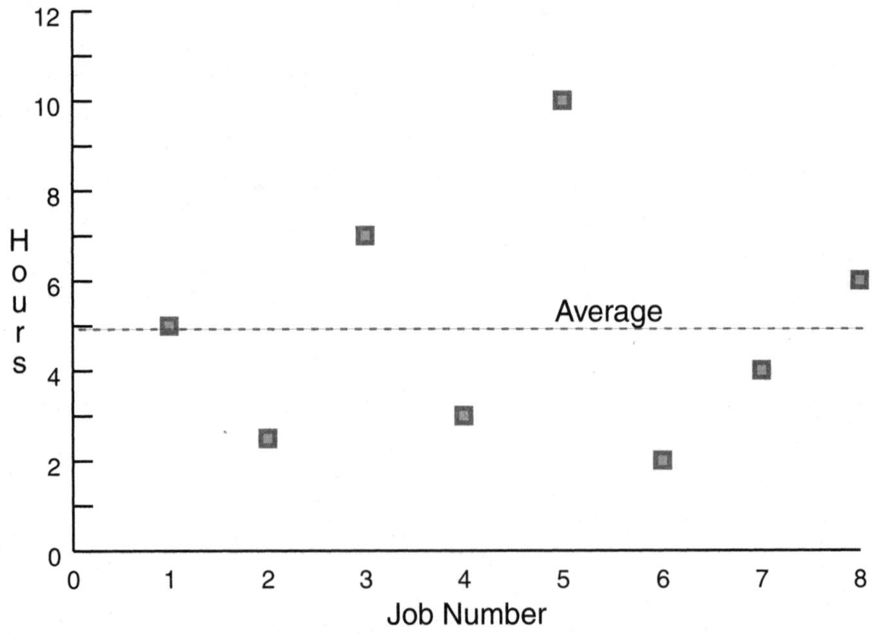

Figure 4.3 *Cycle time chart showing high variability.*

4. Pick the queue that represents your biggest bottleneck and form a *bottleneck task force*. Help the task force use queuing theory to find ways to reduce the queue. Measure the results.

5. Ask finance to assign an accountant to every development team, and have the accountant work with the team to develop a simple economic model showing the cost of delay, the cost of reduced features, the cost of maintenance, and so on.

Chapter 5

Empower the Team

BEYOND SCIENTIFIC MANAGEMENT

When Henry Ford introduced the Model T Ford in 1908, it was so successful that Ford had to invent continually better, faster ways to manufacture the car. The first moving assembly line was introduced in 1913, and by 1927, the River Rouge plant in Dearborn, Michigan, turned iron ore into finished cars in just 28 hours. Ford produced almost 17 million Model T's, converting the country from horses to suburbs in just two decades.

Touring an Auto Factory, circa 1915

Let's take a quick tour of Ford's Highland Park, Michigan, plant in 1915.[1] The 7,000 assembly-line workers here speak 50 languages and very few speak much English. How they do know what to do? Here's what our tour guide tells us:

"A few years back, Frederick Taylor came out with this idea called scientific management.[2] The idea is that you divide all the assembly jobs up into little pieces and figure out how each little piece should be done, and then you teach a worker to do just that one thing. This way, you can train a person in ten minutes without having to say a word. Of course, it takes a whole lot of engineers to figure out all the jobs.

"But that's okay, because the craft shops that used to make automobiles had to close up shop—their cars cost too much compared to the ones we make on

1. See Womack, Jones and Roos, *The Machine That Changed the World,* 31.

2. Taylor's *Principles of Scientific Management* was originally published in 1911.

the assembly line. So now those craft shop workers are our engineers. They're the smart ones. They go out with stopwatches, time each job, and tell the workers how to work faster.

"If they didn't do that, you'd be amazed at how slow the workers would be. But, hey, if we can speed up the assembly line, we make more money, and that means we can pay everyone more. Just last year Ford doubled everyone's salaries to $5 a day. Most people around Detroit are lucky to make $11 a week."

Ford's assembly line began the era of the industrial engineer and supervisor telling people how to do their jobs and rewarding them with pay. At first the pay was impressive, but after a while workers began to realize that the demeaning jobs they took to get established in a new country were not temporary, but had trapped them with high pay. Unions grew strong, and a pall of dissatisfaction settled on the industry.

It's interesting that report cards started to appear in our schools in the 1910s, just about the time that scientific management was gaining credibility in industrial production. Eventually, performance appraisals became the report cards of industry. For decades, it was taken as a given that pay is the most effective motivator for workers and grades are the best motivators for schoolchildren. It wasn't until the 1970s that these assumptions began to be challenged.[3]

In the 1980s, it became apparent that manufacturing techniques pioneered by Toyota—later called lean manufacturing—could produce high-quality products faster and cheaper than scientific management techniques. With both its motivational and operational theories called into question, managers began to move beyond scientific management.

So began a series of programs with names like MBO, TQM, Zero Defects, Optimized Operations, Service Excellence, ISO9000, Total Improvement Program, and Customers First, all aimed at enriching the work environment and the bottom line. Introduced with great fanfare, occasionally successful, the vast assortments of programs generally produced mediocre results. All too often, these programs did not change the reality of how work got done. Frequently, the programs increased the intensity of factors leading to job dissatisfaction (policy, supervision, administration) instead of increasing factors that contribute to job satisfaction (achievement, recognition, responsibility).[4] While this is not the fault of the program, it is a common side effect.

---

3. See Herzberg's classic "One More Time: How Do You Motivate Employees?"

4. The list of motivators and demotivators is from Herzberg, "One More Time: How Do You Motivate Employees?"

CMM

The best known software development improvement program is the Capability Maturity Model, or CMM. As with other programs, CMM has had a range of results, from dramatic success to disappointment. CMM has been used as a certification program similar to ISO9000, especially by software development firms seeking to do business in other countries. Insofar as it has been used as a certification program, CMM has had an impact similar to ISO9000. Both tend to create bureaucracy and make change difficult, even though it is not the intention of either program to do so.

ISO9000 programs should not be thought of as process improvement programs, because they have a bias toward documenting and thus standardizing existing processes rather than improving the processes. Since ISO9000 programs can create a bias against change, it is best to implement them after fundamental improvements have been made.[5] Similarly, when CMM programs are implemented with a focus on documentation and conformance to a particular best way to do a job, they may standardize on less than ideal practices and create a bias against change. Thus they may be better implemented separate from—and after—process improvements.

A bias against process change is not the most difficult issue with programs such as ISO9000 and CMM. As frequently implemented, these programs tend to remove process design and decision-making authority from developers and put it under the control of central organizations. Developers often equate people from the central organization to the stopwatch wielding industrial engineers from the days of scientific management who know the *one best way* for them to do their job. Lean thinking capitalizes on the intelligence of frontline workers, believing that they are the ones who should determine and continually improve the way they do their jobs.

Watts Humphrey, who led the early development of CMM, believes that software development cannot be successful without disciplined, motivated people.[6] We wholeheartedly agree. We respectfully disagree, however, on the practices most likely to produce success. We do not believe that focusing on getting things *right the first time* is appropriate for a design environment; instead, experimentation and feedback are more effective.[7] We believe that the critical factor in motivation is not measurement,[8] but empowerment: moving decisions to the lowest possible level in an organization while developing the capacity of those people to make decisions wisely.

5. Imai, *Gemba Kaizen*, 60.

6. Humphrey, *Winning with Software*, 3.

CMMI

CMM is scheduled to be replaced with the Capability Maturity Model Integration (CMMI) suite by the end of 2003. After developing several maturity models, the Software Engineering Institute (SEI) combined them into CMMI, which promotes a single generic description of *mature* for software development, systems engineering, product development, and other disciplines. Unfortunately, it appears that the software-specific nature of CMM's key process areas (KPAs) will give way to a generic measure of maturity, one with its roots in military procurement.

The CMMI definition of maturity is based on two assumptions:

- *Assumption 1:* A system is best managed by disaggregating it into identifiable work products that are transformed from an input to an output state to achieve specific goals.[9]
- *Assumption 2:* A mature organization is one in which everything is carefully planned and then controlled to meet the plan.

These assumptions sound rather like scientific management to us. We have a different model of what maturity means:

- *Lean Assumption 1:* A mature organization looks at the whole system; it does not focus on optimizing disaggregated parts.[10]

---

7. Ibid.; "To truly accelerate development work and optimize time-to-market, your people must do their jobs the right way the very first time" (p. 10). "Require detailed and complete plans, review these plans, and then negotiate commitments with the people who will do the work" (p. 39). Humphrey calls this "rational management." It seems to us that rational management has a tendency to foster sequential development and it does not deal well with uncertainty. Highsmith's "optimization paradox" discusses how increasing the focus on prediction and control induces failure in uncertain environments. See Highsmith, *Agile Software Development Ecosystems,* 187.

8. Humphrey, *Winning with Software,* 106–107, has a strong focus on measurements. Austin, *Measuring and Managing Performance in Organizations,* 109–110, discusses why measurement-based practices such as management by objectives, and capability evaluations are largely inappropriate for knowledge workers. See also Chapter 7, "See the Whole," in this book.

9. CMMI-SW states: "The process supports and enables achievement of the specific goals of the process area by transforming identifiable input work products to produce identifiable output work products" (p. 36). In Koskela and Howell, "The Underlying Theory of Project Management Is Obsolete," we find a strong argument against this transformation theory. Lean thinking is based on a flow theory, not a transformation theory.

10. See Chapter 7, "See the Whole."

- *Lean Assumption 2:* A mature organization focuses on learning effectively and empowers the people who do the work to make decisions.

Fred Brooks, in *The Mythical Man Month,* quotes Earl Wheeler, retired head of IBM's software business: "The key thrust [of recent years] was delegating power down. It was like magic! Improved quality, productivity, morale." He also quotes Jim McCarthy of Microsoft: "I can't emphasize enough the importance of empowerment, of the team being accountable to itself for its success."

An organization that respects software developers as professionals will expect them to design their own jobs with proper training, coaching, and assistance. It will expect them to improve continually the way they do their work as part of a learning process. Finally, it will give them the time and equipment necessary to do their jobs well. In a lean organization, the people who add value are the center of organizational energy. Frontline workers have process design authority and decision-making responsibility; they are the focus of resources, information and training.

TOOL 13: SELF-DETERMINATION

The NUMMI Mystery

In 1982, General Motors closed its Freemont, California, plant. No one was surprised; the place was a disaster. Productivity was among the lowest of any GM plant, quality was abysmal, and drug and alcohol abuse were rampant both on and off the job. Absenteeism was so high that the plant employed 20 percent more workers than it needed just to ensure an adequate labor force on any given day. The United Auto Workers local earned a national reputation for militancy; from 1963 to 1982, wildcat strikes and sickouts closed the plant four times. The backlog of unresolved grievances often exceeded 5,000.[11]

Two years later, the same plant was reopened by New United Motor Manufacturing, Inc., or NUMMI, a joint venture between Toyota and GM. Toyota managed the plant but was required to rehire the former GM employees. Eighty-five percent of the hourly workers were from the former GM plant, including the entire union leadership.

Within two years, NUMMI's productivity was higher than any GM plant—double that of the original plant. Quality was much higher than any GM plant and nearly matched Toyota's Japanese plants. Absenteeism was down to about 3 percent, and substance abuse was a minimal problem. In 1991, after 8 years of operation, a total of

11. Adler, "Time-and-Motion Regained," 98.

only 700 grievances had been filed, and 90 percent of the employees described themselves as "satisfied" or "very satisfied."[12]

Clearly, something in the management practices made all the difference to NUMMI employees, and those practices have been sustainable. As the NUMMI plant approaches 20 years in operation, it continues to top all other GM plants in productivity and quality, while employee satisfaction remains very high. Other GM plants have been unable to copy the management practices of NUMMI, although other Toyota-managed plants in the United States have successfully done so with similar results.

Make no mistake about it: Automobile assembly is still difficult, repetitive work. At the NUMMI plant, workers repeat the same actions approximately once a minute, and during that minute, they are busy for 57 seconds. In the old days, they worked for only 45 seconds out of every minute, so they now work a lot harder—and they do exactly the same thing every time. Exactly. If it sounds regimented, it is. Work was regimented in the old GM plant also. In fact, there were 80 industrial engineers who went around with stopwatches designing every single task. Then, they told the workers exactly how to do the task. As you can imagine, the workers did not appreciate being told how to do their jobs.

The first thing the managers at the NUMMI plant did was get stopwatches for everyone, and they taught workers how to design their own jobs. All work at NUMMI is done in teams of six to eight people, one of whom is the team leader. The team designs its own work procedures, coordinating work standards with teams doing the same work on alternate shifts. Management's role is to coach, train, and assist the teams. Engineers are available if the team wants to call on them, but fundamentally, each team is responsible for its own procedures, its own quality, for job rotation within the team, and for smooth flow of parts from upstream and to downstream teams.

Jamie Hresko is a manufacturing manager at GM who was trying to unlock the secret of NUMMI. He took time off from his job to secretly work as an ordinary worker at NUMMI for a month, and he was amazed at what he found.[13] He thought his plant trained and supported line workers, but the extent to which NUMMI workers were the center of attention was well beyond his expectations. It seemed that everyone's job existed solely to help the line workers, and the workers in turn were fully engaged in their jobs. Training was extensive, the atmosphere was friendly and helpful, and it was crystal clear what was important.

So herein lies the puzzle. GM understands that focusing—really focusing—on the worker is the key to success. They can and do send people to NUMMI to find out

12. Ibid., 99.

13. See O'Reilly and Pfeffer, *Hidden Value*, 181–182.

how to do this. And still, they have been largely unsuccessful in doing what they know should be done. Why?

We believe that transferring *practices* from one environment to another is often a mistake. Instead, one must understand the fundamental principles behind practices and transform those principles into new practices for a new environment. In fact, Toyota did not transfer Japanese production practices *en masse* to NUMMI. But it did transfer its belief that the foundation of human respect is to provide an environment where capable workers actively participate in running and improving their work areas and are able to fully use their capabilities.[14] It appears that GM has had a difficult time transferring the same principle to its plants, and thus has failed to unleash the capabilities of front line workers to the same extent as Toyota.

More Than Meets the Eye

A development group at a large company (let's call it the FIX-IT group) became frustrated at working in a chaotic environment, so after a particularly difficult delivery, the group members convinced their manager to give them some time to put some discipline in place. They chose and implemented coding standards, a configuration management system, an automated build process, and a unit testing process.

The FIX-IT group was pleased to have the new disciplines in place, because the members felt they were in a more professional environment and could take more pride in their work. They decided to meet regularly to discuss improvements to their environment. They standardized on templates and checklists that helped them interact better with customers; worked with the database administrator to write scripts for test environments; and added a support person to implement and test the installation process. As time went on, the FIX-IT group delivered software faster and had customers who were happier than those of other groups. The FIX-IT group was also regarded as the best place to work by the developers in the company.

A vice president decided that the success of the FIX-IT group should be replicated in the rest of the company. A staff group was formed to document the processes used by the FIX-IT group and teach them to the rest of the groups in the company. The goal was to create uniform processes so the company could deliver consistent results.

Not surprisingly, the staff group overlooked the principle behind the practices used by the FIX-IT group—the principle that the developers were responsible for defining and constantly redefining and improving their own practices. Since redefining practices did not fit into the goal of uniformity, the staff group consid-

14. See Ohno, *The Toyota Product System*, 7–8.

ered it a bad habit that would have to stop. In addition, the staff group noticed that the FIX-IT group's documentation was sketchy, and some important processes seemed to be missing. The staff group was proud of its discovery that not even the FIX-IT group was perfect.

One year later, the company had a book of documented processes that even the most inexperienced developer could follow. Most development groups ignored the staff group's efforts, including the FIX-IT group, which continued to adapt its own work procedures, focusing on what it considered important. The FIX-IT group continued to produce better software faster and had more satisfied customers than any other group. The attempt to duplicate its success elsewhere, however, was largely a failure.

—A Business Novelette

A Management Improvement Process

Today's organizations are littered with failed improvement programs, whether they go by the name CMM, ISO9000, TQM, Six Sigma, or even Lean. It is notoriously difficult to implement successful improvement programs, and even more difficult to sustain them over time. One program, the Work-Out program, originally developed at General Electric, is different. It was conceived of as a way to change the behavior of middle managers and unleash the know-how of those closest to the work. "In most organizations change efforts come and go—and somehow rarely make a difference. But at GE...one particular change process helped spark a complete transformation—Work-Out."[15]

At a Work-Out, 50 or so workers gather for two or three days and come up with proposals that will help them do a better job. Teams come up with specific proposals for doing away with processes that get in the way and implementing practices that will deliver value faster. Before the Work-Out is over, managers are required to make a yes-no decision on every proposal, either on the spot or within a couple of days. Those who made proposals are expected to be responsible for implementing them—immediately. The combination of simple tools, immediate action, and participation of virtually everyone in the company combined to make Work-Out a uniquely successful improvement program.

In most improvement programs managers tell workers how to do their jobs. In Work-Out the tables are turned; workers tell managers how to let them do their jobs. A Work-Out is a process that teaches managers how to listen to workers, charter them to take action on their ideas, and follow up to be sure that approved proposals are implemented promptly. A Work-Out assumes that workers know how to do their

15. Ulrich, Kerr, and Ashkenas, *The GE Work-Out*, 3.

jobs and focuses management attention on changing the systems that, in the eyes of the workers, prevent them from doing a good job. It is not an accident that this sounds similar to the NUMMI approach.

Treat People Like Volunteers

A new project manager asked me for advice on how to get his team to do what he wanted it to do. I could sense that he had a tendency to give orders to a team that was largely more experienced than he was, and the team's negative reaction was apparent. I had about five minutes to find a way to get him to appreciate how his style was turning off the team; I had to think fast.

"Do you do any volunteer work?" I asked. "Do you coach a sport or anything like that?" It was a gamble.

"Well," he said, "I am the choir director at my church." Jackpot!

"So, how do you get the choir to come to practice? How do you keep them coming? How do you get the choir to sing together?" I asked.

He launched proudly into all the techniques he had developed for dealing with volunteers. I could tell he was a good and popular choir director.

"Okay," I said. "You've just answered your question. Use the same techniques leading your team that you use with your choir, and you will get them to do what you want. If you tell them what to do, you'll fail."

The ill will on the team gradually dissipated and the project was a success.

—Mary

TOOL 14: MOTIVATION

Magic at 3M

Every so often, a group of people will band together to accomplish something great. Excitement fills the air as the impossible challenge is tackled and the unbeatable foe is conquered. Everyone is completely engaged in the task, dedicated to the purpose. Passion and camaraderie create an intense atmosphere in which anything is possible. It's a magical experience people remember fondly for the rest of their lives.

3M is one of those rare large companies in which the magic of engaged teams is easy to find. At any given time, there are dozens of energized, self-organizing groups working on commercializing new products. As a result, 3M has one of the most enviable records of new product introductions in the world, regularly meeting its goal that each division has 30 percent of its sales generated by products introduced in the last 4 years. The torrent of new products has kept the company broadly diversified and continually renewed for decades. This has been going on for over 75 years.

How is this possible? How can a large organization develop such a stream of new products by depending on groups that emerge spontaneously and operate largely outside of management direction? How can such "organized chaos" possibly be sustained over three generations?

3M has a simple, highly effective formula that allows the entrepreneurial spirit to flourish. This formula was put in place by William McKnight, who led the company through its formation and growth from the 1930s through the 1950s. Although he was never on a new product team, he created the soul of a new product development machine. At its heart are small, self-organizing groups that become passionate about a possibility and are allowed to make it a reality. McKnight's vision is captured in quotes such as [16]

> "Hire good people, and leave them alone."
> "If you put fences around people, you get sheep. Give people the room they need."
> "Encourage, don't nitpick. Let people run with an idea."
> "Give it a try—and quick!"

3M puts a great value on scientific research and encourages all of its scientists to be on the lookout for new product opportunities. Scientists are expected to spend 15 percent of their time on projects of their own choosing, preferably new product development projects. This slack time creates an environment in which people have the time to play around with new product ideas. The company has a broad array of forums for scientists to meet each other, exchange knowledge, and discuss interesting ideas. Numerous recognition programs reward scientists for contributions to successful new products. This environment encourages groups to form spontaneously around a new product idea.

New product programs typically start with a champion who has an idea for a new product. The champion recruits volunteers and rounds up enough resources to try out the idea. The environment conspires to encourage teams to form around compelling ideas, and compelling ideas have a tendency to inspire the team. First, the technology is refined, and invariably inventions are made. During this formative time, the group will probably acquire a few sponsoring managers who are expected to keep the project out of sight. Sponsoring managers might help the team recruit members with access to materials and laboratory equipment. Sample products are made and tested with potential customers.

When the team has done enough work to seek official status, it has to pass three simple hurdles: The product must meet a real need, it must use 3M technology, and it

16. Collins and Porras, *Built to Last*, 152.

must have a good profit potential. Two commonly used hurdles are not present: There is no revenue threshold and no need for a strategic fit with existing businesses. The original team members continue to move the product toward commercialization and beyond. If they end up creating a successful business, they can expect to end up running it. Or, they can turn the business over to a division to run so that they are free to create the magic all over again.

The critical invention that allowed all of this to happen was McKnight's invention of an organization that continually evolves from the creativity and initiative of individual employees rather than from the strategic planning of managers.

Purpose

"There is a great deal of evidence that people are hardwired to care about purposes," writes Kenneth Thomas in *Intrinsic Motivation at Work*. "There is also much evidence that people suffer when they lack purpose" (p. 22). Intrinsic motivation comes from the work we do, from pride in workmanship and a sense of helping a customer. Purpose is what makes work energizing and engaging.

People need more than a list of tasks. If their work is to provide intrinsic motivation, they need to understand and commit to the purpose of the work. Intrinsic motivation is especially powerful if people on a team commit together to accomplishing a purpose they care about. There are many things you can do to help a team gain and hold a sense of purpose:

- **Start with a clear and compelling purpose.** Successful teams at 3M always have a champion whose first job is to communicate a compelling vision of the new product's potential in order to recruit volunteers. Team members who commit to a compelling purpose will collaborate with passion to bring their baby to market.
- **Be sure the purpose is achievable.** The fundamental rule of empowerment is to make sure the team has within itself the capability to accomplish the purpose of its work. If a team commits to accomplishing a business objective, it should have access to the resources needed to accomplish that goal.
- **Give the team access to customers.** Talking to real, live customers is a great way for team members to understand the purpose of what they are doing. It becomes meaningful if they can see how their software is going to make life easier for real people. This also gives team members insight into how their individual work fits into the overall picture.
- **Let the team make its own commitments.** At the beginning of an iteration, the team should negotiate with customers to understand their priorities and select the work for the next iteration. No one should presume to tell the team how much work it should be able to finish. The team makes the call, and when the

members commit to a set of features, they are making the commitment to each other.

- **Management's role is to run interference.** A highly motivated team does not need to be told what to do, but it may need to give its leaders some advice. ("If you do not replicate the customer environment, we simply will not be able to test the system adequately.") It will probably need some resources. ("If we don't get more support from a DBA, we won't make it.") It usually needs some protection. ("Kindly tell marketing that no, they can't add five more features to this month's work.") Leaders may not be able to satisfy every request, but the team will maintain momentum if its members know they have someone who is looking out for them.
- **Keep skeptics away from the team.** Nothing kills a purpose faster than someone who knows it can't be done and has plenty of good reasons why. The team does not need to hear it.

In Search of Business Value

As a consultant at a large HMO, I interviewed an IT manager who set out to make a difference for the business units in her company. She believed that the way to do this was through ongoing, close collaboration with business unit managers.

To get started, she asked her team to generate a long list of ideas that might be interesting to business units. She then took the list to business unit managers and used the list to help them imagine the business possibilities that might be generated through different perspectives on information.

With a rough estimate of value from business managers plus a high-level estimate of effort from her team, she found the highest value projects and then helped the business managers to justify these projects.

Working as a team, analysts (some from the business unit, some from the IT organization) defined the details of how the business value could be achieved, focusing as much on changes in business processes as on software development.

As the system was developed, the team worked through each iteration to be sure that the system fit into the business environment and that the business was prepared to use it. Each team was dedicated to achieving the business value behind the system, and because of this, almost all of these systems achieved a business success.

Successful projects generate their own rewards, and developers in the company lined up to work for this manager every time she staffed new projects.

—Tom

Think of a software development team as a multisided polygon, as in Figure 5.1. Each side of the polygon has its goals. The customers would like the system to deliver business value. Analysts or product managers help the customers articulate these features in detail and make them understandable for the developers. Developers estimate the amount of time needed and deliver working software. Testers help ensure that the system meets customer needs by creating comprehensive customer tests. Support people deal with deployment and user training, and make sure the help desk knows how to answer questions. Together, this team has a purpose: Deliver business value.

Figure 5.1 *The team polygon.*

The number of sides of the polygon and the specific disciplines needed to achieve a purpose will vary depending on the type of project. Some customers do not need analysts; others need help translating their broad-brush view into detail that developers can work on. Sometimes testers serve the role of analyst, and vice versa. Domain-savvy developers often serve in the analyst role. The important thing is that analysts do not get in the way of a direct developer-customer communication, but rather, facilitate understanding on both sides.

The Building Blocks of Motivation

Intrinsic motivation is driven by self-determination and a sense of purpose, but it will not flourish in a hostile climate. Research has shown that intrinsic motivation requires a feeling of belonging, a feeling of safety, a sense of competence, and sense of progress.[17]

Belonging

In today's work environment it takes a team to accomplish most purposes. On a healthy team, everyone is clear on what the goal is and is committed to its success. Team members respect each other and are honest with each other. Finally, the team must win or lose as a group. Giving individuals credit for team efforts and fostering competition that creates winners and losers is a good way to kill team motivation. If only a few members of a team get to be winners, the other members learn to look out for themselves, not for the overall good of the team.

Safety

One of the fastest ways to kill motivation is what is called in the U.S. Army a *zero defects mentality*. A zero defects mentality is an atmosphere that tolerates absolutely no mistakes; perfection is required down to the smallest detail. The army considers a zero defects mentality to be a serious leadership problem, because it kills the initiative necessary for success on a battlefield.

William McKnight of 3M was wise enough to understand this in 1949, when he said.[18]

> As our business grows, it becomes increasingly necessary to delegate responsibility and to encourage men and women to exercise their initiative. This requires considerable tolerance. Those men and women, to whom we delegate authority and responsibility, if they are good people, are going to want to do their jobs in their own way. Mistakes will be made. But if a person is essentially right, the mistakes he or she makes are not as serious in the long run as the mistakes management will make if it undertakes to tell those under their authority exactly how they must do their jobs.

---

17. Thomas, *Intrinsic Motivation at Work*, lists the building blocks of intrinsic motivation: choice (self determination), meaningfulness (purpose), competence, and progress (p. 49). In Maslow, Frager, and Fadiman, *Motivation and Personality*, Abraham Maslow presents his classic hierarchy of human needs: physiological, safety, belonging, esteem, and self-actualization.

18. Paraphrased from Huck, *Brand of the Tartan* (p. 239), by 3M at *http://www.3m.com/profile/looking/mcknight.jhtml*, accessed July 25, 2002. Various versions of this remark by McKnight are widely distributed by 3M.

Competence

People need to believe they are capable of doing a good job; they want to be involved in something that they believe will work. It is very motivating to be part of a winning team, very demotivating to believe that failure is inevitable. An undisciplined work environment does not generate a sense of freedom; it creates a sense of doom.

Software development environments must be disciplined in order for work to proceed smoothly, rapidly, and productively. Basic good practices such as using a version controlled code repository, coding standards, a build process, and automated testing are required for rapid development. Also important is a mechanism for sharing ideas and improving designs, perhaps by using pair programming, code reviews, or similar approaches.

A sense of competence comes from knowledge and skill, positive feedback, high standards, and meeting a difficult challenge. A leader who delegates and trusts workers must nevertheless verify that they are on the right track and provide the necessary guidance to allow them to be successful.

Progress

Even a highly motivated team will only work so long before members need to feel they have accomplished something. This reaffirms the purpose and keeps everyone fired up. If there is no other reason to develop software in iterations—and there are many!—this is a compelling reason by itself. Every iteration, the team gets to put its best efforts in front of customers and find out how it has done. Of course, there's some risk that the customer won't be pleased, but it's better to find that out earlier than later. Most often, customers are delighted to see working software that they can actually use. The meaningfulness of the work is enhanced and the team is reenergized.

When a team reaches a particularly important objective, it's time for a celebration. Team members celebrate small accomplishments by congratulating each other. They celebrate medium-sized accomplishments by escaping for a while to have some fun. Important accomplishments should result in public recognition, preferably immediately. Projects should have meaningful measurements that show progress toward the goal posted in a place for everyone to see.[19]

---

19. See the section "Information Radiators" in Chapter 4, "Deliver as Fast as Possible."

The Dirty Coffee Cup

Dee Hock relates how the early management team at Visa confidently committed to the board that it would implement an authorization system in a year. Then, it hired a consultant who told the team it couldn't be done, so the team members decided to do it themselves. The tasks were laid out on a large linear calendar. Someone hung a coffee cup on a string to mark the current date. As tasks were completed, they were removed from the calendar. Any task that got on the wrong side of the string was descended upon by the entire team and quickly conquered. Every day, the string moved, and the tasks were taken off the calendar. When the project was completed on time, the dirty coffee cup got a large amount of the credit.[20]

Long Days and Late Nights

People who are passionately involved in something often find that it dominates their lives. They think about it all the time, and their subconscious takes over when they are not consciously focused on the task. They begin to avoid doing less interesting tasks that interfere with their passion. Their single-minded focus on the task at hand may turn into an obsession.

Passionate teams will put in long hours and late nights in order to accomplish their purpose. There is a lot of debate about whether this is bad or good. After all, the people are doing what they love, and they choose to spend the long hours.

A couple of cautions are in order. First, long hours and late nights are not a sustainable mode of operating, and generally they do not result in better work. People get careless when they are tired; it's often better to quit for the day at a reasonable hour and come back fresh the next day.

Second, excited, passionate teams may create a climate in which people are expected to work long hours and late nights. This is not fair for those who would not choose such dedication but for peer pressure, and it may result in subtle discrimination. Parents should not have to apologize for coaching their kids' teams in the evening. Women should not feel they have to leave the software development profession because they don't see how long hours and family commitments can coexist. Those who love to exercise every day should have time to do it without feeling guilty.

20. Hock, *Birth of the Chaordic Age*, 203–208.

It is better to encourage moderation than heroism. If a dedicated team is working at a sustainable pace and an emergency comes up, the members will rise to the occasion. If they are seriously overcommitted already, they can't respond to an emergency.

TOOL 15: LEADERSHIP

Leadership

"No one has yet figured out how to manage people effectively into battle; they must be led," wrote John Kotter in "What Leaders Really Do." Kotter draws a sharp distinction between managers and leaders, summarized in Table 5.1.

Table 5.1 *Managers vs. Leaders*

Managers	Leaders
Cope with Complexity	*Cope with Change*
• Plan and Budget	• Set Direction
• Organize and Staff	• Align People
• Track and Control	• Enable Motivation

Respected Leaders

It is not an accident that every major new product development program at 3M is led by a *champion*. Innovation at 3M is brought about by excited, motivated teams, and if you look behind a passionate team, you will find a passionate leader. 3M new product development teams are led by a product champion who probably wrote the initial product concept, gathered management support for the program, and recruited most of the team. The champion interprets the product vision for the team, thus representing the customer who, after all, is not even aware of the new product yet. The champion sets the pace of development and determines how decisions are made. A champion is also expected to keep working on a good idea even if the program is killed by management.

A similar role is played by the chief engineer at Toyota, who spends time studying the target market, writes the vehicle concept document, establishes the overall design, sets the schedule, and is responsible, in the end, for the economic performance of the vehicle. In contrast to the coordinating role of a new vehicle manager at U.S. auto companies, the chief engineer has complete responsibility for the vehicle and has the authority necessary to make all program decisions. The Toyota chief engineer has been called a *heavyweight program manager,*[21] but this is a misnomer, because a chief engineer is much more a leader than a manager. Perhaps the correct characterization of a chief engineer is a *respected leader.* The emphasis of the chief engineer role is on setting direction, aligning the organization, and motivating the team.

Product champions at 3M and chief engineers at Toyota have a strong sense of product ownership. In both 3M and Toyota, the product produced by a champion or chief engineer often bears his or her name (Fuji-san's car or Art Fry's Post-It® Notes). At 3M, the champion is largely self-nominating, and the roles in both companies hold great stature. It might seem that a strong sense of ownership would lead chief engineers and champions to exercise a great deal of control over the development of *their* product, but neither of these leaders has direct authority over the people working on the product. They fully understand that leveraging the talents of a large pool of experts is far more effective than trying to control the work. Thus, they lead the development team instead of trying to manage it. It is because of their dedication and passion that champions and chief engineers excel at inspiring technical teams.

Master Developers

In an extensive study of large system design,[22] Bill Curtis and his coauthors found that for most large systems, a single or small team of *exceptional designers* emerge to assume primary responsibility for the design. Exceptional designers exercise leadership through their superior knowledge rather than bestowed authority. Their deep understanding of both the customers and the technical issues gain them the respect of the development team. Exceptional designers are people who are extremely familiar with the application domain and are skilled at communicating their technical vision to the development team. They are usually consumed with the success of *their* systems.

Notice that the exceptional designer identified by Curtis and his colleagues has the same characteristics we noted in a respected leader such as a chief engineer or product champion. In software development we have used terms such as *systems engineer, chief programmer,* and *architect* to designate the role of the exceptional designer. For purposes of this book, we use the term *master developer* to designate the role of respected leader of a software development project.

The role of a master developer is essential. However, it is not necessary to identify a master developer at the beginning of every project. For small systems, a master developer will tend to emerge in a self-organizing team. Even in large systems, Curtis

21. Sobek, Ward, and Liker, "Toyota's Principles of Set-Based Concurrent Engineering"; Clark and Fujimoto, *Product Development Performance.*

22. Curtis, Kransner, and Iscoe, "A field Study of the Software Design Process for Large Systems," 1272.

and colleagues found that exceptional designers exercised leadership because of their knowledge, not because they were designated leaders. If a master developer is appointed, be sure that the person is a respected leader who will empower the team. A chief architect who does not collaborate with the developers can prevent the emergence of the right kind of design leadership.

Master developers have extensive experience in the domain and the technology; they understand both the customers and developers. They understand the system's constraints, interactions, unstated requirements, exception conditions, and likely direction of change. They look at the system from a fairly high level of abstraction, yet can drill down to the complexity and detail that both developers and customers must cope with. They have the wisdom to guide market tradeoffs in product development and business tradeoffs in internal development. If a development team does not have this kind of a leader, it will seek one out, because teams understand that such leadership is a key to making their efforts a success.

Since master developers are perceived as the most knowledgeable people, they become the focal point of communication.[23] Organizations with architects who serve in an advisory role will find that these architects are not likely to serve in the role we define as master developer. Master developers are part of the team, enmeshed in the details of the work. They provide the leadership necessary for the team to make good decisions, make rapid progress, and develop high-quality software.

The master developer is like the conductor of a musical group, coordinating the efforts of the musicians and helping them to play together.[24] Some teams are like jazz bands, so they need a leader who encourages improvisation. Some teams are like symphony orchestras, so they need a leader who keeps everyone on the same sheet of music. Conductors have to be deeply familiar with each instrument and with the music, yet they don't play in the band or tell the musicians what to do. They let the music provide detailed guidance; their job is to bring out the best in the musicians, both individually and as a group.

---

23. Ibid., 1272.

24. Ohno, *The Toyota Production System*, describes the metaphor of workers as members of a sports team and managers as coaches who help the team reach peak performance (pp. 23–25).

The Fuzzy Front End

A consistent criticism of iterative approaches is that they do not provide for design prior to the beginning of programming. We suspect that this misconception is an indication of a deeper concern; the underlying issue is most likely a difference of perspective on the level of design detail desirable prior to beginning other areas of development. Those with a bias toward sequential development would like to see all design done prior to the start of programming. Agile approaches recognize that architectures evolve and mature; the practical approach is to provide for an emerging design rather than try to stop it.

The real question is, When has enough design been done for developers to start working? This is where master developers fit in—they are the ones who make the call. It is the responsibility of master developers to judge the level of initial conceptual design necessary at the beginning of concurrent development, facilitate the emergence of the design as development proceeds, and assure that there are no downstream surprises that should have been anticipated.

Development should begin as soon as a conceptual design is articulated at a high level. A single team working on a modest problem might start with development immediately and allow a master developer to emerge. A multiteam system will require more coordination. Some domains might lend themselves to immediate experimentation; others may have concerns, such as safety or security, which require more consideration. Quite often, the architecture of a system is predetermined or obvious from the nature of the problem, other times there are several architectural options to be considered.

Some organizations prefer to have a standard process for dealing with the fuzzy front end of product development, which is fine; but a hope that a standard process will enable less experienced designers to come up with a great design is misguided. As Fred Brooks notes, "Great designs come from great designers. Software construction is a creative process. Sound methodology can empower and liberate the creative mind; it cannot enflame or inspire the drudge."[25] For a large system that requires a new architecture, we agree with Brooks:[26] "Design must proceed from one mind or a small group of agreeing minds." The best approach for designing a new architecture is to put a few of your wisest people together and have them start working on it.[27]

25. Brooks, "No Silver Bullet: Essence and Accidents of Software Engineering."

26. Brooks, *Mythical Man Month*, 233.

27. Hohmann, *Beyond Software Architecture*.

Where Do Master Developers Come From?

Master developers grow into their role through extensive experience in the technology and domain being addressed by the system, coupled with excellent abstraction and communication skills. There is no substitute for experience. As Pete McBreen explains in *Software Craftsmanship,*[28] learning the skill of software development is like learning a craft. New programmers start as apprentices to master craftsmen. As they become skilled, they teach other apprentices and eventually journey to work with other master craftsmen. Journeymen disseminate ideas and develop broad skills, eventually becoming master craftsmen themselves.

Leaders only flourish in organizations that want them to be there. An organization has to value leadership in order to develop leaders. We notice that organizations that hold technical leaders in high esteem seem to have plenty of these leaders grow up from the ranks. They have a built-in leadership apprenticeship program because they have an assortment of different programs where people can learn the craft of leadership. They often have *dual ladders,* which allow technical leaders to achieve the same status and pay as supervisors and managers.

People respond to the expectations of their management. Software development leaders will not flourish in an organization that values process, documentation, and conformance to plan above all else. An organization will get what it values, and the Agile Manifesto[29] does us a great service in shifting our perception of value from process to people, from documentation to code, from contracts to collaboration, from plans to action.

Project Management

Against this backdrop, let's examine the role of a project manager in agile development. Often, the software project manager does not have a technical background and is generally not responsible for developing a deep understanding of the technical aspects of the project. Thus, the project manager usually does not play the role of master developer.

On the other hand, agile development is based on short iterations in which team members make their own commitments and monitor their own progress toward meeting those commitments. Although a high-level list of features may be arranged

28. See McBreen, *Software Craftsmanship,* 82. We like Luke Hohmann's guidance: "Staff one journeyman for important projects. Staff one master for mission-critical projects. Staff one realist for every three optimists" (*Journey of the Software Professional,* 310-311).

29. *www.agilemanifesto.org.*

into a long-range iteration release plan, this plan does not drive day-to-day work. Pull systems structure the work itself to signal to developers what to do, so in a properly structured lean environment, a project manager does not assign tasks or monitor their completion. If the team is empowered to make its own decisions, what is the job of the project manager?

The 22 tools in this book help to define the role of project leadership in agile software development. Project leaders start by identifying waste and sketching a value stream map of the current development process, and tackle the biggest bottlenecks. They coordinate iteration planning meetings and daily status meetings, provide information radiators, and help the team get the resources it needs to meet commitments. They coordinate multiple teams by insuring that synchronization is regular and thorough. They ensure that the development environment has standard tools, such as source control and automated testing, and make sure that refactoring and integrated acceptance testing are being done. They work with accounting to create financial models so that the team can make good tradeoff decisions. They provide a motivating environment and keep skeptics at bay, organize celebrations and send the team home at night.

Project leaders play an important role in an agile project; it's just not the role they learned at their project management class. Instead of scheduling with Pert and Gantt charts, they create a release plan with frequent milestones and keep the focus on meeting iteration commitments. Instead of worrying about scope creep, they worry about creeping elegance; instead of worrying about change approval processes, they worry about change-tolerant design practices. They make sure that testing and integration are part of development instead of a separate and later event. They make sure that the people involved in deployment, training, and customer support are fully involved from the start.

Lean Project Management Training

Most of the topics covered in a traditional project management course are not what an agile project leader needs to know. We recommend an alternate toolkit for project leaders:

1. Seeing Waste
2. Value Stream Mapping
3. Feedback
4. Iterations
5. Synchronization
6. Set-Based Development
7. Options Thinking
8. Last Responsible Moment
9. Making Decisions
10. Pull Systems
11. Queuing Theory
12. Cost of Delay
13. Self Determination
14. Motivation
15. Leadership
16. Expertise
17. Perceived Integrity
18. Conceptual Integrity
19. Testing
20. Refactoring
21. Measurements
22. Contracts

TOOL 16: EXPERTISE

Nucor[30]

Nucor opened its first steel mill in South Carolina in 1968, just as the steel industry in the United States was entering troubled times. Even as the rest of the industry decayed, Nucor's sales grew 17 percent per year for the next 30 years, while maintaining some of the highest profit margins in the industry. Having started from scratch 35 years ago, Nucor is the largest steel producer in the United States, with over $4 billion in sales. Nucor was the first mini-mill company to make flat-rolled steel and the first to commercialize thin-slab casting. It did not invent these processes; every steel

30. Information in this section is from Gupta and Govindarajan, "Knowledge Management's Social Dimension: Lessons from Nucor Steel." See also Christensen, *The Innovator's Dilemma*, 101–108; and Collins, *Good To Great*.

company had access to the same technologies. It was simply the best at adopting breakthrough technologies, beating its competitors by years.

Nucor employees at all levels have a clear goal: productivity. Incentives based on work group productivity are the core of Nucor's compensation plan. Interestingly, Nucor avoids the suboptimization of typical measurement systems by basing incentives one level higher than you would expect.[31] A plant manager is not paid based on his or her plant's productivity, but on the productivity of all plants; workers' incentive pay is based on the productivity of a group of 30 or 40 people. However, Nucor does not simply reward productivity; it makes sure that everyone has the opportunity and the expertise to become more productive.

Nucor's competitive advantage is a pervasive expertise in building and running steel mini-mills and in adopting the best technology available as early as possible. This expertise is not an accident. First, Nucor hires intelligent, motivated people. Then, it trains them continuously across many functions. Finally, it encourages experimentation by individuals and self-organizing teams, tolerates failure, and aggressively spreads the knowledge gained through experimentation throughout the company.

Nucor attributes its incredible track record to its ability to develop expertise in all workers and its ability to tap into and spread this expertise throughout the company. Nucor has learned that knowledge is shared in two ways: Some knowledge can be codified and shared by documentation, but much knowledge is tacit knowledge that will only be shared through conversation. Therefore, it involves production workers in the selection of equipment, transfers people frequently both within and between plants, and sends a crew of experienced workers to a new plant to help it start up.

Xerox[32]

Xerox has some 25,000 repair technicians fixing copying machines, and the company had developed extensive documentation on how to repair a balky machine. Researchers at Xerox Palo Alto Research Center (PARC) were working on artificial intelligence, and they considered replacing the paper documentation used by repair technicians with an electronic system. Luckily, they asked the technicians who often gathered for lunch in the PARC cafeteria what they thought of the idea. The technicians told them the paper documentation was useless for the tough problems they encountered. The way they solved vexing problems was by finding out how other technicians had fixed similar problems.

31. See "Tool 21: Measurements" in Chapter 7.

32. Information in this section is from Mitchell, "Share...and Share Alike." See also Brown and Duguid, "Balancing Act: How to Capture Knowledge Without Killing It."

The PARC researchers were intrigued, so they studied various groups of repair technicians and found that, indeed, the way all of the technicians solved tough repair problems was by trading war stories at informal gatherings. They decided to start up a database of tips for technicians, but found managers were opposed to the idea. It was felt technicians did not have enough expertise to provide valuable tips to each other, and besides, managers knew that the way to insure quality of service was through a standardized process.

Management resistance was a fortunate turn of events, because the database of tips was developed underground, largely by PARC researchers and technicians in France. Together they developed a way to have technicians test the tips, combine and edit them, and post the good ones into a database along with the name of the person submitting the tip. Tests showed that the tip system increased productivity by 10 percent in two months. Word spread through the underground that the system was really useful, and technicians who would not have trusted yet another management initiative were begging for the system.

What PARC researchers discovered is that technicians across the company had developed small *communities of expertise* to deal with difficult repair problems that fell off the map of the official documentation. Together with PARC, technicians found a way to spread the community across the company. In effect, the technicians developed a *community of scientists* who discovered solutions through experimentation, wrote up the results, and submitted them for publication. The tips were reviewed and replicated by peers, and published with due credit in a database widely used by the community. Useful tips gained wide peer recognition for the technician who submitted it.

In a paper summarizing the effort, PARC director John Seely Brown notes that the technicians developed a community of expertise similar to the way scientists develop such communities. Scientists work in small groups and circulate ideas through peer review and publication. Most scientists don't get paid for scientific articles, but they earn status and "bragging rights" among their peers.[33] The same dynamic seems to be the motivator in the open source community.[34]

Communities of Expertise

Software development is a complex endeavor with many areas of specialized knowledge. On the one hand, there is the technical knowledge—there are database experts and user interface experts, embedded code experts and middleware experts. On the other hand, there is a great deal of domain knowledge—if your company writes

33. Brown and Duguid, "Balancing Act: How to Capture Knowledge Without Killing It."

34. See Raymond, *The Cathedral and the Bazaar.*

health-care software or security software, it is important to develop expertise in these domains. If you are going to have a competitive advantage in the marketplace, you need to have areas of expertise in your organization that don't exist in competing companies. Even if your organization serves a customer internal to your company, you would do well to understand what particular expertise your group brings to the company that can't be obtained by outsourcing.

The traditional way to develop communities of expertise in a company is to divide the organization into functions that match the core competencies needed by the organization. Each function hires and trains people, establishes standards, and develops expertise for its particular competency. Functions supply staff to value-adding teams that develop a product or system under the guidance of a program leader.

There are inherent problems with this matrix structure. First, there is the potential for workers to feel split loyalties when they have two managers to satisfy, and second, there is the danger that one side of the matrix will dominate the other. However, successful matrix structures exist in many companies, and a close look at these companies reveals that success is determined by the way managers view their jobs. In companies with successful matrix management, functional managers view their jobs as mentors and teachers. They make sure that there are masters who help to develop journeymen and apprentices through a progressive series of work assignments with appropriate support and coaching. At the same time, matrixed value-added team leaders view their jobs as enablers and motivators who gather resources and remove obstacles, and as guides who represent the voice of the customer to the team.

For example, at 3M, new scientists are hired into a function, where they work daily with colleagues who have deep knowledge of their specialty—be it making ultra-clear polymers or the weathering of clear plastics or designing precise optical structures to bend light. When these scientists get together on a product team to design an ultra-bright traffic sign material, they bring to the project the collective knowledge of their disciplines. Functional managers at 3M are skilled in their discipline and see their jobs as teacher and mentor. They are rewarded if their function contributes in a meaningful way to bringing innovative new products to market. Thus, functional managers encourage and help their people to contribute their expertise to new product development programs.

The Toyota product development organization is also a matrix organization. The chief engineers lead the team, but the deep technical expertise needed to design a car resides in the functions. Engineers stay in the same function for perhaps a decade before they are considered really experienced body or engine or layout engineers. During this time, they are taught and mentored by managers who are experts in their area. Functional managers at Toyota are respected in their fields, and they have the stature to act as a counterbalance to a chief engineer at times when major tradeoff decisions must be made.

Matrix organizational structures are very useful for providing communities of expertise, but even if a company does not use a matrix structure, it is imperative to have communities of expertise. The first step is to identify the technical and domain-specific competencies that are critical to the organization's success. These might include competencies such as database administration, user interface design, security, architecture, embedded programming, testing, and safety analysis. Many companies then create forums—monthly meetings, newsletters, speakers—for these communities. If there are not enough people in a critical area (say, database administration) to form an internal community, then external communities of expertise are usually available.

Standards

Software development needs standards. Naming standards, language standards, code checkout and check-in standards, build standards, and so on are pretty much required for a well-functioning development team. Standards are usually developed by the relevant community of expertise or, when necessary, by the program team. However, it is usually better for a program team to work with existing standards than to develop their own. One way to discover where a community of expertise is needed is to identify where standards are lacking.

What State Do You Live In?

When I order something on the Web, I frequently encounter the dreaded but ubiquitous state drop-down box. I live in Minnesota, so all I want to do is type two keystrokes—MN—in the field for my state. But no! I have to use a drop-down box.

For years, I tackled this problem by moving my hand from the keyboard to the mouse. I clicked on the drop-down box and got a list with a scroll bar, which I clicked a couple of times (Darn! Too far, have to back up....) and then clicked on Minnesota. I assure you, this takes a whole lot longer than typing MN.

A few months ago I learned I could type M in the field and get Maine, then use the down arrow four times to get Maryland, Massachusetts, Michigan, and Minnesota. But wait. Some drop-down lists have Maine, Manitoba, Marshall Islands, Maryland, Massachusetts, Michigan, Micronesia, *then* Minnesota. I kid you not.

Just recently, I learned that I could type M in the box five times and get Minnesota. Who would have guessed? I've been entering MN in drop-down boxes for a decade, and I didn't know that. I must admit that typing five M's beats using a mouse, but it's not nearly as good as just typing MN. For one thing, I often hit the M an extra time or two, and there's no easy way to back up.

Why do I encounter that annoying state drop-down box almost every time I place an order on the Internet? Clearly, someone wants to be sure that I don't mistype MN. Since M and N are right next to each other on the keyboard, I rarely get them wrong. But I do find that I come from Mississippi rather too frequently. Or Micronesia.

When I encounter a state drop-down box, I figure that it was put there by someone in California or Washington, because those folks get their state by simply typing the first letter, so they just don't understand. And I assume that the offending company does not have minimum acceptable standards for user interfaces, because if it did, it would not dare throw a 50-item drop-down list at a customer about to place an order.

—Mary

A 50-state drop-down box is an example of a common user interface design where standards seem to be lacking.[35] Such an affront to users would not survive in a company with a user interface or usability *center of excellence,* where learning occurs and expertise develops through experimentation and knowledge sharing. If you find areas where standards seem to be lacking and sloppy work is evident, foster communities of expertise and ask the communities to develop standards. Developers appreciate reasonable standards, especially if they have a hand in developing them and keeping them current.

And customers appreciate standards even more.

TRY THIS

1. At the end of each iteration, do a process check with the team. Asks two questions:
   a. What is slowing you down or getting in the way of doing a good job?
   b. What would help things move faster, better, cheaper?
   Make a list of *bad* and *good* practices. Decide which items on the first list can be eliminated and which on the second list can be implemented. Then make it happen. Don't do this just once—repeat it after each iteration.
2. Make sure that the development team starts each iteration by writing down the goal of the iteration. The goal should be one or two sentences that give the iteration a theme related to the business value it will deliver. Post the goal in a prom-

35. See more usability annoyances in Johnson, *GUI Bloopers*.

inent spot and refer to it when the team is struggling with a tough decision.

3. Use pair programming or design reviews within the framework of software craftsmanship. Encourage pair programming for the expertise sharing it provides. If design reviews are held, assure that the agenda and tenor of the meeting focus on learning and sharing expertise rather than on ferreting out mistakes.
4. Ask each person on the development team to write down one specialty area in which the team is low on expertise. List everyone's answers and look for a pattern. Have team members pick their top candidate and see which one gets the most votes. Then work with the team to come up with a plan to make that expertise more available to the team. You might use the following strategies:
    a. Buy everyone who is interested a relevant book and meet once a week at lunch to discuss a chapter.
    b. Find a guru in the specialty in question and have him or her pair with various team members, as availability permits, so they can strengthen their skill in the area.
    c. Set up a three-person subcommittee to establish team conventions for the area in question. Be sure they evaluate any corporate or industry standards in preference to designing their own.

Chapter 6

Build Integrity In

INTEGRITY

In the late 1980s Kim Clark of the Harvard Business School set out to examine how some companies could consistently develop superior products. He studied the automotive market because cars are highly complex and development requires hundreds of people over dozens of months. He looked for critical differentiators between average and high-performing companies, and found that the key difference was something he called product *integrity*. He found that product integrity has two dimensions: external integrity and internal integrity.[1] In this book, we rename these two dimensions: *perceived integrity* and *conceptual integrity*. *Perceived integrity* means that the totality of the product achieves a balance of function, usability, reliability, and economy that delights customers. *Conceptual integrity* means that the system's central concepts work together as a smooth, cohesive whole.

1. Clark and Fujimoto, *Product Development Performance*, 30. Clark and Fujimoto define the terms as follows: "Product integrity has both internal and external dimensions. Internal integrity refers to consistency between the function and structure of a product—e.g., the parts fit well, components match and work well together, layout achieves maximum space efficiency. External integrity is a measure of how well a product's function, structure, and semantics fit the customer's objectives, values, production system, lifestyle, use pattern, and self-identity."

Perceived Integrity

Perceived Integrity: Google

I like Google. I use it several times a day. I've tried other search engines, especially new ones trying to compete with Google. But somehow their search results are never as good as Google's. I didn't always use Google. In the early days I read reviews of search engines and tried many of them. But shortly after Google started searching PDF files, I became a permanent fan.

There are a lot of things I like about Google. I like the speed. I like the way results are displayed. I like having the Google toolbar on my browser. Google translates Web sites for me. I don't have to use my ad blocker to keep Google from annoying me. And it's free.

But what I really like about Google is that I don't have to spell everything perfectly. Google detects typos and politely asks if I might have meant *error* instead of *eror*. I find myself disappointed when I do any other kind of search, because I have to remember to watch my spelling.

I imagine Google has lots of other features that I like, but I'm not even aware they're there. It seems to me that the designers were *inside my head* when they designed Google. I certainly couldn't have told them what I wanted in a search engine. Somehow, they just knew. How did they do that?

—Mary

In our opinion, Google gets high marks for *perceived integrity*. Perception is in the eyes of the beholder, so Google might not strike you as such a great service. But you have your favorite software tools. Sometimes you come across software that suits you so well that you think the designer must have been *inside your head*.

Perceived integrity is affected by the customer's whole experience of a system: how it's advertised, delivered, installed, accessed; how intuitive it is to use; how well it deals with idiosyncrasies; how well it keeps up with changes in the domain; how much it cost; how timely it is; how well it solves the problem.

The measure of perceived integrity is roughly equivalent to market share, or perhaps a better term might be mindshare. If you had to rebuild your computer tomorrow, loaded with only the software you regularly use, how many products would you load? If you wiped out all your bookmarks, which ones would you add back immediately? These are the products and services you perceive to be relevant to your life, the products with perceived integrity.

Conceptual Integrity

Conceptual Integrity: Two Airline Reservation Systems

I have a lot of frequent flier miles, and I make a lot of airline reservations; some are regular reservations, and some are frequent flier reservations. Until recently, my local airline had two completely different reservation systems—one for making regular reservations and one for making frequent flier reservations. Every time I made frequent flier reservations, I wondered, "Why couldn't they just let me use their regular reservation system? I'm doing the same thing; I just pay with different currency."

The system for regular reservations is identical to a system used at a popular travel Web site. It is pretty clear this component is from an outside vendor, so it didn't have the capability to deal with the idiosyncrasies of paying for a ticket with frequent flier payment miles. Thus, the airline developed its own reservation system for frequent fliers.

The inconsistency had an explanation, and no doubt an economic justification. Nevertheless, the dual reservations systems demonstrate a lack of conceptual integrity in the airline's reservation service.

Just recently, I was pleasantly surprised to discover that the frequent flier system had been completely integrated into the regular reservation system. Clearly, the airline had recognized the dissonance and eliminated it.

—Mary

Conceptual integrity means that a system's central concepts work together as a smooth, cohesive whole. The components match and work well together; the architecture achieves an effective balance between flexibility, maintainability, efficiency, and responsiveness. When a single airline Web site has two different reservation systems, this is a clear indication that two distinctly different design concepts are being used for the central concept of *make a reservation.*

Conceptual integrity is a prerequisite for perceived integrity. When a system does not have a consistent set of design ideas, usability will suffer, because the user does not have a single metaphor for the application, strategies for doing the application, and user-interface tactics.[2]

Conceptual integrity emerges as the system evolves and matures. In the airline example, the regular reservation system has undergone several generations of growth and change, and as a separate component, it has maintained conceptual integrity.

2. See Brooks, *The Mythical Man Month*, 255.

However, when placed side by side with a completely different reservation system, the overall reservation process did not have conceptual integrity, and this created a dissonance that was perceived by a user who used both systems.

Although conceptual integrity is necessary for perceived integrity, it is not sufficient. If the most elegant architecture in the world does not do an exceptional job of meeting users' needs, users will not notice the underlying conceptual integrity. It is for this reason that a system's architecture must evolve and mature; perceived integrity will change over time, and thus the underlying architecture must do so also. As new features are added to a system to maintain perceived integrity, the underlying capability of the architecture to support the features in a cohesive manner must also be added.

The Key to Integrity

The fundamental thesis of Kim Clark and Takahiro Fujimoto's book *Product Development Performance* is that integrity is achieved through excellent, detailed information flow. Perceived integrity is a reflection of the integrity of the information flow from customers and users to developers. Conceptual integrity is a reflection of the integrity of the upstream/downstream technical information flow. See Figure 6.1.

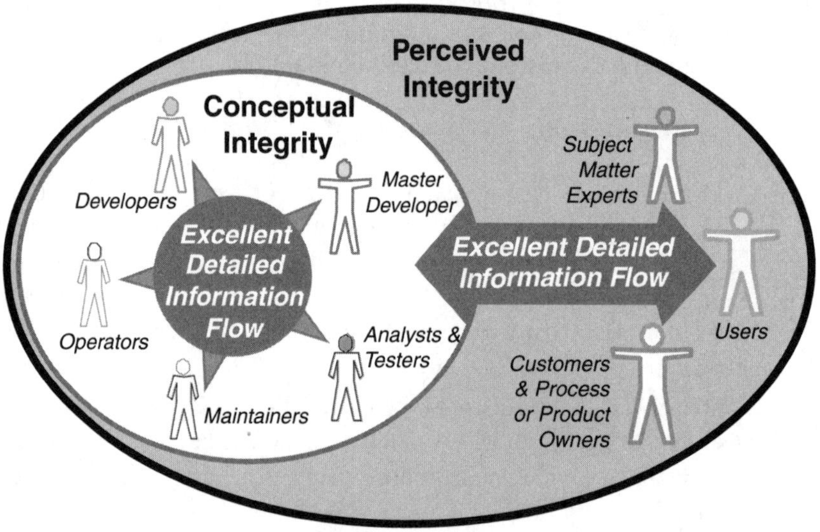

Figure 6.1 *Information flow produces integrity.*

The way to build a system with high perceived and conceptual integrity is to have excellent information flows both from customer to development team and between the upstream and downstream processes of the development team. The information flow must take into account both the current and potential uses of the system.

This is consistent with the findings of Bill Curtis and his colleagues in "A Field Study of the Software Design Process for Large Systems," which concludes that the three fundamental requirements for improved software development performance are

- Increased application domain knowledge across the entire software development staff.
- Acceptance of change as an ordinary process and the capability to accommodate emergent design decisions.
- An environment that enhances communication to integrate people, tools, and information.

TOOL 17: PERCEIVED INTEGRITY

Decisions that affect perceived integrity are made every day, mostly at the lowest levels of the development organization. Companies that consistently achieve perceived integrity have a way of constantly keeping customer values in front of the technical people making detailed design decisions. In most Japanese automakers, this is done by a chief engineer, who has developed a vision of what the target customer segment wants in a car. The chief engineer spends a lot of time walking around, talking with the engineers as they make tradeoffs, making sure that these engineers have a good idea of what the customer will find important. If the vision of perceived integrity isn't refreshed regularly, the engineers have a tendency to get lost in the technical details and forget the customer values.

Chief engineers are among the most highly skilled engineers in the organization. They have added to their engineering skills the ability to understand their target customer base and create a vision of a car that these customers will buy. In addition, they must have the leadership skills necessary to transmit this vision on a daily basis to the people making detailed decisions and tradeoffs. The chief engineer is responsible for the technical architecture of the car, including all the technical details. However, it is understood that a car is too complex a system for a single person or a small group to design, so the role of the chief engineer is to facilitate tradeoffs that will create the optimum perceived integrity as the design of the vehicle emerges. Therefore, the chief engineer must understand what the engineers are grappling with as they proceed with the many tradeoffs they must make, in order to help them understand how their decisions will affect the integrity of the product.

Sequential software development attempts to transmit the concept of perceived integrity to programmers through a multistage process. First, requirements are gathered from customers and written down. Then, these requirements are subjected to analysis, usually by people other than those who gathered requirements. Analysis is an attempt to understand, in more technical terms, what the requirements mean, using various diagrams or models. Traditionally, analysis is not supposed to deal with implementation details; it is simply a step in refining the requirements. The analysis is then used to design how the software will actually be implemented. This is typically done by yet a different group of people. The design is then turned over to still another group, the programmers, who are supposed to write the code.

What's wrong with this picture? First, as we all know, customers of a software system are generally not able to define what they will perceive as integrity any more than they are able to describe accurately what they want in a car. Customers know what their problems are, but quite often, they can't describe the solution. They will know a good system when they see it, but they can't envision it beforehand. To make matters worse, as their circumstances change, so will customers' perception of system integrity.

The problems with sequential development do not go away even if customers can envision and someone can document an accurate set of requirements. Requirements are traditionally written down and handed off to a team of analysts, which does an analysis and hands off the results to designers, who design the software and hand off the results to programmers. It's the programmers who are going to be making day-to-day decisions on exactly how to write the code. They are two or three documents away from an understanding of the customer perception of system integrity. At each document hand-off, a considerable amount of information has been lost or misinterpreted, not to mention key details and future perspectives that were not obtained in the first place.

Where is the equivalent of the chief engineer? Where is the master developer who understands both what the customer will value and what kinds of tradeoffs the programmers have to make? Who will refresh the programmers' minds about what the customer really wants and guide them over time as they make tradeoffs to insure that the result is a system with integrity? If a process does not provide an accurate, detailed information flow from the customer to the developers, the resulting product will lack perceived integrity. It is hard to imagine that this kind of information can be transmitted through multiple iterations of documents handed off to multiple layers of people.

So what is the alternative? There are several techniques that can be used to establish first-class customer–developer information flows:

- Smaller systems should be developed by a single team that has immediate access to the people who will judge the system's integrity. The team should use short iterations and show each iteration to a broad range of people who will know integrity when they see it, so they can make course corrections based on feedback.

- Customer tests provide excellent customer–developer communication.
- Complex system should be represented using a language and a set of models that the customers understand *and* the programmers can use without intervening refinement.
- Large systems should have a master developer who has deep customer understanding and excellent technical credentials, and whose role is to facilitate the design as it emerges, representing the customer's interests to the developers.

These approaches are not mutually exclusive. Even top-notch master developers benefit from frequent iterations, just as chief engineers benefit from frequent and increasingly detailed prototypes. No matter what other communication techniques are used, customer tests should be prepared that convey examples of how the system works. These tests help customers understand how the system will behave so developers can be sure that their work satisfies the customers' expectations.

Model-Driven Design

In *Domain Driven Design* Eric Evans advocates *model-driven design,* that is, the construction of a domain model such that software implementation can flow directly from this model. Domain models must be both understood and directly usable by the customers or customer representatives and by the developers actually writing the code. Evans advocates this domain model as a ubiquitous language; that is, developers and customers alike should use the same words to mean the same things; typically, the words should come from the customers.[3] This is the only way the two sides can talk meaningfully and that the customers can validate the developers' understanding of their problem. Developers will have additional deeper models of technical infrastructure issues, but all business rules, business process, and domain-related issues will be implemented and validated from the jointly evolved domain model level. There are many ways to model anything. The joint modeling ensures that the results will be both a correct representation of the domain issues and at the same time be effectively implementable in software. Model-driven design is a valuable approach for complex systems, as it lets everyone speak the same language.

Models capture how the system appears to the user, how it will deal with meaningful concepts and rules, and how it provides value. The right kind of model will de-

3. See the discussion of ubiquitous language in Evans, *Domain Driven Design*.

pend on the domain and how its details might best be abstracted into a concise format.

A Matrix Model

After spending a couple of weeks trying to understand a complex entity registration system, I realized that the entire system boiled down to 25 entities and about 150 transactions that could happen to the entities. This meant there were almost 4,000 possible combinations, although in reality, many of the combinations were invalid, and many valid combinations resulted in the same action.

I created a matrix with entities across the top and transactions down the side. If a square in the matrix was filled in, that meant the entity-transaction pair was valid. The filled-in squares pointed to the actions required for that entity-transaction pair. This model of the system ended up as a 23-page spreadsheet, which fully described the business rules, right down to the details of how to populate user interface screens.

The customer loved this matrix model and spent a great amount of time assuring that every detail was correct. The programmers could understand the model and program directly from it. When a question arose, the developers and customer pored over the matrix together to clarify the point, sometimes improving the model a bit. When the question was resolved, the matrix was updated. It was the only requirements document we used.

—Mary

We have used a collection of models to support excellent customer–developer information flow during development of complex systems:

- **A conceptual domain model.** This might be a class model of the basic entities in the system, whether they are events, documents, transactions, representations of physical items, or whatever. Or it can be a matrix like the one described in the sidebar. Whatever its form, the domain model must include both the key concepts in the users' mental models and the relationships among these concepts. It should not be highly detailed or comprehensive but rather needs to focus on the key ideas and concerns. It is meant to capture the users' understanding of the system's domain.
- **A glossary.** This defines the terms found in the domain model and ensures a consistent language for the team. It is the ubiquitous language advocated by Evans. It can exist in the heads of the team, arising from ongoing team conversations, or it could be a written document if everyone cannot be collocated to share in the

conversations. It contains any semantics, rules, and policies of the domain not captured in the domain model. *All terms should be in domain language, not technical language.*

- **A use case model.** The domain model and glossary are static views of the domain. A use case model is a dynamic view of the system and is useful for capturing tacit knowledge about what *usability* really means in this domain. It organizes and details the customers' goals and subgoals for interacting with the domain model and drives the workflow and navigation.
- **Qualifiers.** Early implementations of a system are often coded and tested in a development environment, where it is difficult to simulate all of the interactions and loads that the production system might experience. Developers should understand what *multiplier* or *quantifier* might be applied to the basic functionality to achieve business value. This would include number of users, acceptable response time, required availability, projections for growth, possible business impact of defects, need for aggressive security or safety, and so on.

The developers writing the business layer and presentation layer of the code should use these models directly, without translation. When either is speaking of the same concept, both customers and developers should use the same words, generally words drawn from the domain or a metaphor of the domain. If models are translated or different language is used, a large amount of information will be lost or garbled. In addition, software directly reflecting the domain model will be more robust to changing business needs than software with significantly different internal structures chosen for purely technical reasons.

One way to determine if a model is useful is to observe whether it is kept up to date. Some believe that it is important to keep a model up to date so that it can be used, but we think the opposite is true. When a model ceases to be useful, it will no longer be maintained. It is okay to create models that are useful for a time and eventually fall into disuse. But it is a waste to create and maintain models simply because it seems like a good idea. You know you have devised a useful model when it is eagerly referenced and maintained.

When models are used, they should be viewed at a level of detail appropriate to engage the customer or customer representative. The best way to do this is to start with a high-level abstraction and add detail when it is time to begin implementation of a particular area. For example, with the matrix model in the sidebar, there was one top-level matrix that exploded into detailed business rules. As each category of business rules came under development, the spreadsheet concerning those business rules was fleshed out in detail.

People can deal with only a limited number of concepts at a time, so in a complex software system, communication will of necessity be limited to only a handful of concepts at a time. The key to communication about complex systems is to hide details behind abstractions when a broad picture is desired and move to lower levels of abstraction to flesh out the details. Models are useful tools for creating abstractions and enabling communication on broader topics. Iterations are the key mechanism to trigger the movement from abstractions to implementation of details.

Tests are the best way to remember the details of what was agreed to and ensure that the features continue to work as the system evolves. Returning to the matrix model, both working code and acceptance tests were produced from the spreadsheets during each iteration. At the end of an iteration, the customer checked to see that the general concept was acceptable, while a suite of regression tests was used to demonstrate that the new business rules were correct and that previously implemented business rules still worked correctly.

Maintaining Perceived Integrity

Even good customer–developer information flows may not capture the strategic need for applications to change in the future. Most software systems are dynamic over time; well over half of the spending on an application will occur after it goes into production.[4] Systems must be able to adapt to both business and technical change in an economical manner.

One of the key approaches to incorporating change into an information infrastructure is to ensure that the development process itself incorporates ongoing change. One of the fears of those considering an iterative development approach is that later iterations will introduce capabilities that require change to the design. However, if a system is built under the paradigm that everything must be known up front so the optimal design can be found, then it will probably not be adaptable to change in the future. A change-tolerant design process is more likely to result in a change-tolerant system.

Maintaining institutional memory about a system is key to assuring its long-term integrity. There have been many attempts to use documentation created during design to do this. However, design documentation rarely reflects the system as it was actually built, so it is widely ignored by maintenance programmers. If this is the only purpose documentation serves, it was a waste to create it. One way to maintain intuitional memory about a system is to make the developers responsible for ongoing up-

4. The percentage of software lifecycle cost attributed to maintenance ranges between 40 percent and 90 percent. See Kajko-Mattsson et al., "Taxonomy of Problem Management Activities."

dates. Alternately, the developers and maintenance programmers can work jointly over a period of time to transfer tacit knowledge. You can also create an as-built model of the system after it is developed. But the best way to maintain institutional knowledge about a system and keep it maintainable is to deliver a suite of automated tests along with the code, supplemented by a high-level overview model created at the end of the initial development effort.

TOOL 18: CONCEPTUAL INTEGRITY

Conceptual integrity means that a system's central concepts work together as a smooth, cohesive whole. The components match and work well together; the architecture achieves an effective balance between flexibility, maintainability, efficiency, and responsiveness. The architecture of a software system refers to the way in which the system is structured to provide the desired features and capabilities. An effective architecture is what gives a system conceptual integrity.

How is conceptual integrity achieved? In designing a complex machine like an automobile, hundreds of engineers are involved over a period of about three years. Hundreds of specialized parts are developed by specialized engineering groups, and thousands upon thousands of detailed decisions and tradeoffs are made. The key to achieving conceptual product integrity in an automobile is the effectiveness of the communication mechanisms developed among these groups as all of these decisions are made.[5]

An automobile's architecture is not something that is decided at the beginning of a development effort. True, a car has an engine, a body, a drive train, and so forth. But layout and styling engineers have very different ideas about how a car should look. And manufacturing engineers have quite a different view how new parts should fit together than do the engineers who design the parts. In a very real sense, the architecture of the automobile emerges as these groups work together. If they work together effectively, the product will have conceptual integrity.

There are two key practices used by automotive companies to achieve conceptual integrity. First, the use of existing parts immediately removes many degrees of freedom and thus reduces the complexity and need for communication. When a new car has novel body styling and a new engine, it helps to use a proven suspension system.

The second practice automotive companies use to achieve conceptual integrity is to use *integrated problem solving* to assure excellent technical information flow. As we noted earlier, Clark and Fujimoto's research showed that conceptual integrity is a re-

5. Clark and Fujimoto, *Product Development Performance*, 30–31.

flection of the integrity of the upstream and downstream technical information flow in the product development process.[6] Product development is a system of interconnected problem-solving cycles, and frequent problem-solving cycles that effectively span upstream and downstream engineers are common practice in automotive companies with high product integrity.[7]

Integra Integrity

My 2002 Integra has an elegant but simple vent system for directing airflow from the dashboard. This seemingly minor touch makes the car "feel right" whenever I drive it. It contributes nicely to the overall theme of the Integra: high performance at reasonable cost. The designer of the vent system certainly understood the Integra theme.

But a system that is so functional, yet so apparently inexpensive, was not designed by a single person in isolation. The designer must have gotten input from a number of people. Many related factors must have been considered. First, there had to be close synchronization with airflow engineers, because the airflow is excellent. Then, someone had to be thinking about parts pricing, manufacturing cost, assembly techniques, and finally, maintenance.

If developing this vent system had been simple, then other cars would have this elegantly functional system. I get the feeling that many people had to be talking to each other to get this detail just right.

—Tom

Just what does integrated problem solving mean in practice? It means that[8]

- Understanding the problem and solving the problem happen at the same time, not sequentially.
- Preliminary information is released early; information flow is not delayed until complete information is available.
- Information is transmitted frequently in small batches, not all at once in a large batch.
- Information flows in two directions, not just one.

6. Ibid., 30.
7. Ibid., 206.
8. Ibid., 211.

- The preferred media for transmitting information is face-to-face communication as opposed to documents.

Without integrated problem solving, designers decide in isolation what combination of features and capabilities will provide the best value to customers. When design is completed, a large batch of information is sent from the designers to those who must decide the best way to develop that value at acceptable cost and speed. This "throw it over the wall" approach might be diagramed as in Figure 6.2.

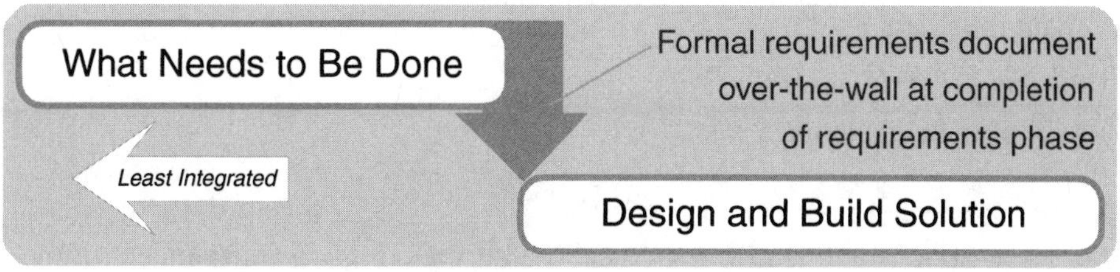

Figure 6.2 *Requirements before design.*

With integrated problem solving, illustrated in Figure 6.3, the picture changes to one of early, frequent, and bilateral communication. This rich, bilateral communication deemphasizes control mechanisms in favor of face-to-face discussions, small batches, speed, and flow.

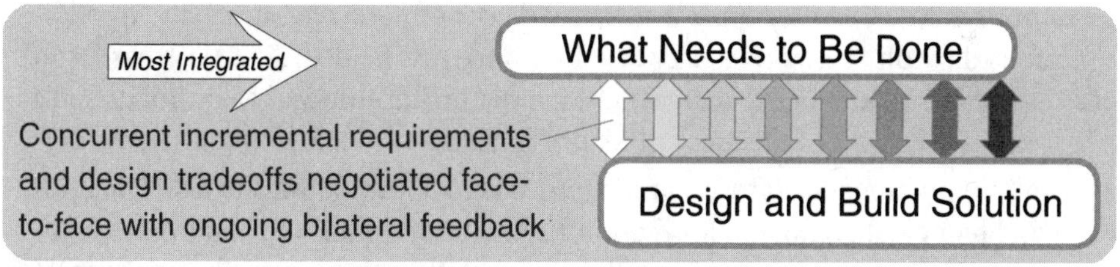

Figure 6.3 *Concurrent requirements and development.*

Software Architecture Basics

Car architecture starts with the basics: an engine, a body, a drive train, and so forth. Similarly, software architecture for most complex systems usually starts with the standard pattern of architectural layers. Layers give a solid foundation to system architecture. The basics in software development are[9]

9. See, for example, Fowler, *Patterns of Enterprise Application Architecture*, 20.

- Presentation (user interface)
- Domain (business logic)
- Data Source (persistence, messaging)

Some authors identify additional layers:[10]

- Presentation (user interface)
- Services (transaction management)
- Domain (business logic)
- Translation (mapping, wrappers)
- Data Source (persistence, messaging)

Lower layers should not depend on higher layers—so, for instance, the database does not know about the business logic, and the business logic is independent of the user interface. It should be possible to test each layer independently from other layers by simulating the behavior of other layers. Layers provide high cohesion within the layer and separation of concerns between the layers, two fundamental architectural patterns in software design. These two patterns are used iteratively to achieve system integrity.

The conceptual structure of each layer is another area that needs early consideration. Particular attention should be paid to the presentation layer, since conceptual integrity in user interface design is a primary driver of perceived integrity. In addition, it can be difficult to modify a user interface once it is fielded, since it is harder to change user habits than it is to change code. Larry Constantine and Lucy Lockwood's book *Software for Use* gives excellent guidance in usage-centered design.

One of the functions of software architecture is to allow systems to adapt to both business and technical change in an economical manner. Since you can't build complete flexibility into a system, you should try to group things that are likely to change together and hide them from the rest of the system. Putting things that vary together—by making them a component or service—and hiding them from the rest of the system allows changes to be made that have only local impact and do not disrupt huge parts of the system. Several books discuss how to do this, including excellent

10. See, for example, Hohmann, *Beyond Software Architecture*.

texts by Evans,[11] Fowler,[12] Larman,[13] and Martin.[14] If you have done this wisely, the system should be easier to change in the future.

Even while designing to accommodate change, watch out for the temptation to spend too much time puzzling over what a system might need in the future in order to design a great architecture from the start. As we have seen, predicting the future tends to be a waste of time and resources. It is better to take a breadth-first approach and get the basics right. Then, let the details emerge and plan on regular refactoring to keep the architecture healthy.

Emerging Integrity

How can you be sure that a good architecture will emerge? How can you be sure your system will have conceptual integrity? The practices used in automotive product development can be equally effective in software development.

First, use existing parts when possible. This means use off-the-shelf software when possible. It means putting a wrapper around legacy databases if you can. Use standards such as XML and Web-browser clients. Allow users to export data to spreadsheets and manipulate it. By fixing as many points of the system as feasible with existing software and standards, you reduce the communication required, clearing the path for better communication on the remainder of the system.

Second, use integrated problem solving. This means getting started on writing software before the design details are finalized. Show partially complete software to customers and users to get their feedback. Make sure developers have access to customers or customer representatives to get questions answered as soon as they arise. Run usability tests on each feature as soon as it is developed. Develop and run customer tests throughout each iteration, not just at the end. Use the *synchronization* and *set-based design* tools described in Chapter 2, "Amplify Learning," to increase communication among multiple or dispersed teams.

Third, be sure there are experienced developers involved in all critical areas. There will probably be a great difference between a user interface designed by someone who understands how to design and test for usability and someone who does not. Stored procedures written by developers with little experience with database transactions are not likely to be as robust as those written by developers who have dealt with

11. Evans, *Domain Driven Design*.

12. Fowler, *Patterns of Enterprise Application Architecture*.

13. Larman, *Applying UML and Patterns*.

14. Martin, *Agile Software Development*.

database lockups. A person writing embedded code to control a machine for the first time will not have the same appreciation of timing problems as someone who has had a few machines run away on her. Certainly not everyone developing a system can or should be highly experienced, but a complex system requires developers on the team who understand the complexities of various technical areas in the system as well as the patterns generally used to deal with those complexities.

Finally, complex systems require the leadership of a master developer with the skills to facilitate collaborative efforts across multiple development teams. For example, assume there are different technical teams working on the user interface and the database. As developers on each team make decisions and tradeoffs, it is important to integrate their problem-solving efforts with each other as well as with the needs of the customer. The communication necessary to assure this happens would be the responsibility of the master developer.

TOOL 19: REFACTORING

Engineering historian Henry Petroski has written extensively about how design actually takes place.[15] Engineers start with something that works, learn from its weaknesses, and improve the design. Improvement comes not just from meeting customer demands or adding features; improvements are also necessary because complex systems have effects that are not well understood at design time. Suboptimal choices are an intrinsic part of the process of engineering complex designs in the real world. It is not reasonable to expect a flawless design that anticipates all likely contingencies and cascading effects of simple changes. Design researcher Donald Norman notes that it takes five or six attempts to really get a product right.[16]

Most of the concerns we hear about iterative development involve fears that an iterative approach will result in an ineffective architecture or design. Where do people get the idea that all good design happens at the beginning of a project? Many people involved in developing products understand that great designs evolve over time. The more complex the system, the more important design evolution becomes.

This thinking is echoed in lean manufacturing practices, where continuous improvement is a key strategy. No one expects a manufacturing process to be perfect—it is simply too complex. Instead, production workers are expected to *stop the line* when things are not perfect, find the root cause, and fix it before continuing with manufacturing. The Toyota Production System started out with a few practices, which were

15. See, for example, Petroski, *Design Paradigms*.

16. Norman, *The Design of Everyday Things*, 29.

continuously improved by thousands of production workers over decades. Even today, this effective, comprehensive manufacturing system is still being improved.

We need to adopt the attitude that the internal structure of a system will require continuous improvement as the system evolves. Just as manufacturing processes are continuously improved by production workers, so must a software system be continuously improved by developers. In fact, you are using many software products that have been through multiple releases; no doubt, the design of each product has been improved several times. Refactoring—improving the design as the system develops—is not just for commercial software. Without continuous improvement, any software system will suffer. Internal structures will become calcified and fragile. In a surprisingly short time, the system will cease to be useful.

Keeping Architecture Healthy

The need for refactoring arises as architecture evolves and matures, and new features are requested by users. New features can be added one at a time to the code, but generally new features are related, and often it would be better to add an architectural capability to support the new feature set.[17] This often comes about naturally as a refactoring to remove duplication when you add the second or third of a set of related items.

Entering Addresses

I was working on a data entry application that started with the entry of a name and address. We put in the code for a name and address. Later, the application was expanded, and now we had to enter names and addresses in five different places. Each place had a slightly different twist. In one place, only a Minnesota address was valid, in another place there had to be a country code, in a third place the address was to default to a previous field, in the fourth place the address needed to provide for multiple names.

At this point the address entry features were crying out for a general-purpose address entry capability in the architecture, one that could handle field defaults, multiple entries in a field, field validation, and optional fields. Rather than code each feature, we needed an architectural capability for address entry.

—*Mary*

17. See Hohmann, *Beyond Software Architecture*, for a discussion of adding architectural capabilities to support features.

If features such as address entry are added to the system in several different places with a different twist at each place, the system will lose conceptual integrity. Resist the temptation of the brute force approach and add the architectural capability. If you let crud build up in the system, its integrity will begin to degrade, and you will eventually have to pay the debt.[18] Regular refactoring is what keeps systems healthy over time.

A Reward for Developers

Microsoft keeps the same team working on a product such as Excel over multiple releases. After the team has worked hard to complete a release, the members are rewarded with a couple of months in which they are allowed to clean up the underlying structures of the code that bothered them the most while working on the release.[19]

Maintaining Conceptual Integrity

There are several good books and other sources of information on refactoring,[20] so we will not attempt to cover the same ground. Instead, we highlight the key characteristics of a system with conceptual integrity. When a system begins to lose these characteristics, it's time to refactor.

1. **Simplicity.** In almost every field, a simple, functional design is the best design. Experienced developers understand how to simplify complex code, and in fact, most software development patterns are aimed at bringing simplicity to a complex system.
2. **Clarity.** Code must be easy to understand by all those who will eventually work with it. Every element should be named to communicate clearly what it is or does without the need for comments. Well-understood naming conventions, using a common language, code clarity, simple notation, encapsulation, and sparse, focused comments are but a few of the techniques that contribute to easily understood code.

18. Ibid.

19. Cusumano, *Microsoft Secrets,* 280–281.

20. See Fowler, *Refactoring*; Beck, *Test-Driven Design*; Shalloway and Trott, *Design Patterns Explained*. See also *www.refactoring.com*.

3. **Suitability for Use.** Every design has to accomplish its intended purpose. A fork that is difficult to eat with is not well designed. A user interface that is not intuitive is not suitable for a consumer Web site. When performance has degraded to an unacceptable level, the issue should be promptly addressed even if it means changing the design.
4. **No Repetition.** Identical code should never exist in two or more places. Repetition indicates an emerging pattern and should send up a flare calling for design clarification. When changes have to be made in more than one place, the possibility for error grows exponentially, so duplication is one of the biggest enemies of flexibility. The evil of duplication extends beyond code. Every piece of knowledge should have a single, authoritative, ambiguous representation in the system.[21].
5. **No Extra Features.** When code is no longer needed, the waste involved in maintaining it is large. If it is there, it has to be stored, compiled, integrated, and tested every time the code is touched. Get rid of it![22] The same is true of just-in-case features that anticipate possible future needs. Anticipating the future is usually futile and consumes valuable resources. You can take an option on the future by delaying decisions, but don't predict the future by providing extra features before they are needed.

Good design evolves over the life of a system, but this does not happen by accident; poor code does not get better by being ignored. When a developer finds something wrong with the code base, something that interferes with the smooth flow of development or its smooth execution, then she or he should *stop the line*—stop adding new features. The team should take the time to find and fix the root cause of the problem before proceeding with more development.

Useful refactoring requires a good sense of design. Inexperienced teams have been known to change code repeatedly without improving the design; we have heard complaints that some teams spend too much time perfecting unimportant details. However, we have also heard experienced designers say that the one mistake they made in developing a system was not refactoring aggressively enough. Clearly, the amount of refactoring that is appropriate for a system is a design judgment.

---

21. See Hunt and Thomas, *The Pragmatic Programmer,* 26–33, on the DRY (Don't Repeat Yourself) principle.

22. This is very difficult to do with user-visible features of software products; somewhere, some user probably has come to depend on the feature. This emphasizes the need for not adding just-in-case features in the first place.

Isn't Refactoring Rework?

Conventional wisdom holds that sequential development should result in better products with less risk, while overlapping design and development will lead to expensive and time-consuming *rework*. On the contrary, as we discussed in detail in Chapter 3, "Decide as Late as Possible," concurrent development usually results in better, cheaper products, faster and with less risk. Concurrent development means that the design of the product emerges throughout the development process. Improving a design during the development process is most certainly *not* rework; it is good design practice.

Okay, you say, but there isn't time to stop development to improve the design. We would argue that there isn't time *not* to refactor. Work will only go slower as the code becomes complex and obscure. As suggested by Figure 6.4, incurring a refactoring debt will kill team productivity. Just like advertising, refactoring doesn't cost, it pays. No one at Toyota would think that stopping a line to find and fix a problem slows things down. They know that focusing on relentless improvement makes the line go faster.

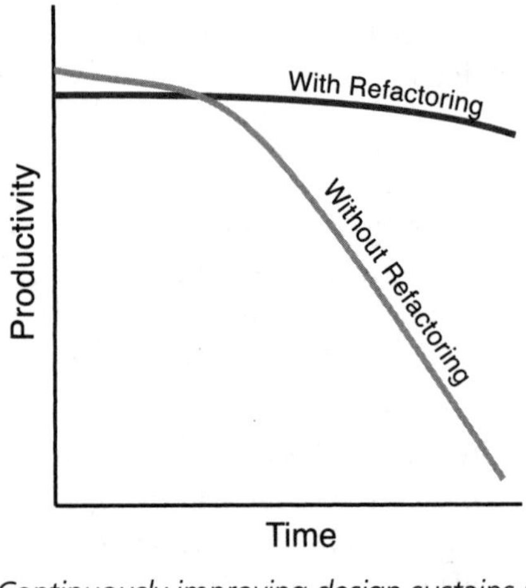

Figure 6.4 *Continuously improving design sustains productivity.*[23]

Refactoring is not waste; on the contrary, refactoring is a key method for avoiding waste in providing business value to customers. A well-designed code base is the foundation of a system that can respond to the needs of customers both during development and throughout the useful life of the system.

23. This is the inverse of the cost of change curve. Changes will happen. If your practices and discipline keep the cost of change low, your productivity will be sustained even when change happens.

A key tool that goes hand in hand with refactoring, and in fact makes refactoring possible, is automated testing. This is covered in the next section.

TOOL 20: TESTING

Imagine a complex assembly machine that puts together videocassettes. It has 15 assembly steps, each followed by a test step: position, test, position, test.... At one step, a robot puts a part in place; at the next step a sensor checks to be sure that the part is there. As you move down the manufacturing line, you find that every time something is done, a test follows to be sure it was done correctly. These tests assure that there are no missing or misaligned parts and that all the parts fit together as the product is being assembled. When a videocassette passes these tests, you know it was put together the way it was designed.

During manufacturing, a representative sample of videocassettes is pulled off the line and put into a test bed to be sure that each functions smoothly and plays back high quality video in a variety of machines currently in use by consumers. These tests show that the videocassettes will work correctly when they are actually used.

In software development, we also test that design intent is achieved and that the system does what customers want it to do. When developers write code, there should be a test to be sure that each feature works as intended and that all of the pieces work together. These tests have been categorized as unit tests, system tests, and integration tests. As we move from programming one module at a time to programming entire capabilities and features, the distinction between unit, system, and integration tests has less meaning. A better name for these tests might be *developer tests,* because their purpose is to assure that code does what the developer intended it to do.

Tests to be sure that the system does what customers want have been called acceptance tests, but this term has traditionally been used to refer to tests that run at the end of development. A better name for tests that make sure that a system does what customers intend is *customer tests,* since their purpose is to assure that the system will do what customers expect it to do. Customer tests are run throughout the development, not just at the end.

Tests play several pivotal roles during the software development process. First, tests unambiguously communicate how things are supposed to work. Second, they provide feedback on whether the system actually works the way it is supposed to work. Third, tests provide the scaffolding that allows developers to make changes throughout the development process, making tools such as *last responsible moment, set-based development,* and *refactoring* useful in practice. When development is done, the test suite provides an accurate representation of how the system was actually built. Finally, by developing and maintaining test suites for all systems in production, making changes to production systems that interact with each other can be done safely by running a full suite of tests for all related applications.

Communication

When a product is released to manufacturing, tests are released along with it to tell the manufacturing organization exactly what constitutes an acceptable product. In the same way, developer tests convey exactly how the system is supposed to work internally, while customer tests convey by example exactly what customers need an application to do.

Customer tests can be a viable replacement for, or supplement to, most requirements documents. Suppose a developer has a conversation with a customer about details of a feature. The conversation should not be considered complete until it is expressed as a customer test. Whether the test is written by a customer representative, tester, or developer, it is a precise description of how the feature should work for the customer.

Now imagine a quick design session among developers determining how the feature will be implemented. The implementation is not complete until the design details are exercised by developer tests. By documenting the design in tests, developers can write code with a clear understanding of exactly what it is supposed to do. This is a good way to refine thinking and help developers write code with conceptual integrity.

There are alternatives to writing tests as a communication device prior to coding, but there is no alternative to writing tests to demonstrate whether the system does what it is supposed to do. So, you may as well get double duty out of tests by using them to document what the system is supposed to do, just as manufacturing often uses tests to convey product specifications.

Feedback

When a developer writes code, she or he should get immediate feedback about whether the code works as intended. In other words, there should be a test for each mechanism the developer implements. In fact, developers will find a way to test their code as soon as it is written anyway; this is how code is developed. Why not capture that test and use it? You are going to test the system anyway, so you may as well capitalize on the fact that development is a cycle of experiments with a successful test at the end of each cycle.

The reason you are developing software in short iterations is so that you can provide feedback about how the system works to the customers or customer representatives and get their input on how to proceed. In order to get that feedback, you need to show them what the software developed during the iteration does for them. In other words, you need a set of demos or scripts that demonstrate the developed functionality. These need to be understood by customers well enough to be sure that everything they care about is successfully implemented in the iteration. So, why not have testers on the team to write customer tests during each iteration? Since you are going to demonstrate features at the end of the iteration anyway, you may as well capture the demonstration in tests.

As long as you've got them, developer and customer tests should be automated as much as possible[24] and run as part of the daily build. If the tests are not automated or if they take too much time, they won't be run often enough. Big batches of changes will be made before testing, which will make failure much more likely, and it will be much more difficult to tell which change caused the tests to fail.

Scaffolding

Scaffolding is a supporting framework that allows workers to do things that would otherwise be dangerous. If you develop software in *iterations*, delay decisions until the *last responsible moment*, and use *set-based development* and *refactoring*, you are going to be making serious changes to code once it has been written. This is dangerous, as we all know, because changes tend to have unintended consequences. Any nontrivial system requires that hundreds of thousands of details must all be correct at the same time. Many of these details interact with each other in ways far too complex to anticipate. The larger the code base, the more devious the interactions might be. To make changes safely, there must be a way to immediately find and fix unintended consequences. The most effective way to facilitate change is to have an automated test suite that tests the mechanisms the developers intend to implement and the behavior the customers need to have. A test suite will find unintended consequences right away, and if it is good, it will also pinpoint the cause of the problem.

In this sense, automated test suites are scaffolding that provides safety and access to the builders of the software system as they complete the construction of a partially built edifice. You can't effectively use the other tools in this chapter without this scaffolding. It may seem like writing tests slows down development; in fact, testing does not cost, it pays, both during development and over the system's lifecycle.

When you think about it, the tests are there for you to find, formalize, and automate, because developers somehow check their work as they code, and ways are found

---

24. For a discussion on deciding when to automate tests, see Marick, "When Should a Test Be Automated?"

to demonstrate to customers how the system works at the end of iterations. The thing you need to do is capture those tests, make sure they are correct and complete, put them under version control, automate them, consider them as part of the released product, and continue to use and improve them. You might end up with as many lines of test code as of product code, but the benefit will far outweigh the cost.

As-Built

The Importance of As-Built Drawings

At the end of July 2002, news stories told of the dramatic rescue of nine men from the flooded Quecreek coalmine near Somerset, Pennsylvania. The men were trapped deep in the mine after they drilled into an abandoned mine full of water.

Drawings of the abandoned mine had not been updated to show a large cavern that was dug just before the old mine was closed. An updated map was subsequently found, but it was not available to the miners as they worked. So they drilled into the water-filled cavern, not knowing it was there.

Mining is not the only industry with inaccurate maps. It's a safe bet that your city does not have accurate as-built maps of its underground infrastructure. For that matter, few buildings have accurate as-built or as-maintained drawings.

It doesn't come as a surprise that it is difficult, if not impossible, to maintain accurate as-built documentation of software. Heroic attempts are made to do this with safety-critical software, but as the coalmine accident shows, there can always be lapses. However, if a system has a comprehensive test suite that contains both developer tests and customer tests, those tests will in fact be an accurate as-built reflection of the system. If the tests are clear and well organized, they are an invaluable resource for understanding how the system works from a developer's and a customer's point of view.

The other thing a test suite does is give an indication of the health of the as-built system. Defect counts, types, and trends are a very good indication of whether a system is converging, when a product is ready to ship or deploy, and how robust the system is.

The bottom line is, you should have complete, automated (as far as practical) suites of developer and customer tests. They should be subject to the same discipline in design, semantics, versioning, builds, synchronization, and refactoring as the system itself. If there doesn't seem to be enough time, the first thing to do is reallocate the effort used in requirements documentation to writing customer tests. Require developers to write and automate their own developer tests, while providing training and coaching in test development and automation. You will get more payoffs from an effective test program than from most other investments you might make.

Maintenance

The software industry needs to find a way to make software easy to change after it is running in production, since well over half of development occurs after initial release. Furthermore, making changes to production software has to be economical—that is, changes must be made relatively quickly and at a reasonable cost. There are many ways to make software more changeable—layering, clumping, and hiding potential variability; components; use of commercial software; and so on. It is also a good idea to have the development team retain responsibility for application maintenance to preserve domain learning. All of these techniques are important, but we must add one other mechanism that to the list: maintaining a set of comprehensive tests throughout the lifecycle of the system. If a scaffolding of tests was built during development, all you have to do is re-erect the scaffolding and proceed with the changes. Then, the system can be safely repaired and refactored throughout its useful life. Scaffolding is as useful for maintenance as it was for the original construction.

Let's say you have a complex system with many applications using common services—a common database, middleware, or hardware, for example. You know enough about complex systems by now to suspect that a change in any one application could have an adverse reaction on an unrelated application. Since you don't have a reliable set of as-built documentation, you have to figure out for yourself how all the systems actually work before you can safely change any of them. No wonder maintenance is so difficult.

What you need is the test suite for each application, developed as scaffolding for change during development. These tests, assuming you keep them healthy, constitute an accurate set of as-built documentation for all the applications in your environment. If each application has an up-to-date test suite to prove its integrity, you can test the entire environment before a change is released.

TRY THIS

1. Pick one of your current systems and find out if it has a common language. Chat with the customers and write down a glossary of what they consider key terms that they use when talking about the system. Take this glossary to the development team and find out if they use the same words or if they have a technical translation for some domain terms. Next, ask the developers to identify in the code the names they use for each word in the combined glossary. Finally, see if

there are any key classes in the systems that are not represented in the glossary. If you detect that there are two or three different vocabularies in use, explain to the development team why it is important for them to use the domain language, even among themselves.

2. Hold a team meeting and invite any of the following people who normally would not be there. People who will
   a. test the system
   b. deploy the system
   c. train the users
   d. be responsible for operating the system in production
   e. work at a help desk for the system
   f. maintain the system
   g. develop or maintain any system accessing the same data

   Have the assembled group brainstorm any concerns they have about the system under development. Then, use prioritization to pick the three most important issues. Form a joint committee of interested parties to address the three issues. Meet again in two weeks to be sure the three issues have been resolved, and repeat the process.

3. Put five sheets of flip chart paper on the wall in the team room. Label the top of each sheet:
   a. Simplicity
   b. Clarity
   c. Suitability for Use
   d. No Repetition
   e. No Extra Features

   Ask each developer to note on the appropriate piece of paper anything in the current system that does not seem to meet the standard. For instance, if they detect repetition, they would note the culprits on the *No Repetition* sheet. When refactoring has removed an offending item, it is crossed off the list. At the end of the iteration, let the team take a day or two to clean up the worst offenders on the charts.

4. Estimate the average cycle time of the following:
   a. Time from writing feature until developer test is run.
   b. Time from writing feature until it is integrated into system and automated developer test suite is run.
   c. Time from writing feature until customer test is run.
   d. Time from writing feature until usability test is run.
   e. Time from writing feature until deployment.

Next, write down a target cycle time for each item. Attack this list from top to bottom: Work with the team to come up with a plan to bring each cycle time down to its target number, and one by one, close the gap.

Chapter 7

See the Whole

SYSTEMS THINKING

A system consists of interdependent and interacting parts joined by a purpose. A system is not just the sum of its parts—it is the product of their interactions. The best parts do not necessarily make the best system; the ability of a system to achieve its purpose depends on how well the parts work together, not just how well they perform individually.

Systems thinking looks at organizations as systems; it analyzes how the parts of an organization interrelate and how the organization as a whole performs over time. When this analysis is done by constructing a computer simulation of the organization's behavior, it is called system dynamics. System dynamics analysts construct a computer model by interviewing people to discover the organization's operating policy for making decisions and the feedback loops within the organization. Analysts generally find broad agreement within an organization on how decisions are made, and they find that most people make consistent decisions based on appropriate data. However, the computer simulation usually reveals surprising unintended consequences of seemingly correct policies, pointing out that that the broader impact of local policies is not well understood.

Systems dynamics guru Jay Forrester reports that a computer model based on known policies in a company often predicts the very difficulties that the company has been experiencing. He notes that the policies established to solve a problem will often exacerbate the problem, creating a downward spiral: As a problem gets worse, managers apply even more aggressively the very policies that are causing the problem.[1]

1. Forrester, *System Dynamics and the Lessons of 35 Years*.

We often see this dynamic in software development. When an organization experiences software development problems, there is a tendency to impose a more "disciplined" process on the organization, usually one with more rigorous sequential processing: Document requirements more completely, obtain written customer approval, control changes more carefully, and trace each requirement to the code. If an organization lacks basic development discipline, the imposition of a rigorous sequential process may initially improve the situation. Systems thinking warns that just because things get better does not mean the "cure" is the right one. The delayed effects of a sequential process in an evolving environment will eventually take their toll; it will become increasingly difficult to keep the system in line with current customer needs. At that point, pushing an even more rigorous sequential process will initiate a downward spiral.

One of the basic patterns in systems thinking is called *limits to growth*.[2] Even as a process produces a desired result, it creates a secondary effect that balances and eventually slows down the success. If you continue to push on the same process for increased success, you will amplify the secondary effect and start a downward spiral. Instead of pushing growth, find and remove the limits to growth.

Finding and removing the limits to growth is the fundamental teaching of the theory of constraints.[3] The idea is to seek out and remove the current constraint to growth, recognizing that the constraint will move to another place once the current constraint is addressed, so this is an ongoing process. In fact, policies from the past may actually become today's constraints.[4]

A second basic pattern in systems thinking is called *shifting the burden*.[5] In this pattern, an underlying problem produces symptoms that can't be ignored. However, the underlying problem is difficult to confront, so people address the symptoms instead of the root cause of the problem. Unfortunately, the quick fix allows the underlying problem to grow worse, unnoticed because its symptoms have been covered up.

Lean thinking uses *five whys*[6] to counter the tendency to shift the burden to symptoms rather than addressing the root cause of a problem. The five whys work like this: Say you have a problem with an increasing number of defects. You ask *why* the defects occur and find out that a new module has been added that has unintended consequences. Next, you ask *why* the new module generates defects in other modules.

---

2. Senge, *The Fifth Discipline*, 95.
3. See Goldratt, *The Goal*, and *Theory of Constraints*.
4. See Goldratt, *Necessary But Not Sufficient*, 125, 210.
5. Senge, *The Fifth Discipline*, 104.
6. Ohno, *The Toyota Production System*, 17.

You find out that it was not tested. You ask *why* it was not tested and find out that the developers were under pressure to deliver it before it was tested. You ask *why* there was such pressure and find out that someone thought that developers work better with hard deadlines, so an artificial deadline was enforced. But you are not done. You have at least one more *why* to ask before you arrive at the root of the problem. You ask *why* someone felt that artificial deadlines were necessary and find that the manager has an intense fear of software schedule overruns. So, you spend time with this manager explaining how the backlog burndown chart[7] works and how it shows that the system is converging, and slip in an explanation of how the unreasonable schedule pressure is actually increasing defects and prolonging the schedule.

A third basic pattern in systems thinking is *suboptimization*. The more complex a system, the more temptation there is to divide it into parts and manage the parts locally. Local management tends to create local measurements of performance. These local measurements often create systemwide effects that decrease overall performance, yet the impact of local optimization on overall results is often hidden. We discuss this pattern in depth in the next section.

TOOL 21: MEASUREMENTS

Lance Armstrong won the Tour de France each year from 1999 to 2003, yet he won only a few of the daily stages:

1999: Won 4 out of 21 stages
2000: Won 1 out of 21 stages
2001: Won 4 out of 21 stages
2002: Won 4 out of 21 stages
2003: Won 1 out of 21 stages

Armstrong knows that winning the race is not about winning stages. If he had focused on winning each stage, his chances of winning the race would have been slim to none. The Tour de France is not a race where winning each day is an attainable objective. Of course, if a rider could win every day, he certainly would win the race. But bicycle racers know that trying to win every stage is a very bad strategy. The idea is to keep ahead of every else's overall time, not to exhaust oneself by trying to beat a fresh new competitor every day.

We have a tendency to decompose a big job into smaller tasks, sort of like the stages of the Tour de France. It seems obvious, then, that the way to get the best overall result is to optimize the results of each individual job, because we believe that if we get top measurements on each task, they will add up to the top measurement on the job. But just like the Tour de France, optimizing every task is often a very bad strategy.

7. See Chapter 2, "Amplify Learning," Figure 2–6.

Machine Utilization

At our video tape manufacturing plant, we used big, expensive machines to make video tape. Very expensive. Each product made on these machines had to help pay for the machine. The monthly depreciation of a machine was charged to products based on their time in the machine.

We never knew exactly how much our products were going to be charged for machine time. If a machine spent half a month undergoing maintenance, the monthly depreciation was spread across only half the usual number of products, so a product made on the machine that month was charged twice as much.

Machine costs were a big part of unit costs, so obviously the way to lower unit costs was to run the machine flat out all month, spreading its monthly depreciation across as many units as possible. And that's what we did. That's what everybody did. It only made sense.

But running a machine flat out is sort of like trying to win every stage of the Tour de France—it gives good numbers in the short run, but they don't add up to final profits. Why? When a machine runs flat out, it builds up inventory. A pile of stuff is needed in front of the machine to keep it busy, and a pile of stuff collects at the back of the machine as it makes stuff that isn't really needed. These mounds of inventory clog the arteries of the plant and make it very inefficient.

That's what we learned when lean production came to our plant in the 1980s. One of our sister plants went from shipping in 6 weeks to shipping in 6 days, using one-tenth the floor space, and making better product while they were at it. When we stopped trying to make every machine as productive as possible, profits improved.

The culprit was measurements. We were rewarded for high machine utilization and low unit costs. Our accounting system also perversely rewarded us for keeping inventory high, because inventory comes out on the asset side of the books. When we decided not to make anything until it was needed, we reduced machine utilization, increased unit costs, and lowered assets. Our cost accountants were not happy to see all of these numbers move in the "wrong" direction.

Cost accounting theory told our accountants that the total cost of production equals the sum of the costs of each operation.[8] It took them a while to understand that low unit cost and high utilization did not necessarily increase profitability, and in fact often had a negative effect on it.[9]

—Mary

8. See Koskela, *An Exploration Toward Production Theory and Its Application to Construction.*

9. This is the subject of *The Goal,* by Eliyahu M. Goldratt.

Local Optimization

We recently encountered a testing department that is measured on the applied ratio of testers, that is, the percent of the available testing hours that are recharged to other departments. To drive applied ratio numbers up, the department manager keeps the number of testers low and lets a big pile of work stack up ahead of every tester to be sure everyone always has plenty of work to do. The customer departments with systems to test have to wait a long time for testing, which increases their cycle time, reduces their feedback, and generally results in poorer quality products with more defects. This drives up the amount of testing needed, thus driving up the workload of the testing department.

Focusing on applied ratio in testing is the same as focusing on machine utilization in manufacturing. Although manufacturing managers and their accountants have learned that this is a suboptimizing measurement, this testing department and its accountants has yet to learn the same lesson.

One of the more challenging problems in measuring performance is that measurements occur at local levels, but maximizing local measurements is often at crosspurposes with optimizing the organization as a whole. Yet it is often not apparent that local optimization is hurting the entire organization, as in the case of the testing department. The costs of accumulating inventory—whether it is work waiting to be done or extra features added just-in-case—are hidden to the measurement system. The economic benefit of the rapid flow of value through the value stream is also hard to measure, yet increasing flow is an excellent way to identify and eliminate the waste created by suboptimizing measurements.

Focusing exclusively on local measurements has a tendency to inhibit collaboration beyond the area being measured, because there is no reward for it. Using the testing department again, the testers were not measured on their ability to collaborate with developers and help decrease defects, so they probably didn't get involved in improving the development process. As we saw in Chapter 5, "Empower the Team," Nucor addresses this issue by basing incentives on measurements one level higher than one would expect. If we applied the same concept in this case, developers and testers would be jointly recognized for a low defect rate, giving them more incentive to collaborate.

Why Do We Suboptimize?[10]

While Lance Armstrong knows not to try to win every stage of a bicycle race, sub-optimizing behavior is not so obvious to others. The detrimental effects of local mea-

---

10. See also Austin, *Measuring and Managing Performance in Organizations*, Chapter 14.

surements on overall performance are usually hidden, and so we persist in using suboptimized measurements out of superstition and habit.

Superstition

Superstition is an unsubstantiated association of cause and effect. Some superstitions are harmless. For instance, you wear your red shirt and your team wins. In fact, every time you wear your red shirt, the team wins, and when you forget, it loses. You know your red shirt isn't causing the team to win, but you'd like to think it is.

Some superstitions are more harmful. For instance, when the applied ratio of testers is high, profits go up. You assume a high applied ratio goes straight to the bottom line. When applied ratio goes up further and profits fall, you attribute the fall to something else. You have a superstition that high applied ratio means high profits.

Habit

The testing department manager may be optimizing applied ratio out of habit—that's the way the department has always been run. The typical project measurements of cost and schedule control are often done out of habit also. You might not really believe they are the most important measurements of a project's success, but they are what everyone measures, so they must be important.

The Unimportance of Cost and Schedule

I led several new product development programs at 3M, and I never thought much about cost and schedule. Development costs that occur before a product is released to the market are not tracked to the product.

New-to-the-world products are expected to be based on inventions, and everyone knows you can't schedule an invention. For such a product, the cost of delay is relatively low, because there is no competition to take the market away. There is great eagerness to get the product on the market as fast as possible, and a simple version of the product is often test-marketed as early as possible. Still, schedule is simply one of a number of tradeoffs considered by the development team.

For line extension products, schedule is often driven by a marketing request to place the new product in an annual show. The development team works very hard to accommodate such a request, with the clear recognition that if a product does not pass quality tests, it misses the show.

What really drove our new product development programs was the P&L our team accountant developed early and updated often. This and the marketing plan told us the whole story—where we needed to reduce unit cost, when we had to introduce the product, how many features we needed at introduction, how to make tradeoffs. Who needs cost and schedule control when you are navigating from a business plan?

Many people are jarred by the idea that a company that develops new products so successfully does not manage product development projects by cost or schedule. Why? They have fallen into the habit of thinking that cost and schedule are the important things in managing a project. It's hard for them to think of these as suboptimizing measurements. Yet a focus on cost and schedule would have distracted us from our ultimate objective: Develop and commercialize a profitable new product that meets a customer need and has a competitive advantage.

—Mary

Measuring Performance

"When you try to measure performance, particularly the performance of knowledge workers, you're positively *courting* dysfunction." These are particularly strong words from Tom DeMarco and Timothy Lister in the forward to Rob Austin's book *Measuring and Managing Performance in Organizations*, but if you read the book, you might have second thoughts about measuring performance.

Austin's theory makes a lot of sense.[11] His premise is that people will try to optimize the measurements that their performance is measured against. So far, you probably agree. The problem is, it is very difficult to measure *everything* that is important with knowledge work, especially where each effort is unique and uncertainty reigns. You probably agree with that too. So you measure what you can—that should make enough things work right that you will get the overall results you want, right?

Not exactly. The basic rule that you get what you measure still holds. If you cannot measure everything that is important, partial measurements are very likely to turn into suboptimized measurements. If you can't measure *everything* that is necessary to optimize the overall business goal, then you are better off without the suboptimizing partial measurements. Otherwise, you are in serious danger of encouraging suboptimized behavior.

Our culture is adverse to this conclusion; performance measurements seem so fundamental to the way we do business. Austin notes that since most managers want to use performance measures, they try to create measurements that will cover *everything*. They do this in three ways:[12]

1. **Standardize.** Standardize by abstracting the development process into sequential phases and standardize on how each phase should be done. Then, measure conformance to the process.

11. Ibid., Chapters 5 to 10.

12. Ibid., 103–104.

2. **Specify.** Create a detailed specification or plan, measure performance against plan, and find variation from the plan.
3. **Decompose.** Break big tasks into little tasks and measure each individual task.

If Austin is right on this, traditional software development management practices come from a desire to measure complex, unstructured work by disaggregation. Unfortunately, such measures will most likely encourage suboptimizing behavior because they still do not measure *everything* that is important. The way to be sure that *everything* is measured is by aggregation, not disaggregation. That is, move the measurement one level *up,* not one level *down.* Recall that Nucor measures group, not individual, productivity; 3M measures profitability of the business created by a product, not its development costs.

Information Measurements

Measurements are important for tracking the progress of software development. For example, defect counts are very important in gauging the readiness of software for release. However, information measurements, not performance measurements, should be used for this purpose. Information measurements are obtained by aggregating data to hide individual performance. A defect measurement system is a performance measurement system if it attributes defects to individuals; it becomes an informational system if it aggregates defects by feature. Austin is quite explicit that it is important to aggregate performance measurements rather than attribute them to individuals.[13]

But why shouldn't defects be tracked by developer? Wouldn't that help developers improve their level of performance? The problem with attributing defects to developers lies in the assumption that individuals personally cause the defects. It was once thought that factory workers personally caused quality defects, and if they would only be more careful, there would be fewer defects. Then, we learned from the quality movement in the 1980s that less than 20 percent of all quality defects are under the worker's control; the rest are rooted in the prevailing systems and procedures, which are under management control, not worker control.[14]

We submit that the same insight is true in most software development environments: The vast majority of defects have their root cause in the development systems and procedures, and trying to attribute defects to individual developers is a case of

13. Ibid., Chapter 13.

14. This is attributed both to Joseph M. Juran and to W. Edwards Demming. See Juran, *Juran's Quality Handbook,* and Demming, *Out of Crisis.*

shifting the burden. We are not looking for the root causes of the problems if we trace defects to individuals; rather, we are hiding them. The way to find the root cause of defects is to encourage the entire development organization to collaborate in seeking them out. Attributing defects to individuals discourages such collaboration, while aggregating them into informational measurements that are not traced to individuals assists in finding their cause.

TOOL 22: CONTRACTS

Can There Be Trust Between Firms?

We often hear the lament, "Agile development sounds good, but how does it apply to me? I have to work under contract." Without doubt, the biggest barrier to using agile practices is the sharp line between one firm and another. Each firm is expected to look out for its own interests, with the understanding that the other firm will be doing the same thing. It would seem, then, that the only safe approach is to write an airtight contract, because people move to new jobs, rules change, and then the only thing that matters is what's in the contract.

Actually, there is a better way, one that was pioneered by Toyota when it started working with U.S. suppliers in 1988 and was documented by Jeffrey Dyer in *Collaborative Advantage*. Of course, Toyota negotiated contracts with its suppliers, but the contracts were not the primary vehicles that protected the suppliers' interests. In a surprisingly short time, suppliers developed *trust* in Toyota, and in 1998, Toyota was rated by auto suppliers as the most *trusted* automaker in the country, scoring twice as high as General Motors.[15] *Trust* in this case has a specific meaning:

- The extent to which the automaker can be trusted to treat a supplier fairly.
- The extent to which the automaker might try to take unfair advantage of the supplier.
- The automaker's reputation for fairness among the supplier community.

This kind of trust does not come from individuals trusting each other. Suppliers may trust an individual purchasing agent completely. But they can't trust that the same person will be there a year later, or that whoever is there still will be playing by the same set of rules. Suppliers developed "a greater trust in the fairness, stability, and predictability of Toyota's routines and processes."[16]

15. Dyer, *Collaborative Advantage,* 90.

16. Ibid. 100.

Dyer notes that suppliers share proprietary information with Toyota, confident that it will not find its way to their competitors, as sometimes happened with General Motors. Suppliers invest in specialized equipment for Toyota, knowing that Toyota does repeat business with its suppliers 90 percent of the time, while they had only a 50 percent chance of repeat business from GM. Suppliers let Toyota experts into their plants to teach them the Toyota Production System, understanding that Toyota will not demand price reductions based on their findings, as GM has been known to do.[17]

It's not that Toyota doesn't look out for its own best interests; it's just that Toyota understands that a strong supplier network is far more beneficial to its interests than short-term gains that come from taking advantage of a supplier. Toyota, in the United States, obtains about three-quarters of its components from suppliers, while U.S. automakers obtain less than half of their components from suppliers. Yet Toyota spends half as much money and half as much time on procurement as GM. In addition, suppliers are more productive and produce better quality in manufacturing cells devoted to Toyota.[18] As an organization, Toyota is keenly aware that partnership relationships rather than arm's-length relationships with the bulk of its suppliers better serve its best interests.

Another company that achieves high value from partnerships with suppliers is Dell, which thus far has outperformed and outlasted most of its competitors in the highly competitive market of selling personal computers. To do this, Michael Dell focused company efforts on understanding the perception of value in high-margin customer segments and then delivering that value as rapidly as possible. This means the company does not focus on making hardware or software; that would be a distraction. Instead, Dell has worked to establish sophisticated win-win arrangements with its suppliers, which operate to the mutual benefit of both parties.[19]

But Software Is Different

You might be saying to yourself that good supplier relationships are important when the supplier is developing something it can manufacture many times over, like a disk drive or a taillight. But in software, we develop a system only once; it is complex and expensive; it is subject to many changes; and if not done right, the financial impact can be tremendous. Where is the parallel to *this* in manufacturing?

At the beginning of Chapter 3, "Decide as Late as Possible," we discussed the large and expensive metal dies used to stamp out vehicle body panels. The cost of

17. Ibid., 94, 97, 101–103.

18. Ibid., 5–7.

19. See Magretta, "The Power of Integration: An Interview With Michael Dell."

these dies accounts for close to half of a new model's capital investment. They are complex, expensive, and subject to many changes, even after the design is supposedly frozen. Correcting a mistake made in cutting a die is very time consuming and it's expensive to start over again. Yet in the late 1980s Toyota developed dies for half the cost and in as little as half the time using concurrent development practices, compared to the typical U.S. company using sequential development. Moreover, the resulting dies gave Toyota a significant cost advantage in the manufacturing process.[20]

Tool and die makers are supplier companies in both the United States and Japan. U.S. automakers waited until the design specs were frozen, and then sent the final design to the die cutting supplier, which triggered the process of ordering the block of steel and cutting it. Changes had to be approved and officially sent to the supplier by the purchasing department. Since suppliers had to bid low to get the job, they made most of their profits from the change orders, which amounted to 30 percent to 50 percent of the die cost.[21]

In Japan, the tool and die suppliers start working on a die at the same time the car design is started. Die cutters are expected to know what a die for a part will involve, and they are in constant communication with the designer. Suppose that a body engineer wants a change made. The body engineer goes directly to the die-cutting shop, discusses the proposed change with the die engineers, checks production feasibility, and together they decide what to do. The die shop makes the changes in the milling machine and keeps on cutting the die. Paperwork and approvals follow later.[22]

In Toyota, tool and die contracts are *target-cost* contracts; the supplier and automaker agree on the total target cost of the tools, including all changes. Typically, changes add 10 percent to 20 percent to the base cost, and this is covered in the original contract. If the target cost cannot be met, the parties negotiate who is to bear the added cost, and generally, Toyota ends up with the larger share. This kind of arrangement gives the engineers in *both* companies incentives to work together to keep the cost within target.

In the United States, toolmakers had fixed-price contracts that went to the lowest bidder, so they viewed engineering changes as profit-making opportunities.[23] To contain costs, automakers put a rigorous change approval process in place, similar to the change approval processes found in many software development contracts. When you

20. See Clark and Fujimoto, *Product Development Performance,* 187, 234–237; see also Womack, Jones, and Roos, *The Machine That Changed the World,* 111.

21. Clark and Fujimoto, *Product Development Performance,* 187.

22. Ibid., 236–237.

23. Ibid., 187.

look at the overall result, the U.S. approach almost doubled the cost and time necessary to make a die.[24] Moreover, it resulted in a lower quality die.[25]

We believe that the overall impact of many contracting and scope control policies in software development is in the same ballpark. That is, a fixed-price contract with a vendor hoping to profit from changes, combined with rigorous change approval mechanisms to contain cost, may approximately double the cost and time it takes to develop the software, while producing a lower quality result.

The Purpose of Contracts

Dyer defines *trust* as "one party's confidence that the other party...will fulfill its promises and will not exploit its vulnerabilities."[26] Many people think that the reason for contracts is to substitute for this trust. Conventional wisdom says that all eventualities should be spelled out in a contract so the parties cannot possibly take advantage of each other.

Many enterprises find it almost impossible to select suppliers using a process that values good faith or to write contracts that assume that the other party will act in good faith. It is widely held that the purpose of contracts is to limit the natural tendency of one party to take advantage of the other party as it looks out for its own interests.[27] However, if damaging behavior can be limited through the relationship rather than the contract, all manner of benefits in terms of speed, flexibility, cost, and information exchange can result. Unfortunately, these benefits are counterintuitive and difficult for a public official to explain to a newspaper reporter.

Let's take a step back and examine why companies work with suppliers in the first place. As our world gets more complex, there is a great value in specializing. If you were going to have a rare kind of surgery, you would want to go to a hospital that specializes in it. If Dell wants the best video display card, it collaborates with the company that makes that card. If you want the best software for a particular area, you are likely to seek out the companies that are experts in providing that kind of software.

Another reason to outsource software development is to reduce costs and improve the likelihood of success. For example, an organization might find that salaries

24. Ibid., 187, 234–237; see also Womack, Jones, and Roos, *The Machine That Changed the World,* 111.

25. Due to superior die quality, typical Japanese stamping in 1990 took five shots per panel, compared to seven in the United States, saving manufacturing time (Clark and Fujimoto, *Product Development Performance,* 186).

26. Dyer, *Collaborative Advantage,* 88.

27. Thompson, *"Public Economics and Public Administration."*

at a vendor are lower than their own salaries. Or it might negotiate a fixed price for a system that is lower than the internal cost to do the same work. It may find that an experienced software development vendor might have skills sets that are not available internally.

Let's examine the cost side of the equation. Money actually paid to vendors is only part of the story. In addition, there are transaction costs—the cost of selecting potential vendors, negotiating and renegotiating agreements, monitoring and enforcing the agreement, billing and tracking payments. As we demonstrated in the die-cutting example in the previous section, the cost of trying to control changes can add huge hidden costs to a contract, and you can expect such costs to escalate in an evolving domain.

Dyer finds that the second kind of costs, transaction costs, dominate most vendor-supplier relationships.[28] So, when evaluating the cost of outsourcing, it is imperative that all costs are considered: direct costs, obvious transaction costs, and hidden costs that come from arm's-length relationships and change intolerance. These costs will be especially high in an environment that is going to change despite heroic efforts to keep change at bay.

Let us turn our attention to the third cost of outsourcing, the lost opportunity cost that may result if the communication bandwidth between customer and vendor is narrow. As we saw in Chapter 6, "Build Integrity In," system integrity depends on broad, early, and frequent communication between customer and developer. Lack of communication between customer and vendor is a frequent cause of system failure.[29] Bear this in mind if increasing the chance of success is a reason for outsourcing.

Contracts that focus on keeping parties from taking advantage of each other have a lot of built-in control mechanisms and communication gates that have a tendency to raise costs and reduce the collaboration critical to success. Contracts that focus on supporting collaboration are more likely to reduce costs and result in successful contracts.

Fixed-Price Contracts

Let's examine the most commonly used contract designed to protect the customer, the fixed-price contract. Sometimes corporate budgeting cycles and related processes require fixed-price contracts. For many government entities, the law requires fixed-price contracts—often awarded to the lowest bidder. As we saw in the die-cutting example, this practice encourages vendors to bid low and make their profit on changes. Another motivator for fixed-price contracts is the desire of a customer to transfer risk

28. Dyer, *Collaborative Advantage,* 91–96.

29. See Ripin and Sayles, *Insider Strategies for Outsourcing Information Systems,* 43, 58–59.

to the vendor. In practice, the customer can't really transfer the bulk of the risk. If the contract doesn't work out, the customer will suffer.

As we noted in Chapter 2, "Amplify Learning" it is a good idea to develop software in short iterations driven by immediate customer needs, developing high-priority features first and stopping when resources run out. However, this approach is very risky for vendors working under fixed-price contracts, because they frequently have difficulty obtaining customer agreement that the work is done when the money runs out. Therefore, vendors tend to protect themselves by creating a detailed specification and keeping it under strict change control, charging extra for any changes. The result may be a substantial increase in cost or a very disappointed customer.

Fixed Price—Unhappy Customers

"I ran a software development company which prided itself in not exceeding the price and schedule quoted at the beginning of an engagement. In a three-year period, we had 78 projects, and 77 of them were delivered on time, on budget, and in scope. Then I surveyed the customers and found out that none of them was happy! The systems that we delivered did not solve their problems. Sure, we had protected ourselves by being on time, on budget, and in scope, but in doing this, we could not deliver what the customers really wanted. That's why I sold my business."

—A colleague (who wishes to remain anonymous)

Risk should be born by the party best able to manage it, and in a fixed-price contract, risk is seemingly transferred to the vendor. If a problem is technically complex, then the vendor is most likely to be in a position to manage the associated risk, so it is appropriate for the vendor to assume the risk. However, if a problem is uncertain or changing, then the customer is in the best position to manage the risk, so fixed-price contracts should be avoided. If a fixed-price contract cannot be avoided, then the customer should be willing to incur a substantial cost beyond the fixed price, due to the certainty of changes.

Fixed-price contracts may involve significant risk in estimating the cost prior to doing any work. A competent vendor will include this risk in the bid. A vendor that does not understand the complexity of the problem is likely to underbid. The process of selecting a vendor for a fixed-price contract has a tendency to favor the most optimistic—or the most desperate—vendor.[30] Consequently, the vendor least likely to understand the project's complexity is likely to be selected. Thus, fixed-price contracts tend to select the vendor most likely to get in trouble.

Therefore, it is quite common for the customer to find a vendor unable to deliver on a fixed-price contract. By the time this becomes apparent, the customer rarely has the option to choose another vendor, so the customer must often come to the rescue. Alternately, the vendor may attempt to recoup its loss through change orders, which leads the customer to aggressively avoid any change to the contract. Faced with no other way to recover a loss, a vendor will be motivated to find ways to deliver less than the customer really wants.

A fixed-price contract is biased in favor of the customer at the expense of the vendor, making it necessary for vendors to aggressively protect their interests, at the expense of the customer. It is not a climate in which organizational trust has much soil in which to grow.

Time-and-Materials Contracts

"Customers should prefer flexible-price contracts to fixed-price contracts where it is cheaper for the customer to deal with uncertainty than it is for the contractor to do so or where the customer is more concerned with the ability of the contractor to provide a product that works than with price," writes Fred Thompson in "Public Economics and Public Administration."

The flexible-price contract, also known as a time-and-materials or time-and-expenses contract, is designed to deal with uncertainty and complexity, but it does not do away with risk; it simply shifts it from the vendor to the customer. In the 1970s, the U.S. Department of Defense (DoD) experienced some very high-profile bailouts on fixed-price contracts, so it began to use more time-and-materials contracts in situations where the government was better able to manage the risk.

On the downside from a vendor perspective, time-and-materials contracts offer less security than fixed-price contracts. However, these contracts are usually considered a good deal for vendors for as long as they last. In fact, vendors generally have little incentive to be efficient, because the longer the work takes, the more money they make. To control self-serving behavior on the part of time-and-materials vendors, DoD developed extensive vendor control mechanisms, which contributed to the development of the discipline of project management.

Time-and-materials contracts mark a significant increase in contract transaction costs. Companies with DoD contracts not only hire administrators to oversee compliance with contract requirements, they also add accountants to sort out allowable and unallowable costs. High transaction costs would be reasonable if they added value,

30. Thompson, "Public Economics and Public Administration" in *Handbook of Public Administration*.

but in fact transaction costs are by definition nonvalue-adding costs. Thompson notes, "Controls contribute nothing of positive value; their singular purpose lies in helping us to avoid waste. To the extent that they do what they are supposed to do, they can generate substantial savings. But it must be recognized that controls are themselves very costly."

One way to avoid the high cost of controls is not to use them. Thompson suggests that when the costs of controls are high, it might be better to keep work inside a vertical organization, where presumably administration will control self-serving behavior. Unfortunately, vertical integration does not always work to minimize control costs. In fact, many organizations find themselves using DoD-style project management controls internally. It seems incongruous that cost, schedule, and scope control mechanisms that add cost but not value and that were invented to prevent contractual parties from taking advantage of each other would come to dominate development inside of companies—the very place where they should not be needed.

Time-and-material contracts can be used for agile software development as long as the contract allows for concurrent development and collaboration between the parties. The first step is to change the control mechanism from one that favors sequential development to one that favors concurrent development. After establishing a conceptual design and the overall capability of the system, sketch out a tentative release plan and begin iterations as soon as possible so the customer can see working code and offer concrete, timely feedback. As velocity becomes established, modify the release plan and level of resources if necessary.

The problem with time-and-material contracts is that once the system is partially deployed, the customer is dependent on the vendor, while the vendor has limited incentive to reduce costs. Agile development mitigates this bias in favor of the vendor by having the vendor deliver value for the money spent at the end of every iteration. Each iteration, the customer schedules the most valuable remaining features, insists on delivery of working, integrated code, and evaluates the value delivered. This gives the customer the option to terminate the contract at any point and still obtain value for the investment up to that time.

When you think about it, concurrent development is a safer approach for time-and-materials contracts than is sequential development and its associated controls. Exchanging incremental value for incremental pay protects both vendor and customer. However, this approach requires that the project management systems commonly used for sequential development be set aside. More importantly, there must be ongoing collaboration between working-level people in the vendor and customer shops.

Multistage Contracts

Multistage contracts attempt to deal with the unknowns and risks inherent in fixed-price contracts, matching the risks to the dollars spent over time. There are two types of multistage contracts: those intended to lead to a large fixed-price contract and those that retain their multistage character throughout.

Multistage contracts that morph into large fixed-price contracts start with one or two short contracts for learning enough about the problem to enable a fixed-price bid on the overall system. Usually, only one vendor is involved, so this kind of contract is not generally appropriate when bidding is required.[31] Assuming the vendor remains the same throughout, the customer and vendor increase their learning, reducing the risk of big surprises on either side. However, the incentive to freeze the specification and not allow changes in the final stage is, if anything, higher. There will be less sympathy for a change in the specification if the vendor was paid to get it right in the early stages. Thus, this type of multistage contract retains the problems of a fixed-price contract if uncertainty or change is involved after the body of the contract is awarded.

The second type of multistage contract, which retains its multistage character throughout development, presents a good opportunity for agile development, because it is easy to adapt to iterative development. However, these contracts are not without risks, the biggest risk being that each party has frequent opportunities to abandon the relationship. Multistage contracts create what might be called a bilateral monopoly,[32] that is, both sides come to depend on each other. If one party ends its involvement, the other party may have a lot to lose.

One way to mitigate the risk posed by the bilateral monopoly in multistage contracts is to deliver value with each increment in proportion to the money spent. As in time-and-material contracts, it is a good idea to implement the highest priority customer features first and deliver working, integrated code with each iteration.

Another way to mitigate the risk of termination in a multistage contract is to address the risk through the relationship—that is, the parties develop a trust that the

---

31. Sometimes, multistaged, fixed-price contracts are set up so that one vendor is selected to write a specification, and that specification is let out for bid. In this case, there is a decision to make: Is the vendor who wrote the specification allowed to bid? Behind the question lies the assumption that this vendor has obtained superior knowledge that is not found in the specification. Of course, this is the case because a great deal of domain knowledge is tacit knowledge that cannot be transferred in writing. If the vendor who wrote the specification is not allowed to bid, then all of its tacit knowledge has been wasted, and to the vendors allowed to bid on the contract, this is no different from a single fixed-price contract.

32. See Thompson, *Handbook of Public Administration*.

relationship will continue as long as expected value is delivered. In *Agile Software Development Ecosystems,* Jim Highsmith discusses delivered-feature contracts (pp. 74–75). These are fixed-schedule, variable-scope contracts in which the customer evaluates the value delivered after each iteration. If the work is acceptable, the contract continues into the next iteration. Although there is no contractual obligation for both parties to continue working together, their trust in each other builds at the same rate that their dependence upon each other deepens.

Multistage contracts will rapidly get expensive if a contract must be negotiated for each stage. Thus, these contracts are usually governed by a master contract negotiated at an early stage, with work orders executed against the master contract for each iteration.[33]

Tailoring Multistage Contracts to the Domain

Tim works in a company that sells cutting-edge software to large companies. The software supports innovative hardware that is constantly evolving. In such a changing environment, you would think that development would be kept internal, but such is not the case. Small, venture-funded startup companies develop new techniques faster than Tim's company can internally. It is Tim's job to contract with these small companies to develop portions of the software his company will sell.

One of the big issues in contract negotiations is ownership of intellectual property, which tends to make contract negotiations arduous and not something you would want to do every few weeks. Yet the technology is changing so fast that Tim's company doesn't know exactly what it wants a supplier to do beyond the next three or four months. Further, the small companies are eager to have extended contracts to show their venture funders.

The first principle Tim employs is to split the risk by splitting development into two contracts. The first contract is for proof of concept, and the second is used to finalize the product. Prior to negotiating the first contract, there is a short (2 to 3 week) collaboration period between both parties, using a time and materials contract, to establish an overall plan. This makes the first contract easier to negotiate.

Since the first contract is for a proof of principle or "rough draft," the supplier has full responsibility for the system from architecture to implementation. This is a fixed-price contract, and the supplier is usually expected to work for cost plus a small profit, with the assumption that success at this stage would lead to future profits. This contract can be canceled if it is not proceeding satisfactorily.

33. See Pitette, "Progressive Acquisition and the RUP: Comparing and Combining Iterative Processes for Acquisition and Software Development"; see also Wideman, "Progressive Acquisition and the RUP," Parts I and II.

Assuming the first contract goes well, Tim's company has learned enough about the vendor's work to commit to buying a minimum number of days on a time and materials basis. Of course, given the rapidly changing technology, Tim's company does not attempt to specify exactly what is to be done, but generally it finds that it can keep its vendors usefully occupied at the guaranteed level of commitment. During this second contract, Tim's company takes over more responsibility in guiding development, since the objective is to deliver a quality product without defects.

Once the software is released, the vendor is expected to provide a warranty, for example, 3 months of free defect fixes, to ensure it delivers high quality by delivery date. For additional warranty, Tim prefers a fixed-price support fee with a guaranteed service level. Tim is careful to separate warranty requests from upgrade requests, even when the vendor is contracted with separately to provide upgrades.

—Based on conversations and email with Tim Ocock

Target-Cost Contracts

The problem with traditional fixed-price contracts is that they encourage self-serving behavior on the part of the customer and defensive behavior on the part of the vendor. The problem with traditional time-and-materials contracts is exactly the opposite: They encourage self-serving behavior on the part of vendor and defensive, control-oriented behavior on the part of customers. What we need is a middle ground, one in which risk is shared and both parties have incentives to look out for the overall interests of the joint effort.

There are no canned answers to the contract dilemma, because in the end, no contract can fully prevent parties from taking advantage of each other. Contracts do not create confidence that the other party will honor its commitments and not exploit vulnerabilities (Dyer's definition of trust). There are, however, contract forms that make it easier for parties to share in the problems and rewards brought about by their relationship. One example is a target-cost contract. While the target-cost contract is not a panacea, it is at least a platform on which a partnership can be built.

Target-cost contracts are structured so that the total cost—including changes—is the joint responsibility of the customer and vendor. What makes a target-cost contract different from a fixed-price contract is that if target cost is exceeded, both parties will end up paying more, and if total cost is under the target cost, both parties will share in the benefits. What makes a target-cost contract different from a time-and-materials contract is that vendors do not gain added profit if they work longer, but they may receive a benefit if they are under cost or schedule.

In a target-cost software development contract, the parties start with a general agreement of what is to be accomplished, recognizing that the details cannot be known until mutual work is done. They then come to an agreement on the target cost for the system and agree upon a schedule. In this type of contract, the target cost is understood to be very important, so the design and detailed features will be focused on meeting the target cost. There is a commitment on the part of both parties to meet target cost, and this is understood to require a joint effort of both the technical people and users on both sides.

A target-cost contract recognizes that the actual costs will not necessarily be the same as the target costs, so it provides for a fair allocation of any costs over the target costs, or a fair sharing of any benefits if costs are below target costs. These contracts must give the customer an incentive to keep demands for features in line with target costs, while giving the vendor incentives that favor completing the work under the target cost. Usually, the customer incentive is provided for by a clause triggering equitable cost-sharing negotiations should the actual cost vary significantly from the target cost. One of the following usually provides for the vendor incentive:

- **Cost plus fixed fee:** The target cost does not include profit for the vendor; a separate fee is included to provide vendor profit. The fee is generally paid after the work is successfully completed. If total cost exceeds target cost, the vendor works at cost for the remainder of the contract. If total cost is lower than target cost, the vendor receives a higher profit margin. A bonus for coming in below target cost may be included.
- **Profit not to exceed:** The target cost includes the vendor profit. The vendor agrees to reduce rates and exclude profit after the target cost is reached. If total cost exceeds target cost, the vendor works at cost. However, in this case the vendor has no incentive to come in under target cost unless there is a bonus for early completion.

The most valuable part of target-cost contracts is that they more accurately communicate management intent to the frontline workers of both parties and encourage them to work together to achieve this intent. If cost expectations are not made clear to the working teams from the beginning, the resulting design is unlikely to meet the target. Target-cost contracts must leave the details of the scope to the discretion of the technical teams, because reducing scope is the most fertile ground for cost control.

Target-Cost Contract Example

The customer had a fixed budget for the project, and that was not going to change. It wanted two data entry applications moved to a Windows environment, plus a Web front end developed so that its customers might enter some of their own data. The legacy database needed to be modified to support current practice or converted to a new database system.

The problem was initially divided into four components: two applications, the database, and the Web interface. A team was formed for each component and given a budget expressed in terms of staff days. Team membership included the customer manager responsible for the area, a master developer, an analyst/tester, and an operations/help desk representative. Each application team got 35 percent of the budget, the database team got 15 percent of the budget, and the Web team got 10 percent of the budget. Five percent was held in reserve for contingencies.

Each team was chartered to figure out how to develop and deploy its portion of the system within budget. As teams developed a preliminary release plan, they started making tradeoffs immediately to keep within their staff-day budgets. The application teams realized that their jobs would be a lot easier if the database were converted rather than wrappered, but the database team did not have enough staff hours in its budget. The DBA convinced the application teams that they would be better off with a lower budget and more sophisticated database support, so each application team gave the database team a portion of its budget.

With that decided, the teams got to work on iterations, with highest priority items first. The database team was particularly devoted and quickly began populating two new development databases with sample legacy data, one for each application. It would merge the two databases later.

The application and Web teams had a useful database starting with the first iteration, so they had a reasonably good rendition of the main data entry screen at the end of the first iteration. Each iteration resulted in working, tested software, but all teams decided to delay moving the system into production until a more complete system was available. There was no good way to integrate the old and new systems, so going into production would require more or less complete functionality. However, it was agreed that the applications could go live independently and that the Web front end could follow either application.

As time went on, the applications and Web teams discovered they all needed the same financial features, so they agreed to pool some of their staff days and charter a subteam to develop the joint financial functions.

As the budgets approached 50 percent depleted, the teams took a close look at their velocity and got a good picture of how they were doing on their staff-day targets. They did some hard thinking about what they really needed. At this point, it was especially important for the customer managers to feel obligated to negotiate. If this had been a fixed-price contract, they probably would not have felt the need to dig deeply to find features they could do without. However, the customer managers felt responsible for meeting their team's staff-day targets, and being managers, they were used to that. So, they were quite aggressive in discarding features.

With 70 percent of its budget used up, one application team decided it was ready to go live and spend the remainder of its budget after startup. The team found that deployment was more difficult than expected, especially because of the new financial features. But after all the problems were resolved, it still had 10 percent of its budget left to deal with issues uncovered by production. At about the same time, the Web team went through an easy startup, which was lucky, because it was almost out of staff-days.

The remaining application team had a challenging problem with the legacy database, but on the bright side, the other application team had gotten the financial system working. The team burned up 90 percent of its budget before going live, and needed some of the 5 percent contingency to complete deployment. This left the team with scant funds to do any improvements after production started, so it seemed likely it would have to wait until the next budgeting cycle and get a special allocation.

Fortunately, the local maintenance programmers had been involved in the effort, and they were ready to take over more responsibility. Their time was not charged to the project, so they could work on the system without jeopardizing the budget. They were able to add critically needed features with some guidance from the original developers, and in the process they became confident of their ability to support the system.

—A Business Novelette

Target-Schedule Contracts

Sometimes schedule is more important than cost, although cost is rarely unimportant. If the number of people working on the system does not change and no components are purchased or licensed, then target cost and target schedule are the same thing.[34] Software product companies often meet hard schedules for product upgrades by fixing the resources and the schedule, and working on the highest priority items first. When time runs out, the low-priority features are left undone, but the release meets the overall intent of product marketing.

In the same way, a target-cost contract can usually be run as a target-schedule contract by fixing the resources and schedule. Features should be addressed in priority order, and each iteration should deliver working, tested, integrated, deployable

---

34. If components will be licensed or purchased, see Hohmann, *Beyond Software Architecture.*

software. Well before the deadline, the software should actually be deployed. Then, iterations can continue to deal with issues that arise in production. With this approach, the completed work will be on schedule and on budget by definition, and the delivered features should meet the overall intent of the contract.

If schedule really is the only thing that is important, then a target-schedule contract is more appropriate than a target-cost contract. This allows the team to add resources or license components as needed to meet the schedule. The more degrees of freedom that a target contract leaves to the workers, the easier it will be for them to figure out how to meet the target.

Shared-Benefit Contracts

Target-cost and target-schedule contracts set up an environment in which teams work effectively across company boundaries because it is clear that both companies will share the risks and rewards of the work. This is the key to collaborative contracts; the people doing the work must perceive that both parties have a stake in the results of their efforts. A *profit-sharing contract* is another effective mechanism for sharing risks and rewards if you are developing products for sale. Tim Ocock's company (see sidebar, "Tailoring Multistage Contracts to the Domain") frequently uses profit-sharing contracts.

In a *co-source contract,* both companies share responsibility for developing a system, and the vendor is also expected to transfer its expertise to the customer. A co-source contract is successful if the vendor works itself out of a job by helping the customers develop the capability to do the work themselves. Co-sourcing is a fundamentally collaborative approach, so co-source contracts do not tend to create motivation for self-serving behavior. Bruce Ferguson's company (see sidebar "Agile Contracts Make Business Sense") prefers to use a co-source arrangement whenever possible.

Agile Contracts Make Business Sense

Bruce is the vice president of sales in a company that prides itself on using agile practices to develop systems in large companies. Its preferred approach is to co-source the work—that is, half of the work will be done by Bruce's company and the other half by people in the client company. In this case, Bruce's company quite often does not manage the project, although it has a project leader for its team who works closely with the client project manager.

Bruce finds that no two situations are the same, so one needs to take an agile approach to establishing a contract for software development. The first thing to determine is whether the client is sold on an agile approach, whether they can be sold, or at least whether they can trust an agile approach. Bruce works from three levels of estimates: ballpark, budgetary, and bull's eye. He notes that everyone starts with a ballpark estimate. It's when you get to the budgetary estimate that you switch to an agile focus and convince people that they will get more for their money if they do not attempt to define all of the functionality and do all of the planning up front. Bruce finds that 60 percent to 70 percent of the time, he can sell an agile approach.

Bruce notes that an agile approach must be sold at a high enough level to influence procurement practices, so it is important that the person agreeing to try an agile approach is willing to champion the agile approach to his or her management. If people back down from an agile approach when they encounter difficulties, then they haven't really been sold on the approach.

Bruce tries to avoid tying pricing to deliverables; if pricing is tied to a deliverable, it must be a very small chunk of work. This is the essence of an agile approach, and it often runs counter to the procurement practices of the client. However, if a person high enough in the client company has agreed to use an agile approach, then these procurement and legal issues will be addressed by that champion.

If the client has gotten to the point of agreeing to an agile approach at a level sufficiently high to precipitate a change in procurement practice, then Bruce can rely on the client to put together an appropriate contract. The secret is not in the contract wording itself, but in having a sponsor at a high enough level who understands that the company can benefit more by allowing the system to evolve rather than be specified in detail at the beginning.

Bruce has found that once a client has experienced an agile project, the nature of the contract is not much of an issue for subsequent agile projects. Results talk!

—Based on conversations and email with Bruce Ferguson

The Key: Optional Scope[35]

We have noted several types of contracts that can work for agile software development:

- Time-and-material contracts using concurrent development with highest priority features implemented first and working, integrated code delivered at each iteration so that the customer may easily manage cost by limiting scope.
- Multistage contracts using a master contract and work orders to release each iteration, with similar emphasis on concurrent development, highest priority features first, and working, integrated code delivered at each iteration.

35. See Beck, "Optional Scope Contracts."

- Target-cost contracts, which charter the frontline workers of both parties to work together to come up with a solution to the problem that meets a target cost, giving them the freedom to limit scope as a primary mechanism to achieve the target cost.
- Shared-benefit contracts that assume the parties will modify what they are doing as time goes on to achieve mutual benefit.

There is a common theme here: All of these contracts are mechanisms that avoid fixing scope in detail. This should not come as a surprise. Jim Johnson of the Standish Group noted 64 percent of the features in a typical system are rarely or never used, suggesting that the most fertile ground for productivity improvement in software development lies in not implementing features that are not needed.[36] As Barry Boehm and Philip Papaccio noted in 1988,[37] the best way to develop low-cost, high-quality software is to *write less code*. Chartering a software development team to accomplish a purpose within cost and schedule constraints is about the same as asking them to figure out which features to leave out of the system.

Conventional wisdom holds that specifying and controlling scope in a contract is necessary to protect an organization from self-serving behavior on the part of the other party. However, the effect of this protection is a suboptimized value stream. Although it seems counterintuitive, rigid control of scope tends to expand, not reduce, the scope. This in turn leads to a significant increase in the cost of the features as well as the cost of the control system. The bottom line? Organizations that use outsourcing as a way to save money will save more money overall if they collaborate with vendors by using some form of optional scope contract.

Establishing a partnership relationship with vendors generally happens at the initiation of the customer, and it is not as simple as using any specific form of contract. Both parties need a clear understanding of the value they could bring to each other if they focus on mutual benefit instead of individual benefit. Partnerships require consistent practices so partners develop confidence that commitments will be honored and vulnerabilities will not be exploited, even if individuals change. This in turn requires creative agreements that do not try to cover every eventuality, but instead provide ways to deal with unpredictable future events in a manner that both sides will perceive as fair and equitable.

---

36. Johnson, "ROI, It's Your Job."

37. Boehm and Papaccio, "Understanding and Controlling Software Costs."

TRY THIS

1. Make sure your defect measurement system is an informational measurement system rather than a performance measurement system.
   a. Are defects traceable back to the developer who caused the defect? Why? If there is no good reason, then eliminate the person's identity from the defect reporting system; don't even collect the names.
   b. If there is a reason why you need a developer's identity (e.g., the developer must fix the code), then be sure that an individual developer is the only one who sees the reports related to his or her work. Aggregate all defect reports; do not publicly display or manage from defect measurements sorted by developer.
2. Whether you outsource or are a contractor, the first step to using agile methods under contract is to figure out a way to make scope optional. Ask your legal team to scour the available literature on methods to provide adequate protection to your company without using a fixed-scope specification.

Chapter 8

Instructions and Warranty

CAUTION—USE ONLY AS DIRECTED

Toolkits are usually packaged with instruction sheets and a warranty card, which most of us try to ignore. After all, a tool isn't very user-friendly if you have to read how to operate it. Worse, most instruction sheets start out by listing everything that can go wrong if you use the tools incorrectly. Following this time-honored pattern, we begin the instructions for this lean toolkit with a disclaimer.

- If today's problems come from yesterday's solutions,[1] then tomorrow's problems will come from today's solutions. Avoid creating a pendulum that swings from high ceremony to low ceremony and back; look for the balance point of the lean principles.
  - **Eliminate waste** does not mean throw away all documentation.
  - **Amplify learning** does not mean keep on changing your mind.
  - **Decide as late as possible** does not mean procrastinate.
  - **Deliver as fast as possible** does not mean rush and do sloppy work.
  - **Empower the team** does not mean abandon leadership.
  - **Build integrity in** does not mean big, upfront design. .
  - **See the whole** does not mean ignore the details.

1. Senge, *The Fifth Discipline*, 57.

- One team's prescription is another team's poison. Do not arbitrarily adopt practices that work in other organizations; use the thinking tools in this book to translate lean principles into agile practices that match your environment.
  - The "right" amount of feature analysis and traceability depends on the nature of the system and the probability of change. *Caution:*
    - Putting a rocket into orbit is different than approving a loan.
    - Fixing legacy code is different than creating a Web brochure.
  - The "right" amount of user interaction design depends on the users of the system, their background, and how they might use the system. *Caution:*
    - The perceived integrity of the system rests on the user interface.
    - It's a lot more difficult to refactor users than it is to refactor code.

INSTRUCTIONS

The standard disclaimer is followed by instructions, which illustrate a few basic applications of the tools. Here we give instructions for applications of the lean toolkit within individual spheres of influence, in different size companies, and for different types of work.

The 22 tools in this toolkit should be used to translate the seven lean principles into agile practices that will work in your organization. Many books and articles describe alternate agile practices and techniques in some detail. How you use these will differ depending on your sphere of influence, the size of your company, and the type of work you do.

Sphere of Influence

Lean principles break down barriers, and thus they work best when a senior leader champions them. However, they can be adapted and applied to any level of an organization. Senior management support helps, but it is not essential for lean principles to work. Instead of waiting for lean thinking to descend from above, use it to change your corner of the world. Practice the *Art of the Possible.*[2]

2. This phrase is from Ken Schwaber.

- **Understand lean thinking.** Develop a clear idea of how the lean principles might work in your environment and what kinds of improvements they might bring about.
- **Create a coalition.** Find like-minded souls, especially among your peers, and form a study group. Create a group consensus about how to translate the principles into agile practices that make sense and will have an impact on your problems.
- **In the face of resistance, address the fear.**
  - Resistance indicates a perceived threat to a largely unconscious belief system, one that has no doubt successfully guided the organization in the past. A organization's belief system leads to actions that reinforce the beliefs, creating a self-fulfilling prophecy that tends to blocks out new ideas.[3]
  - Resistance is a sign that you have triggered a fear. This isn't all bad; it means you have injected a new idea into the system, which is the first step to changing the belief system.
  - Recognize that resistance is a symptom, and the cause lies in the belief system that is being threatened. You need to uncover and address the belief system that underlies the fear.[4] Of course, this isn't easy, because the belief system has no doubt led to success in the past, so it will fight back with many varieties of self-fulfilling prophecies.
  - You have some help these days, because the belief in the fundamental validity of sequential software development is being called into question and has already been dismissed in highly successful product development organizations.
- **Accommodate with minimum waste.** If you can't eliminate unnecessary documentation and reports, do them at as high a level as possible. Try to keep your plan at the release level—you have to do that much planning anyway. Write summary documentation—if you write things that ordinary people can comprehend in a short time it might help keep people out of your hair. Write design summary documents for maintenance support only after you have finished your coding—otherwise you're going to have to write them twice.
- **In the face of indifference, get started.** If you are facing indifference rather than resistance, you might take this as tacit approval and simply start using agile practices in your sphere of influence. Or, if you have a small coalition of like minds, the group might develop a good story about how agile practices can benefit your organization, get a hearing, and ask for a chance to try things out on a larger scale.

---

3. Jeffrey Goldstein, *The Unshackled Organization,* 85.

4. See Goldstein, *The Unshackled Organization,* Chapter 6–8 for ideas on how to do this.

- **In the face of support, act.** Don't let your sponsor down. Get moving!
- **Think big; act small; fail fast; learn rapidly.** Once you actually get started, use lean principles to implement lean principles. And good luck.

Large Company

If you work in a large company, you probably have an improvement program or two to deal with: Six Sigma and CMM are but a couple of examples. Realistically, these programs are probably not going to go away, so instead of fighting them, try to leverage them. No doubt these programs were put into place to cure yesterday's ills, and if they are causing you problems, it's probably a case of overcompensation.

- **Exploit Six Sigma.** There are two different flavors of Six-Sigma programs: one for production and one for development. The production flavor focuses on reducing variation; the development version focuses on ensuring fitness for use. Make sure your program is the one focused on development, and if it isn't, build a coalition and lobby hard to get it changed. Once you are using the right program, bring your development approach in line with customer expectations, emphasizing that change tolerance is a key customer expectation. Turn your local black belt loose on getting unlimited access to real customers, on assisting the customers to define and communicate what is really critical to quality, and on improving your testing capability. Find out how your Six-Sigma program incorporates the GE Work-Out concept and exploit that to move the focus of decision making to the development teams.
- **Work with CMM.** If you are dealing with CMM, recognize that each key process area (KPA) in CMM addresses a factor that has caused problems in some software development project in the past. Agile approaches effectively address virtually all of these factors in some way, and therefore a competent assessor should recognize a well-implemented agile ecosystem at CMM level 3 or higher.[5] The approach may not be traditional, but it works. CMM is not supposed to dictate approach, but only assess if the existing approach addresses known software development failure modes.
- **Be wary of CMMI.** CMMI is slated to replace CMM by the end of 2003. Unfortunately, it is designed to cover many areas beyond software development, and thus it is based on a more general set of underlying fears, mostly ones that have arisen in the course of military procurement.

5. Mark Paulk, a senior member of the technical staff at SEI and project leader for CMM version 1.1, reached this conclusion in "Extreme Programming from a CMM Perspective."

If you are faced with CMMI, we suggest you learn about the struggles of the U.S. military acquisition organization to become more agile. Over the past decade, a series of directives and regulations have attempted to bring the same lean thinking to DoD acquisition, which makes U.S. military logistics among the best in the world. In late 2002 Deputy Secretary of Defense Paul Wolfwoitz canceled earlier attempts and tried again to "...create an acquisition policy environment that fosters efficiency, flexibility, creativity, and innovation."[6] He lists 30 principles and policies behind the new defense acquisition system. At the top of the list are many of the principles and tools found in this book: decentralized responsibility, processes tailored to each program, learning and innovation, reduced cycle time, collaboration, a total systems approach.

Incorporating lean principles into the military procurement system practices has proven to be a daunting task. However, by tracking the efforts, you can come up with a good set of justifications for adopting lean principles in your organization.

- **Be careful with PMI.** The Project Management Institute (PMI) sponsors a certification program for project managers. PMI's teachings are based on the same theories as CMMI: namely, that work should be decomposed and tasks managed individually, that creating and following a plan is the essence of project management, and that scope control is fundamental. This view of project management tends to encourage local suboptimization. As noted in Chapter 2, "Amplify Learning," it often creates a downward spiral in managing the scope of a project: The harder you try to manage scope, the more scope customers require. While many good techniques can be learned in the course of obtaining PMI certification, its theoretical foundation tends to be incompatible with lean thinking.[7]

Small Company

If you work for a small company, you probably are wondering how to put disciplines in place and where to find the time to do it. Discipline is fundamental to good software development, but the traditional disciplines of software engineering and project management are not necessarily the most effective approaches. Don't bring in a cure that will be worse than the disease.

---

6. See *http://dod5000.dau.mil* for more information. Quote is from DEPSESDEF Memo issued October 30, 2002. Downloaded January 26, 2003.

7. See Koskela, "The Underlying Theory of Project Management Is Obsolete."

- **Start with hygiene.** First of all, make sure that you have basic professional software development practices in place: a version-controlled code repository, coding standards, build automation, comprehensive testing, etc.
- **Hire the right people.** Hire for skill and experience. There's no substitute for capable people, especially if you work in a small company.
- **Focus.** Do not try to do too many things at once or to improve everything at the same time. Find the one unique thing that you can do better than anyone else and focus all of your attention on doing that very well. Collaborate with others to provide breadth.
- **Use Work-Out.** The original intent of GE Work-Out was to deal with the very problem you are probably having—not enough time. People usually know what is wrong with their work areas and how to fix things, but they don't have the authority or encouragement to make changes. Managers with the authority don't have the time. Work-Out is a forum that gives people the encouragement and authority to fix their work processes themselves.

Special Work Environments

Not all work environments are alike, and some pose more challenge than others. Here are a few ideas for adapting lean principles to some special environments.

- **Government contractor.** Government contracting is subject to public scrutiny. The benefits of lean approaches are often counterintuitive and difficult to prove to skeptics. These two facts make it challenging to use agile practices in government contracts. However, there is hope, because the U.S. military acquisition organization, along with several of its European counterparts, has come to realize that evolutionary procurement is a better approach. (See previous section on CMMI.) We can only hope that as iterative development becomes acceptable in military contracting, it will become more acceptable for other government agencies at the regional and local levels.
- **When failure is not an option.** Sometimes software can kill people if it malfunctions, and when that is the case, there are many regulations on how to assure the software is failsafe. However, even safety-critical systems can be improved with agile software development approaches. Generally a process that encourages safety evaluations periodically throughout development will be superior to a process that depends upon a one-time safety evaluation at the beginning of a project.[8]

---

8. See Poppendieck, "Using XP for Safety-Critical Software."

- **Embedded software and hardware control.** Whether safety-critical or not, software that controls hardware presents a testing challenge because the hardware is being developed at the same time as the software. Three strategies should be used for this kind of software. First, always build a hardware simulator to test the software as it is developed. Consider the simulator part of the software deliverable. Second, adopt concurrent engineering practices. Develop frequent prototypes involving both hardware and software early and often throughout development. Third, use *set-based development,* described in Chapter 2. Set-based development works like a funnel: Early in development there is wide tolerance for experimentation; as development proceeds the tolerances are gradually narrowed. This is particularly appropriate for embedded software, where tolerance for change will narrow as the hardware design is finalized. For embedded software, it may also be appropriate to increase process formality as development proceeds.
- **Global development.** Development teams will not always be located in the same room, in the same company, or even in the same country. Global development is a fact of life, and agile approaches must adapt to this reality. In Chapter 2 we discuss various methods of synchronization that maximize the communications in dispersed teams. When agile practices are used with global teams, use the frequent milestones of an iterative development cycle to keep people from drifting apart. Invest in collaboration support tools such as shared source code repositories and build systems, collaborative IDEs, and video conferencing. Instant messaging is very useful, but may require some adjustment of work hours when time zones are far apart. Finally, there is no substitute for getting people together in the same room, so plan on team member rotation, focused especially on sharing tacit domain knowledge.[9]
- **Maintenance.** Agile practices rule in software maintenance departments. In fact, these folks are wondering why it took the rest of the software development community so long to figure out how to develop production-ready software.

TROUBLESHOOTING GUIDE

Of course, an instruction sheet should have a troubleshooting guide.

- In case of difficulty, additional applications of the principle *see the whole* are recommended. In particular, apply the following three high leverage practices:
  - When a problem appears, stop everything: find and fix its root cause.

9. See Simons, "Internationally Agile."

- Identify your biggest constraint and direct all effort toward removing it.
- Move your focus *up* one level and optimize the whole system.

WARRANTY

Finally, every toolkit comes with a warranty. Here's ours.

Lean principles are warranted to be tried and proven in many disciplines, and when properly applied, they are warranted to work for software development. Proper application means that all of the lean principles are employed and that thinking tools are used to translate them into agile practices appropriate for the environment. This warranty is invalid if practices are transferred directly from other disciplines or domains without thinking, or if the principles of *empower the team* and *build integrity in* are ignored.

Bibliography

Adler, Paul S. "Time-and-Motion Regained." *Harvard Business Review 71(1):* January–February 1993, 97–107.

Austin, Robert D. *Measuring and Managing Performance in Organizations.* Dorset Publishing House, 1996.

Ballard, Glenn. "Positive vs. Negative Iteration in Design." Proceedings Eighth Annual Conference of the International Group for Lean Construction, IGLC-6, Brighton, UK, July 17–19, 2000.

Battin, Robert D., Ron Crocker, Joe Kreidler, and K. Subramanian. "Leveraging Resources in Global Software Development." *IEEE Software 18(2):* March/April 2001.

Beck, Kent. *Test-Driven Design, By Example.* Addison-Wesley, 2002.

Beck, Kent, and Martin Fowler. *Planning Extreme Programming.* Addison-Wesley, 2001.

Beck, Kent. *Extreme Programming Explained: Embrace Change.* Addison-Wesley, 1999.

Beck, Kent, and Dave Cleal. "Optional Scope Contracts." Unpublished, 1999. Available: http://www.xprogramming.com/ftp/Optional+scope+contracts.pdf.

Beinhocker, Eric D. "Robust Adaptive Strategies." *Sloan Management Review 40(3):* Spring 1999, 95–106.

Boehm, B. W. "Industrial Software Metrics Top 10 List." *IEEE Software 4(5):* September 1987, 84–85.

Boehm, Barry, and Philip N. Papaccio. "Understanding and Controlling Software Costs." *IEEE Transactions on Software Engineering 14(10):* October 1988, 1462–1477.

Boehm, Barry, and Victor R. Basili. "Software Defect Reduction List." *IEEE Computer 34(1):* January, 2001.

Bonabeau, Eric, and Christopher Meyer. "Swarm Intelligence." *Harvard Business Review 79(5):* May 2001, 106–114.

Brooks, Frederick P., Jr. "No Silver Bullet: Essence and Accidents of Software Engineering." Information Processing 1986, Proceedings of the IFIP Tenth World Computing Conference, H.-J. Kugler (ed.), Elsevier Scientific Publishing Company, Amsterdam, 1986, 1069–1076.

Brooks, Frederick P., Jr. *The Mythical Man Month: Essays on Software Engineering,* Anniversary Edition. Addison-Wesley, 1995. Originally published in 1975.

Brown, John Seely, and Paul Duguid. "Balancing Act: How to Capture Knowledge Without Killing It." *Harvard Business Review 78(3):* May–June 2000.

Christensen, Clayton M. *The Innovator's Dilemma.* Harvard Business School Press, 2000. Originally published in 1997.

Clark, Kim B., and Takahiro Fujimoto. "The Power of Product Integrity." In Kim B. Clark and Steven C. Wheelwright (eds.), *The Product Development Challenge: Competing Through Speed, Quality, and Creativity. Harvard Business School Press,* 1994.

Clark, Kim B., and Takahiro Fujimoto. *Product Development Performance: Strategy, Organization, and Management in the World Auto Industry.* Harvard Business School Press, 1991.

Clark, Kim B., and Steven C. Wheelwright. *Revolutionizing Product Development.* Free Press, 1992.

CMMI-SW. "Capability Maturity Model® Integration (CMMISM), Version 1.1, (CMMI-SW, V1.1) Continuous Representation CMU/SEI-2002-TR-028 ESC-TR-2002-028." CMMI Product Team, August 2002. Available: http://www.sei.cmu.edu/pub/documents/02.reports/pdf/02tr029.pdf. .

Cockburn, Alistair. *Agile Software Development.* Addison-Wesley, 2002.

Cockburn, Alistair. *Writing Effective Use Cases.* Addison-Wesley, 2000.

Collins, Jim. *Good to Great: Why Some Companies Make the Leap...and Others Don't.* HarperBusiness, 2001.

Collins, James C., and Jerry I. Porras. *Built to Last: Successful Habits of Visionary Companies.* HarperBusiness, 1994.

Constantine, Larry, and Lucy Lockwood. *Software for Use: A Practical Guide to the Models and Methods of Usage-Centered Design.* Addison-Wesley, 1999.

Coy, Peter. "Exploring Uncertainty." *Business Week,* June 7, 1999.

Crocker, Ron. *Large-Scale Agile Software Development.* In press, 2003.

Curtis, Bill, Herb Kransner, and Neil Iscoe. "A Field Study of the Software Design Process for Large Systems." *Communications of the ACM 31(11):* November 1988, 1268–1287.

Cusumano, Michael A., and Kentaro Nobeoka. *Thinking Beyond Lean: How Multi-Project Management is Transforming Product Development at Toyota and Other Companies.* Free Press, 1998.

Cusumano, Michael A. "How Microsoft Makes Large Teams Work Like Small Teams." *Sloan Management Review 39(1):* Fall 1997, 9–20.

Cusumano, Michael A., and Richard W. Selby. *Microsoft Secrets: How the World's Most Powerful Software Company Creates Technology, Shapes Markets, and Manages People.* Simon and Schuster, 1998. Originally published in 1995.

DeGrace, Peter, and Leslie Hulet Stahl. *Wicked Problems, Righteous Solutions: A Catalogue of Modern Software Engineering Paradigms.* Yourdon Press, 1990.

Dell, Michael, with Catherine Fredman. *Direct from Dell.* HarperBusiness, 1999.

DeMarco, Tom. *Slack: Getting Past Burnout, Busywork, and the Myth of Total Efficiency.* Broadway Books, 2001.

DeMarco, Tom, and Timothy Lister, *Peopleware: Productive Projects and Teams.* Dorset House, 1987.

Demming, W. Edwards. *Out of the Crisis.* MIT Press, 2000. Originally published in 1986.

Dyer, Jeffrey H. *Collaborative Advantage: Winning Through Extended Enterprise Supplier Networks.* Oxford University Press; 2000.

Eisenhardt, Kathleen M., and Donald N. Sull. "Strategy as Simple Rules." *Harvard Business Review 79(1):* January, 2001, 106–116.

Evans, Eric. *Domain-Driven Design: Tackling Complexity in the Heart of Software.* Addison-Wesley Professional, 2003.

Forrester, Jay W. "System Dynamics and the Lessons of 35 Years." In Kenyon B. De Greene (ed.), *A Systems-Based Approach to Policymaking.* Kluwer Academic Publishers, 1993. Available: http://sysdyn.mit.edu/sdep/papers/D-4224-4.pdf.

Fowler, Martin. *Patterns of Enterprise Application Architecture.* Addison-Wesley, 2002.

Fowler, Martin. *Refactoring: Improving the Design of Existing Code.* Addison-Wesley, 1999.

Freedman, David H. *Corps Business.* HarperBusiness, 2000.

Goldratt, Eliyahu M. *Necessary But Not Sufficient.* North River Press, 2000.

Goldratt, Eliyahu M. *Critical Chain.* North River Press, 1997.

Goldratt, Eliyahu M. *What Is This Thing Called Theory of Constraints and How Should It Be Implemented?* North River Press, 1990.

Goldratt, Eliyahu M. *The Goal: A Process of Ongoing Improvement,* 2nd rev. ed. North River Press, 1992. Originally published in 1984.

Goldstein, Jeffrey. *The Unshackled Organization: Facing the Challenge of Unpredictability Through Spontaneous Reorganization.* Productivity Press, 1994.

Guindon, Raymonde. "Designing the Design Process: Exploiting Opportunistic Thoughts." *Human and Computer Interaction 5,* 1990, 305–344.

Gupta, Anil K., and Vijay Govindarajan. "Knowledge Management's Social Dimension: Lessons from Nucor Steel." *Sloan Management Review 42(1):* Fall 2000, 71–80.

Herzberg, Frederick. "One More Time: How Do You Motivate Employees?" *Harvard Business Review 46(1):* January–February 1968.

Highsmith, James A. *Adaptive Software Development: A Collaborative Approach to Managing Complex Systems.* Dorset House, 2000.

Highsmith, Jim. *Agile Software Development Ecosystems.* Addison-Wesley, 2002.

Hock, Dee. *Birth of the Chaordic Age.* Berrett-Koehler Publishers, 1999.

Hof, Robert D. "Q&A with eBay's Pierre Omidyar." *Business Week Online,* December 3, 2001.

Hohmann, Luke. *Beyond Software Architecture: Creating and Sustaining Winning Solutions.* Addison-Wesley, 2003.

Hohmann, Luke. *Journey of the Software Professional: A Sociology of Software Development.* Prentice Hall, 1997.

Howard, William Willard. "The Rush to Oklahoma." *Harpers Weekly 33,* May 18, 1889, pp. 391–394. Available: http://www.library.cornell.edu/Reps/DOCS/landrush.htm.

Huck, Virginia. *Brand of the Tartan: The 3M Story.* Minnesota Mining and Manufacturing Company, 1955.

Humphrey, Watts S. *Winning with Software: An Executive Strategy.* Addison-Wesley, 2002.

Hunt, Andrew, and David Thomas. *The Pragmatic Programmer: From Journeyman to Master.* Addison-Wesley, 2000.

Imai, Masaaki. *Gemba Kaizen: A Commonsense, Low-Cost Approach to Management.* McGraw-Hill, 1997.

Jeffries, Ron, Ann Anderson, and Chet Hendrickson. *Extreme Programming Installed.* Addison-Wesley, 2001.

Johnson, Jeff. *GUI Bloopers: Don'ts and Do's for Software Developers and Web Designers.* Morgan Kaufmann Publishers, 2000.

Johnson, Jim. "ROI, It's Your Job." Published Keynote Third International Conference on Extreme Programming, Alghero, Italy, May 26–29, 2002. Available at: http://www.xp2003.org/talksinfo/johnson.pdf

Juran, Joseph M. *Juran's Quality Handbook,* 5th ed. McGraw-Hill Professional, 1998. First edition published in 1951.

Kajko-Mattsson, Mira, Ulf Westblom, Stefan Forssander, Gunnar Andersson, Mats Medin, Sari Ebarasi, Tord Fahlgren, Sven-Erik Johansson, Stefan Törnquist, and Margareta Holmgren, "Taxonomy of Problem Management Activities." Proceedings of the Fifth European Conference on Software Maintenance and Reengineering, March 2001, 1–10.

Klein, Gary. *Sources of Power: How People Make Decisions.* MIT Press, 1999.

Koskela, Lauri. *An Exploration Towards a Production Theory and Its Application to Construction.* Technical Research Centre of Finland, 2000.

Koskela, Lauri, and Gregory Howell. "The Underlying Theory of Project Management Is Obsolete." Proceedings of the PMI Research Conference, 2002, 293–302. Available: www.leanconstruction.org/pdf/ObsoleteTheory.pdf.

Kotter, John P. "What Leaders Really Do."*Harvard Business Review 79(11):* December 2001. Reprint of article first published in 1990.

Larman, Craig. *Applying UML and Patterns—An Introduction to Object-Oriented Analysis and Design and The Unified Process,* 2nd ed. Prentice Hall, 2002.

Larpé, Michael A., and Luk N. Van Wassenhove. "Learning Across Lines: The Secret to More Efficient Factories." *Harvard Business Review 80(10):* October 2002.

Magretta, Joan. "The Power of Integration: An Interview with Dell Computer's Michael Dell." *Harvard Business Review 76(2):* March–April 1998, 73–84.

Marick, Brian. "When Should a Test Be Automated?" Presented at Quality Week '98, 1998. Available: http://www.testing.com/writings/automate.pdf.

Martin, Robert C. *Agile Software Development: Principles, Patterns and Practices.* Prentice Hall, 2002.

Maslow, Abraham Harold, Robert Frager, and James Fadiman. *Motivation and Personality,* 3rd ed. Addison-Wesley, 1987. First edition published in 1954.

McBreen, Pete. *Software Craftsmanship: The New Imperative.* Addison-Wesley, 2002.

Miller, George A. "The Magical Number Seven, Plus or Minus Two: Some Limits on Our Capacity for Processing Information." *The Psychological Review 63,* 1956, 81–97.

Mitchell, Meg. "Share…and Share Alike." *Darwin Magazine 2(2):* February 2001. Available: http://www.darwinmag.com/read/020101/share.html.

Norman, Donald A. *The Design of Everyday Things,* reissue. Currency/Doubleday, 1990. Originally published in 1988.

O'Reilly, Charles A., III, and Jeffrey Pfeffer. *Hidden Value: How Great Companies Achieve Extraordinary Results with Ordinary People.* Harvard Business School Press, 2000.

Ohno, Taiichi. *The Toyota Production System: Beyond Large-Scale Production.* Productivity Press, 1988. Originally published in Japanese in 1978.

Palmer, Steven R., and John M. Felsing. *A Practical Guide to Feature-Driven Development.* Prentice Hall, 2002.

Paulk, Mark C. "Extreme Programming from a CMM Perspective." *IEEE Software 18(6):* November/December 2001.

Petroski, Henry. *Design Paradigms: Case Histories of Error and Judgment in Engineering.* Cambridge University Press, 1994.

Pitette, Gilles. "Progressive Acquisition and the RUP: Comparing and Combining Iterative Processes for Acquisition and Software Development." *The Rational Edge,* November 2002. Available: http://www.therationaledge.com/admin/archives.jsp.

Poppendieck, Mary. "Lean Programming" (Parts 1 and 2). *Software Development Magazine 9(5, 6):* May, June 2001.

Poppendieck, Mary. "Wicked Projects." *Software Development Magazine 10(5):* May 2002, 72–76.

Poppendieck, Mary, with Ron Morsicato. "Using XP for Safety-Critical Software." *Cutter IT Journal 15*(9*):* September 2002.

Prahalad, C. K., and M. S. Krishnan. "The Dynamic Synchronization of Strategy and Information Technology." *MIT Sloan Management Review 43(4):* Summer 2002, 24–33.

Prahalad, C. K., and M. S. Krishnan. "The New Meaning of Quality in the Information Age." *Harvard Business Review 77*(5*):* September–October 1999, 109–118.

Raymond, Eric Steven. *The Cathedral and the Bazaar.* Posted to Internet: 2000/08/24; accessed: November 12, 2001. Available: http://tuxedo.org/~esr/writings/cathedral-bazaar/cathedral-bazaar/x285.html.

Reinertsen, Donald G. *Managing the Design Factory: A Product Developer's Toolkit.* The Free Press, 1997.

Ripin, Kathy M., and Leonard Sayles. *Insider Strategies for Outsourcing Information Systems: Building Productive Partnerships, Avoiding Seductive Traps.* Oxford University Press, 1999.

Rittel, H., and M. Webber. "Dilemmas in a General Theory of Planning." *Policy Sciences 4,* 1973, 155–169.

Royce, Winston W. "Managing the Development of Large Software Systems." Proceedings, *IEEE WESCON,* August 1970, 1–9.

Schwaber, Ken, and Mike Beedle. *Agile Software Development with Scrum.* Prentice Hall, 2001.

Senge, Peter M. *The Fifth Discipline: The Art and Practice of the Learning Organization.* Doubleday Currency, 1990.

Shalloway, Alan and James R. Trott. *Design Patterns Explained: A New Perspective on Object Oriented Design.* Addison-Wesley, 2002.

Shingo, Shigeo. *Study of "Toyota" Production System from Industrial Engineering Viewpoint.* Japan Management Association, Tokyo, 1981.

Simons, Matt. "Big and Agile?" *Cutter IT Journal 15(1):* January 2002.

Simons, Matt. "Internationally Agile." *Inform IT,* March 2002. Available: http://www.informit.com.

Smith, Preston G., and Donald G. Reinertsen. *Developing Products in Half the Time: New Rules, New Tools,* 2nd ed. John Wiley and Sons, 1998. First edition published in 1991.

Sobek, Durward K., II, C. Allen Ward, and Jeffrey K. Liker. "Toyota's Principles of Set-Based Concurrent Engineering." *Sloan Management Review 40(2):* Winter 1999, 67–83.

Sobek, Durward Kenneth, II. *Principles That Shape Product Development Systems: A Toyota-Chrysler Comparison.* Ph.D. dissertation. University of Michigan, 1997.

Stapleton, Jennifer. *DSDM: Business Focused Development, 2nd ed. Addison-Wesley, 2003.*

Sutherland, Jeff. "Agile Can Scale: Inventing and Reinventing Scrum in Five Companies." *Cutter IT Journal 14(12):* December 2001, 5–11.

Taylor, Winslow. *Principles of Scientific Management.* Harper and Brothers, 1911.

Thimbleby, Harold. "Delaying Commitment." *IEEE Software 5(3):* May 1988.

Thomas Group. National Institute of Standards and Technology Institute for Defense Analyses. *Business Week,* April 30, 1990, 111.

Thomas, Kenneth W. *Intrinsic Motivation at Work: Building Energy and Commitment.* Berrett-Koehler, 2000.

Thompson, Fred. "Public Economics and Public Administration." Jack Rabin, W. Bartley Hildreth, and Gerald Miller (eds.), *Handbook of Public Administration,* 2nd ed. Marcel Dekker, 1998. Available online at http://www.willamette.edu/~fthompso/pubfin/ECON&PA.html.

Ulrich, Dave, Steve Kerr, and Ron Ashkenas. *The GE Work-Out: How to Implement GE's Revolutionary Method for Busting Bureaucracy and Attacking Organizational Problems—Fast!* McGraw-Hill, 2002.

Ward, Allen, Jeffrey K. Liker, John J. Cristaino, and Durward K. Sobek, II. "The Second Toyota Paradox: How Delaying Decisions Can Make Better Cars Faster." *Sloan Management Review 36(3):* Spring 1995, 43–61.

Wideman, R. Max. "Progressive Acquisition and the RUP, Part I: Defining the Problem and Common Terminology." *The Rational Edge,* December 2002. Available: http://www.therationaledge.com/admin/archives.jsp.

Wideman, R. Max. "Progressive Acquisition and the RUP, Part II: Contracts That Work." *The Rational Edge,* January 2003. Available: http://www.therationaledge.com/admin/archives.jsp.

Womack, James P., and Daniel T. Jones. *Lean Thinking, Banish Waste and Create Wealth in your Corporation.* Simon and Schuster, 1996.

Womack, James P., Daniel T. Jones, and Daniel Roos. *The Machine That Changed the World: The Story of Lean Production.* HarperPerennial, 1991. Originally published in 1990.

Yourdon, Edward Nash (ed.). *Classics in Software Engineering.* Yourdon Press, 1979.

Yourdon, Edward. *Death March: The Complete Software Developer's Guide to Surviving "Mission Impossible" Projects.* Prentice Hall PTR, 1997.

Zaninotto, Enrico. Keynote "From X Programming to the X Organization." Third International Conference on Extreme Programming, Alghero, Italy, May 26–29, 2002.

Index

E

Q

R

S

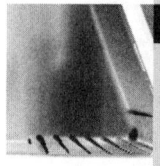